W9-ARG-332

DATE DUE

MAR 2 5 2004	
SEP 1 6 2004	
OCT 2 8 2004	
JUL 0 5 2006	
OCT 0 2 2006	
MAR 0 6 2007	
AUG 1 2 2008	
MAY 1 2 2011	
NOV 0 1 2011	
NOV 1 4 2011	
NOV 2 8 2011	
MAR 1 8 2013	

BRODART, CO.   Cat. No. 23-221-003

THE BEDFORD SERIES IN HISTORY AND CULTURE

The World Turned Upside Down

Indian Voices from Early America

Edited with an introduction by

Colin G. Calloway

University of Wyoming

BEDFORD BOOKS *of* ST. MARTIN'S PRESS

Boston • New York

For Bedford Books
Publisher: Charles H. Christensen
Associate Publisher/General Manager: Joan E. Feinberg
History Editor: Niels Aaboe
Developmental Editor: Louise D. Townsend
Managing Editor: Elizabeth M. Schaaf
Copyeditor: Barbara G. Flanagan
Text Design: Claire Seng-Niemoeller
Cover Design: Hannus Design Associates
Cover Art: Johnson Hall by E. L. Henry. Oil on canvas, 1903. 1993.44. Collection of the Albany Institute of Art. The painting depicts Iroquois Indians in council with British Indian superintendent Sir William Johnson at his home in the mid-1700s. Johnson Hall, in Johnstown, New York, was a regular venue for Indian councils during Johnson's long career in Indian diplomacy. Johnson died there in 1774, in the middle of a council such as the one shown in the painting.

Library of Congress Catalog Card Number: 92–75887
Copyright © 1994 by Bedford Books *of* St. Martin's Press

Manufactured in the United States of America.

8 7 6 5 4
f e d c b a

For information, write: St. Martin's Press, Inc., 175 Fifth Avenue, New York, NY 10010
Editorial Offices: Bedford Books *of* St. Martin's Press, 29 Winchester Street, Boston, MA 02116

ISBN: 0–312–08350–5 (paperback)
ISBN: 0–312–10281–X (hardcover)

Acknowledgments

"Brant Weighs Indian and White Civilization, 1789." Isabel Thompson Kelsay, *Joseph Brant*, Syracuse, N.Y.: Syracuse University Press, 1984. Reprinted with permission.
"The Continuing Conflict Over Land, 1793." *The Correspondence of John Graves Simcoe*, edited by E.A. Cruikshank. 5 vols. Toronto: Ontario Historical Society, 1923–31, pp. 17–19.
"A Native American Theological Debate, c. 1670." *John Eliot's Indian Dialogues*, edited by Henry W. Bowden and James P. Ronda. Westport, Conn.: Greenwood Press, 1980. An imprint of Greenwood Publishing Group, Inc., Westport, Conn. Reprinted with permission.

Acknowledgments and copyrights are continued at the back of the book on page 199, which constitutes an extension of the copyright page.

Foreword

The Bedford Series in History and Culture is designed so that readers can study the past as historians do. The historian's first task is finding the evidence. Documents, letters, memoirs, interviews, pictures, movies, novels, or poems can provide facts and clues. Then the historian questions and compares the sources. There is more to do than in a courtroom, for hearsay evidence is welcome, and the historian is usually looking for answers beyond act and motive. Different views of an event may be as important as a single verdict. How a story is told may yield as much information as what it says.

Along the way the historian seeks help from other historians and perhaps from specialists in other disciplines. Finally, it is time to write, to decide on an interpretation and how to arrange the evidence for readers.

Each book in this series contains an important historical document or group of documents, each document a witness from the past and open to interpretation in different ways. The documents are combined with some element of historical narrative—an introduction or a biographical essay, for example—that provides students with an analysis of the primary source material and important background information about the world in which it was produced.

Each book in the series focuses on a specific topic within a specific historical period. Each provides a basis for lively thought and discussion about several aspects of the topic and the historian's role. Each is short enough (and inexpensive enough) to be a reasonable one-week assignment in a college course. Whether as classroom or personal reading, each book in the series provides firsthand experience of the challenge—and fun—of discovering, recreating, and interpreting the past.

Natalie Zemon Davis
Ernest R. May

Preface

American Indian people often seem to be silent in the history of early America. Since the native peoples who inhabited North America when Europeans invaded the continent were members of oral cultures, most of what we know about them comes from the biased and distorted writings of European-Americans, people who were literate but alien. The voices of Indian women are especially difficult to detect in records written by non-Indian men, who generally did not understand the role of women in Indian societies and usually did not solicit, or did not listen to, women's opinions.

Indian people have certainly been deprived of their voices throughout much of American history, but anyone who has delved deeply into the records of early America knows that they were anything but silent. Many of their words survive for us today, if we know where to look for them and how to read them. The selections in this volume represent a small fraction of the statements made by Indian peoples as they encountered Euro-Americans and struggled to survive in a world turned upside down by their presence.

In some areas of mainland North America, first contacts with Europeans occurred in the sixteenth century. Indian people in Florida, for example, felt the impact of Spanish invasion, European diseases, and Christian missionaries well before 1600. The bulk of the selections in this book, however, comes from the seventeenth and eighteenth centuries, when dealings with the newcomers were most extensive. The selections are from the Indian peoples who inhabited eastern North America, predominantly the area that today comprises the eastern United States. Indians in what is now the southwestern United States also lived in "colonial America," and to exclude them and deny the long Spanish presence in that region helps to perpetuate an Anglocentric, and distorted, view of American history as beginning on the east coast and moving west. Most of our United States history texts and courses still pay far more attention to English colonial America than to Spanish or French colonial America. However, to do justice to the various and complex ways in which Pueblo, Navajo, Apache, Comanche, Pima, Papago, Cahuilla, and other Indian peoples responded to Spanish soldiers, priests, and settlers over several centuries in a different environment would expand enormously the size and scope of this volume. This short collection focuses on the eastern third of the continent, but it does include instances of Indian relations with Spanish, French, and Dutch as well as with English colonists.

The Indian peoples of the eastern woodlands displayed considerable diversity in language, culture, and political systems. However, they had enough in common that anthropologists regularly classify such diverse peoples as the Abenakis, Iroquois, Shawnees, Cherokees, and Chickasaws as members of a common cultural and environmental region. The peoples of the eastern woodlands also shared many experiences in their dealings with Europeans, as these documents reveal.

The collection generally is divided into topical chapters. The Revolutionary and early national periods occupy separate chapters, not because of the importance of the American Revolution in United States history—key dates in U.S. history do not necessarily have the same meaning for Indian people—but because the changes generated by that event had profound consequences for Indian peoples in North America. The Revolutionary era saw a recurrence of many familiar pressures and problems, but it also initiated a new era in which the United States exerted increasing domination over Indian lives. For Anglo-Americans, the colonial period of their history ended in 1776 with the Declaration of Independence or in 1783 with the winning of that independence. The Indians' struggle for independence began much earlier and went on much longer, until at least 1795 when the united tribes of the Old Northwest were finally defeated. The final chapter provides some of their words from this period.

Many of the records made by non-Indians in early America give us valuable information about Native American life; most of the statements made by Indian people comment on how their lives were being affected by Europeans. Just as European documents often presented a one-sided view of the past, so Indian speakers often portrayed Europeans as greedy and aggressive while depicting themselves as innocent victims. Their words offer a valuable corrective to Eurocentric notions of history, but the reality of human encounters was usually more complex than that.

In addition, there was much that Indians chose not to say and much that went unrecorded when they did say it. Whereas Indian people often were vocal about the causes of change and upheaval in their lives, they generally kept quiet about sources of continuity and stability. For example, ancient rituals helped maintain order in the world and tie communities together when all else threatened to tear them apart. Sacred places and practices were not the things to discuss, however, with outsiders who were determined to stamp out what they saw as "pagan superstition." By their silence, native peoples often were able to preserve intact the core of their universe, even as their world turned upside down. The recurrent themes and concerns that run through the chapters—loss of land, war and peace, missionaries and Christianity, the education or reeducation of Indian youth, the inroads made by European technology and European alcohol, political changes within Indian societies—represent a part of Native American historical experiences in early America; they are not the whole story. Nevertheless, Indian peoples had to deal with them and recognized them as crucial issues that needed to be discussed with Europeans.

A NOTE ON TERMINOLOGY

There is no consensus about what is the most appropriate name for the original inhabitants of North America. The names tribal members used to describe themselves often translate into "the people," or "the real people"; there was no need for a collective term embracing all the peoples of North America until Europeans arrived and invented one. Of course, Columbus was confused when he called the natives of these lands *Indians*. Some people insist on using *Native American* and reject *Indian* as a derogatory term. However, *America* is also a word of European invention. Many Indian people today call themselves just that, *Indian people*. In this book, I have identified particular peoples by their tribal names; when talking more generally I have used *Native American, American Indian,* and *Indian people* interchangeably, recognizing that none is entirely satisfactory and that all are, at best, labels of convenience. In addition, to write about "American Native American policy" or "American–Native American relations" creates stylistic problems. In a similar vein, *white* is a term usually best avoided and I have normally used *European, American, colonists,* and so on, preferring such terms as both more accurate and less laden with connotations. On occasion, however, and generally for stylistic reasons, I have used *white* rather than the neutral *non-Indian*. The people who appear in this book distinguished between themselves and *white men,* and it is clear to whom they referred when they used that term.

Historical documents sometimes go through many changes as people copy, recopy, and edit them. Rather than impose another round of changes in an effort to modernize spelling or achieve consistency, the documents in this collection have been reprinted essentially as they appear in the source from which they have been taken.

ACKNOWLEDGMENTS

This book is much the better for the comments of Neal Salisbury, James H. Merrell, James H. O'Donnell III, Peter C. Mancall, Randolph A. Roth, Robert M. Weir, and an anonymous reviewer, all of whom offered constructive criticisms on an earlier version of the manuscript. I am grateful to Ernest May and Chuck Christensen for the invitation to do this book, to Sabra Scribner for the careful attention she gave to the manuscript in its early stages, and to Richard Keaveny for his diligent and enthusiastic assistance in preparing the manuscript for production. Elizabeth Schaaf carefully guided the manuscript through the design and production process; Barbara Flanagan did an excellent job of copyediting; and Phil Roberts, my colleague at the University of Wyoming, took care of the indexing.

Colin G. Calloway

Contents

2. Cultural Conflicts, Contests, and Confluences   43

3. Land, Trade, and Treaties   78

Illustrations

INTRODUCTION

"Times Are Altered
with Us Indians"

A Creek chief died. When the chief was dead, he appeared before Gohan-tone, who said to him, "This land belongs to you and your children forever. This land will be yours forever, but these whites who have just come will overwhelm you and inherit your land. They will increase and the Indian will decrease and at last die out. Then only white people will remain. But there will be terrible times."
—Yuchi legend, paraphrased from George E. Lankford,
Native American Legends[1]

The times are exceedingly altered, yea the times are turned upside down; or rather we have changed the good times, chiefly by the help of the white people.
—Mohegan Indians to the Connecticut Assembly, 1789

A WORLD OF CHANGES

For thousands of years before Europeans set foot in North America, Indian peoples pioneered, settled, and shaped the land. Societies and traditions evolved and changed; civilizations rose and fell. By the time Europeans arrived and believed they had "discovered" America, the original inhabitants had developed long histories, a wealth of stories and legends, diverse political systems and social structures, hundreds of different languages, complex religions and elaborate rituals, beautiful art forms, practical styles of architecture, and far-reaching networks of trade and communication.

They developed effective hunting, fishing, and farming techniques; they cultivated new crops and integrated new foods into their diets; in some areas of the country they built irrigation networks to enable them to grow crops in desert terrain. In many societies, hunters observed rituals that helped them maintain respectful relationships with the animals they hunted. Warfare and diplomacy also followed prescribed protocols.

Communities changed size and shifted location in response to military, political, economic, and ecological pressures. Indian cities like Cahokia, at the junction of major trade routes near what is today East St. Louis, had reached their zenith and were already in decline by the time Europe emerged from its "Middle Ages."

When Europeans penetrated the continent they encountered a wide variety of Indian peoples—Abenakis and Wampanoags in New England, Iroquois in New York, Delawares in New Jersey and Pennsylvania, Shawnees in Kentucky and Ohio, Cherokees in Tennessee and the Carolinas, Creeks in Georgia and Alabama, Choctaws and Chickasaws in Mississippi—and called them all "tribes" as if they were static units. But many of these societies were in flux, and all were descendants of ancient peoples, living on the foundations of civilizations that stretched back to time immemorial. Change was nothing new in North America.

Nevertheless, the changes that followed the European invasion of North America dwarfed what had gone before. As historian James Merrell has described, the invaders created a "new world" for Native Americans, one that demanded continual adaptation and adjustment.[2] The Indian people whose words appear on these pages were living in a world that was literally changing before their eyes. Contact with Europeans did not monopolize their lives and thoughts, but their comments in speaking to Europeans reveal their concerns about the transformations they witnessed and their opinions about Europeans as the primary agents of change.

The most devastating agents of change, however, were invisible to the Indians. Europeans and Africans brought germs and viruses of lethal diseases that were common in the Old World but unknown in America before 1492. Smallpox, plague, measles, yellow fever, pneumonia, tuberculosis, diptheria, influenza, and a host of other diseases spread like wildfire among Indian populations who had little or no immunity to the new killers. Scholars disagree in their estimates of the population of North America in 1492, although many accept a figure of somewhere between five and ten million as a reasonable guess.

The impact of the new diseases on this population constituted one of the greatest biological catastrophes in human history. Whole tribes were wiped out. Others lost 50, 75, 90 percent of their population. Indians from the Hudson River told the Dutch explorer Adriaen Van der Donck in 1656 "that before the smallpox broke out amongst them, they were ten times as numerous as they are now, and that their population had been melted down by this disease."[3] Diseases raced along well-traveled trails and trade routes, killing thousands of Indian people who had not yet laid eyes on a European.

The Pilgrims who landed at Plymouth in the 1620s, in the wake of a

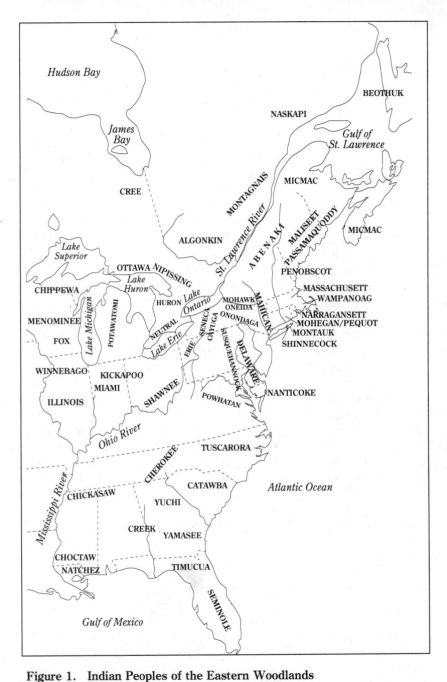

Figure 1. Indian Peoples of the Eastern Woodlands
The map shows the location of selected tribes at the time they first met Europeans. (The Seminoles migrated south to Florida, separating from the Creek Confederacy in the eighteenth century.)

massive epidemic in New England between 1616 and 1619, found the area virtually empty of Indian people. The Pilgrims attributed this circumstance, like most others, to divine providence: God had cleared the land of the "heathen" to make way for His chosen people. Later generations better understood the workings of disease: In the 1760s the British at Fort Pitt gave blankets from the smallpox hospital to Delaware Indians as a form of germ warfare. Europeans who traveled into Indian country frequently saw abandoned villages; the people they met were usually survivors of one or more epidemics. From the fifteenth century to the twentieth century, diseases introduced by Europeans constituted the number one killer of American Indian people. While Indian populations plummeted, the colonial population doubled every twenty-five years in the eighteenth century. By 1790, the year of the first United States census, the original inhabitants of the eastern woodlands had become engulfed in a sea of peoples from Europe and Africa.

Disease disrupted all aspects of Indian life. Normal hunting and planting activities were interrupted, producing hunger and famine, which in turn rendered populations more vulnerable to disease.

The social fabric of Indian society was torn apart as elders, providers, storytellers, clan relatives, healers, and counselors perished. These people were also grandparents, parents, aunts and uncles, brothers and sisters, cousins and children. After an epidemic of smallpox swept through the Wampanoag Indians on Martha's Vineyard in 1645, a Wampanoag sachem named Tawanquatuck described the plight of communities bereft of their elders: "A long time ago they had wise men, which in a grave manner taught the people knowledge, but they are dead, and their wisdome is buried with them, and now men live a giddy life, in ignorance, till they are white headed, and though ripe in years, yet they go without wisdome to their graves."[4] At the very time when Indian societies needed all their resources to deal with the new and growing threat of European invaders, their capacities for resistance were being steadily eroded by recurrent outbreaks of disease. Some communities went under; others merged with neighboring villages as a way of surviving. Epidemics left survivors bewildered and heartbroken.

One reason diseases spread so rapidly was that Indian peoples, who traded extensively among themselves, were eager to trade with Europeans. European traders offered Indians guns, metal goods, woolen clothing, alcohol, and a wide variety of other items in exchange for beaver belts and deerskins. In some of the southern colonies, the English traded for Indian slaves, encouraging tribes to raid their enemies for captives.

Native Americans saw the benefits that the new goods could offer, but they also realized the cost. Traditionally, Indian trading involved exchanging gifts as a way of making and maintaining alliances and friendships. Europeans traded for profit. Many Indian hunters now catered to European market demands rather than the needs of their community and depleted animal populations. They became increasingly dependent on the Europeans for manufactured goods and frequently bought goods on credit, falling into debt to European traders.

Alcohol, bought from traders, caused social chaos, and alcoholism was added to the list of killer diseases imported from Europe. Competition for hunting territories and trade increased intertribal warfare. New weapons of destruction sparked arms races that upset existing balances of power and could be paid for only with beaver pelts and deerskins.

Most Indian peoples in the eastern woodlands were farmers as well as hunters. Corn was the staff of life throughout much of the region, but Indian peoples pursued diversified economies that, prior to their disruption, provided for human needs while imposing minimal demands on the ecosystem. In general, men hunted, fished, and cleared the fields; women did the planting and harvesting. There were times of hunger as well as times of plenty but, compared with European colonists—or even modern-day Americans— Indian peoples in the eastern woodlands seem to have been able to satisfy the necessities of life with relatively light expenditures of time and labor. Indeed, Indians have been called the original "affluent Americans."

Europeans, however, dismissed the Indian way of life as "nomadic," "barbaric," and wasteful, and settlers from England, France, and Holland, where land was in short supply, coveted Indian land. English Puritans invoked the Bible as justification for taking over land and making it productive. Settlers encroached on Indian lands until tensions exploded in bloody wars; when the Indians were defeated, they were forced to give up land as the price of peace. Imperial and colonial governments, land companies and speculators, and individual settlers employed wars and treaties, bribery and coercion, alcohol and corruption to systematically transfer the rich lands of eastern North America from Indian to European hands. Even when land transfers occurred without hostility, Indians realized they were getting the short end of the deal. "The Lands we gave you will last long," Cherokee chief Oconastota told southern Indian superintendent John Stuart in 1767, "but the Cloath & other necessaries with which you Supply us, soon wear out."[5]

In many eastern woodland societies the people held tribal lands in common, although individuals had personal property and sometimes kin groups had stronger claims to certain lands than did other members of the tribe. Europeans, however, insisted on owning the land. Land was now a commodity that could be transferred and property from which others could be excluded. Colonists cut down trees, erected fences, built roads and bridges, and constructed mills and dams, changing the physical appearance of the landscape and rendering impossible the kind of life Indian people had once lived.

Domesticated livestock ate Indian corn and drove away much of the wildlife that survived the ravages of the fur and deerskin trade. Indians in Maryland complained to the colonial assembly in the mid-seventeenth century that "Your hogs & Cattle injure Us[.] You come too near Us to live & drive Us from place to place."[6] Native American affluence gave way to widespread poverty and starvation as the subsistence patterns that had sustained people for centuries now functioned only in truncated form.

Europeans attempted to change the Indians' spiritual world as well as their physical world. Missionaries labored to convert Indian people to Christianity and convince them to abandon beliefs and rituals that had served them well for centuries. Indian reactions sometimes were violent. As early as 1597 Guale Indians on the Atlantic coast of northern Florida killed five Franciscan missionaries; in 1647 Christian Apalachees near modern Tallahassee rebelled and killed three friars.

But with much of their world crumbling around them, some Indian people sought solace in the new religions Europeans offered them. Some became active converts to Christianity, even working as missionaries among their own people. Others, however, did not go that far. Those who did accept elements of Christian teaching and practice did not necessarily cast aside traditional religions. Why could not the Christians' God coexist with their own? Fearing that unconverted Indians would "contaminate" the converts and cause them to revert to "heathen" ways, some missionaries placed their Indian converts in separate communities, isolated from the rest of the tribe. Deep divisions developed in Indian communities between Christians and traditionalists and even between converts to different Christian denominations. Some Indians exploited Christianity as a way to reinforce their own challenges to leaders whose influence rested on traditional spiritual bases.

Christianity was not the only source of political upheaval. Europeans frequently interfered in Indian politics, undermining the authority of established leaders and promoting "client" chiefs who they hoped would do their bidding. Escalating warfare gave greater influence to young war chiefs, who formerly had exercised only limited and temporary authority. Older civil or peace chiefs found it increasingly difficult to control their young men. "Times are altered with us Indians. Formerly the warriors were governed by the wisdom of their uncles the Sachems but now they take their own way," explained an Onondaga sachem during the American Revolution.[7] Europeans complicated the process by funneling guns and gifts into Indian societies through the hands of the chosen chiefs. Client chiefs wore scarlet or blue uniforms, with medals around their necks, as evidence of their allegiance to a European monarch. They fulfilled one of a chief's primary functions—that of generosity—by handing out muskets, blankets, and knives to their followers. They drew additional prestige from their connections to governments in Charleston or Quebec, or even in London and Paris. In return, the client chiefs had to call their men to war. Indian peoples found themselves caught up in more than one hundred years of international wars fought in North America, as first Britain, France, and Spain and then Britain and the United States competed for dominance. U.S. Indian agent George Morgan said at the beginning of the American Revolution that Indians "have been long taught by contending Nations to be bought & sold."[8] Indian warriors served alongside European and colonial armies in campaigns against other European powers. Indian auxiliaries fought other Indians in wars that were not of their making and not in their interest but impossible to escape. The campaigns took Indians away from their villages, their families, and their economic and political responsibilities. Many Indians did not return.

War also hit Indian people hard on their home front. Colonial armies burned Indian crops and villages, spreading hunger and starvation. War shattered individual lives and disrupted community life. Before Europeans arrived, Indian warfare had tended to be small scale, waged seasonally, and marked as much by ritual as by bloodshed. Now generations of Indians grew up thinking that war was a way of life. The image of Indians as "warlike" became fixed in the minds of Europeans, further justifying their destruction and dispossession of native peoples.

War, like disease, destroyed some Indian communities and altered others. Indian people who fled from the fighting took refuge with other Indian communities in safer locations, entered mission villages, or huddled around colonial forts where the garrison provided meager food and shelter. In the mid-seventeenth century, war parties from the Iroquois Confederacy in New York smashed the confederacy of their Huron trade rivals in Ontario and pushed into the territory of other tribes. The survivors scattered throughout the Great Lakes and Ohio Valley, and many villages became virtual refugee camps. In the eighteenth century, as European pressures increased, tribes and communities splintered over issues of war and peace, resistance and relocation. Warriors who fought together often formed new communities. Shawnees lived with Creeks, Cherokees with Shawnees. Some Shawnees migrated across the Mississippi while others remained in Ohio. Many Abenakis from northern New England migrated to Canada; some drifted west to the Ohio Valley and beyond; others clung to their traditional lands. Delawares or Lenni Lenapes from New Jersey kept moving west away from

European settlement. Iroquois villages in New York gave shelter to peoples displaced from homelands farther east; meanwhile other Iroquois migrated west to Ohio and became known as Mingoes.

The European invasion of North America unleashed forces that shattered the world built by Native Americans over thousands of years. At a time when European colonists were establishing new societies in North America, Indian peoples were struggling to survive in a dangerous new world and trying to rebuild amid the ruins of their old worlds. They naturally viewed the history of their relations with Europeans with bitterness, but, contrary to Hollywood stereotypes, they did not suffer in silence. Nor did they succumb without a struggle. Indians who had been defeated militarily often resorted to quieter methods of cultural resistance that exasperated their conquerors. Indian leaders advocated varying strategies to ensure the survival of their people and to keep intact as much of their land base and culture as possible. Different Indian peoples had different experiences and different ways of dealing with European invasion. There was no single Indian response just as there was and is no single Indian voice. The selections in this book reveal some common themes but they also show that Indian peoples responded in various ways and played various roles in America's early history.

INDIANS IN COLONIAL AMERICA

At the end of King Philip's War (1675–76), when the English defeated and scattered the tribes of southern and central New England, Abenaki sachems from the north warned the English in Boston that they still could drive the settlers out of the country since it was "wide and full of Indians."[9]

At this distance, it is hard for us to imagine eastern America as a world in which, despite devastation from war and disease, Indians still were numerous and controlled large areas. Not only do we have to think across the gulfs of time and culture, but our vision is clouded by generations of historians who have written Indians out of our past and by the apparent silence of Indian people in the records customarily consulted by historians.

The roles traditionally assigned to Indian people in our history books involve helping the early settlers celebrate Thanksgiving and then resisting European and American expansion in a series of bloody frontier wars. After the Cherokee and other southern Indians are moved west in the 1830s along the "Trail of Tears," the "Indian" component of our history shifts beyond the Mississippi. There, the Plains Indians act out their prescribed roles of resistance and disappearance as the narrative of nation building gathers pace.

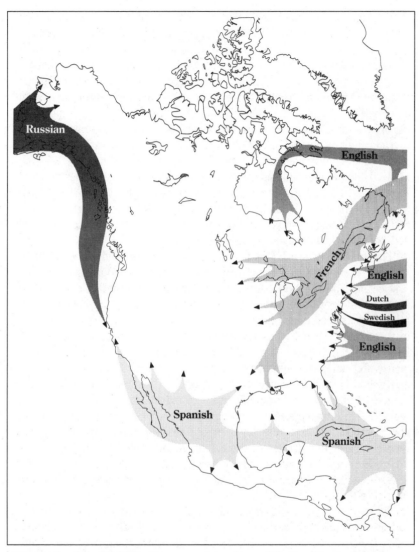

Figure 2. The Multiple European Invasions of Indian North America

Reality was much more complex. Indian peoples did not always fight and they did not disappear. They adapted and survived long after the "Indian wars" and most of our history books had passed them by. Indians remained part of the mosaic of early America, just as they remain part of the mosaic of modern America.

Throughout the colonial era, "Indian country" in eastern North America dwarfed the areas settled by Europeans, and Indian power shaped the continent's history. Europeans relied on Indian allies to help advance their imperial ambitions; colonial armies depended on Indian warriors to bolster their ranks and educate them in forest warfare. Indian protocol governed forest diplomacy and frontier trade. Indian ways figured both prominently and subtly in colonial lifestyles, playing their part in the transformation of Europeans into Americans. European colonists who entered Indian country to trade, hunt, negotiate, or escape the confines of their own society adhered to the customs of the country if they hoped to be successful.

As the world that Indians had made diminished, the boundaries between the Indian and European worlds became increasingly porous. Europeans frequently entered the Indians' world—as captives, traders, missionaries—and some liked it and stayed. But Indians also entered the Europeans' world and participated in the new, emerging societies.

Though our history books do not usually reflect it, Indian people were virtually everywhere in colonial America. They met Europeans when they first set foot on the North American continent at the end of the fifteenth century and served as mapmakers, guides, interpreters, and informants in the European rediscovery of America. They worked as hunters and traders in the commercial networks that linked Indian country to the markets of Europeans. They were allies and enemies in Europeans' wars, and statesmen—and stateswomen—in the diplomacy whose goal was to prevent and end wars. They were converts to and critics of Christianity. They were students, graduates, and dropouts from colonial colleges. They were sailors, whalers, basketmakers, seamstresses, peddlers, trappers, laborers, blacksmiths, carpenters, servants, slaves, prostitutes, teachers, and healers. Indian people walked the streets of colonial towns and villages, and they even visited European capitals as kidnap victims, delegates, and ambassadors. As a result, Indians appear in colonial writings, and their voices echo down to us across the ages.

Many of their roles and experiences receive only the briefest mention in the historical records, however. Mundane, nonviolent, everyday relationships never attract as much attention as do murder and mayhem. Many things simply went unrecorded because they were so much a part of daily life. Inevitably, when Indians and Europeans got together to talk things over, the discussions centered on the areas of friction between them, even when dressed in the rhetoric of friendship. In the late eighteenth century, Moravian missionary John Heckewelder said that the Delawares and other Indians of his acquaintance "loved" to complain of European ingratitude and injustice and did so at such length, in such detail, and with such eloquence that he often felt ashamed to be a white man. Indian speakers before and since have regularly reviewed their experiences since the arrival of Europeans.[10]

SOURCES OF INDIAN HISTORY: WEIGHING THE EVIDENCE

In reading any record, the historian must ask: Who wrote this? Why? For what audience was it intended? What was it meant to achieve? Can I trust it? Is it contradicted or confirmed by other sources, and are those other sources any more reliable? The need for such scrutiny is even greater in dealing with records about or attributed to American Indians, not because Indian people were any less reliable as a source of information but because so much of what they said survives through the filter of European writings. We need to know how long or how well the writer knew the Indians, whether he (or, in very rare instances, she) was sympathetic or hostile to them, and whether he was a reliable observer and an accurate recorder.

Even when Indian speeches were recorded accurately, we cannot accept them as automatically representing a true Indian voice, no matter how impressive those speeches appear. Did the Indian speaker's words reflect the sentiments of other Indian people who were not present at the meeting? Or was the speech intended primarily for a non-Indian audience, phrased to suit European cultural expectations and perhaps even telling the Europeans what they wanted to hear? Interpreters of Indian speeches complicated the problem. Sometimes, depending on the abilities of the interpreters present, a speech would have to be translated into another Indian language first and then into one or more European languages to produce the final version. Even when interpreters at a meeting were competent, sober, and honest (and there were plenty of instances where interpreters were not), how could they put into English or French many Indian idioms and concepts that did not translate across the cultural divide? To do their job effectively, interpreters not only had to know the words, they also had to appreciate different ways of looking at the world. Cadwallader Colden, governor of New York in the early eighteenth century, acknowledged that the English interpreters often did not do justice to Native American eloquence because Indian speakers employed many metaphors "which interpreted by an hesitating Tongue, may appear mean, and strike our Imagination faintly."[11]

Even in translations that rob them of nuances and fluency, Indian speeches display oratorical power and testify to the richness and importance of the spoken word in Native American cultures. Their metaphors and symbolism offer insights into how the speakers conceived of their universe and their place in it. M. Scott Momaday, a Pulitzer Prize–winning Kiowa author and master of the written word, recently had this to say about the oral culture of his ancestors:

> Language was their element. Words, spoken words, were the manifestations of their deepest belief, of their deepest feelings, of their deepest life. When Europeans first came to America, having had writing for hundreds of years and lately the printing press, they could not conceive of the spoken word as sacred, could not understand the American Indian's profound belief in the efficacy of language.[12]

Until lately, Hollywood movies have created an impression that Indians spoke in monosyllabic utterances, breaking away from "how" and "um" only to deliver stock phrases like "white man speak with forked tongue." In reality, Indian orators spoke well and at length. Englishman John Josselyn, who traveled the coast of Maine in the seventeenth century, described the Indian speakers he heard as "poets" who delivered "formal speeches, sometimes an hour long."[13] Samuel Kirkland, a Presbyterian missionary among the Oneida Indians at the time of the American Revolution, attended a council at which the Oneida chief Good Peter "spoke for an hour like an Apollo & with the energy of a son of Thunder."[14] John Norton, an adopted Mohawk of Scots-Cherokee parentage who traveled extensively among the Indian nations early in the nineteenth century, said the Shawnees were "great talkers," had "natural eloquence," and spoke a language that was strong and melodious.[15]

Indian speakers employed rich images and powerful metaphors in their talks, but they also used humor, irony, sarcasm, anger, body language, and dramatic silences. Public speaking was an important part of Indian life, and oratorical prowess a common, respected, and often necessary skill. Indian leaders did not give orders to their people—many North American Indian languages contain no imperative voice—they enlisted their support through persuasion and influence. Many communities reached decisions by consensus, and effective leaders were those who were able to sway opinions by the power of their words. New York Governor Cadwallader Colden said that the Iroquois were "much given to speech making, ever the natural consequence of a perfect republican government; where no single person has a power to compel[,] the arts of persuasion alone must prevail."[16] Henry Timberlake, a young Virginian officer who accompanied a Cherokee delegation to England in 1762, said that the Cherokees were "fond of speaking well, as that paves the way to power in their councils."[17]

One of the most important arenas for discussions between Indians and

Figure 3.   An Indian Orator Addresses the British, Speaking on a Wampum Belt
In this Benjamin West engraving of the peace talks in 1764 following Pontiac's War, an Indian orator speaks to Colonel Henry Bouquet and other British officers.

Europeans was treaty negotiations about land and trade, war and peace. Indians normally attached far greater significance to the words spoken than to the treaties written as a result of those talks. Indian speakers began negotiations by recapitulating what had been agreed upon at earlier meetings and even what the previous speaker had said, as a way of imprinting the spoken words on the minds and memories of the audience. "I cannot write as you do," a Cherokee headman told the governor of South Carolina in 1751. "My Toungue is my Pen and my Mouth my Paper. When I look upon Writing I am as if I were blind and in the Dark."[18] Indian delegates to councils ritually prepared the way for good talks by smoking the calumet, or peace pipe, and offering words of welcome and condolence. They punctuated their speeches by presenting strings and belts of wampum, the shells or beads that acted as a record of proceedings and without which nothing that was said could be considered binding. Treaty councils frequently lasted for days, sometimes weeks.

Europeans, as members of a culture that valued the written word, attached primary importance to the final treaty document rather than to the discussions that preceded it. In order to have a complete record of negotiations, however, they recorded Indian speeches frequently and at length. Indian speeches, translated by European interpreters and written down by European scribes, became part of the formal record of proceedings. Indian words also come down to us from more casual contacts. Traders, travelers, Indian agents, soldiers, missionaries, and others noted conversations they had with Indian people and sometimes quoted the views that Indians expressed in the course of these conversations.

White men did not always speak with "forked tongues," but they sometimes wrote with "forked pens." Indian speakers sometimes pointed nervously or angrily to the men who sat scribbling down their words in treaty councils, knowing from past experience that written words sometimes took on a life of their own. Mohawk Indians complained to Lieutenant Governor James DeLancey of New York in 1754 that even though they could find no one who had sold the land, "we find we are very poor: we thought we had yet land round about us, but it is said there are writings for it all."[19] Other Iroquois told British Indian superintendent Sir William Johnson in 1769: "We have often seen (and you know it to be true) that the White people by the help of their paper (which we dont understand) claim Lands from us very unjustly and carry them off."[20] Indians who later saw records of treaty proceedings sometimes objected strenuously to the written account of events and the statements attributed to them by the Europeans. Many more written accounts of treaty proceedings went unchecked: The Indians knew what they had said and had little inclination or opportunity to see if the Europeans had got the story straight. In some cases, the deeds and treaty documents that Europeans recorded or concocted were no more than legal instruments to dispossess Indian people of their land. They are not always an accurate record of what was said and done in meetings with Indian people, and even less often do they convey a sense of how Native Americans perceived and understood the proceedings.

Sometimes, reported Indian words owed more to imagination than to memory. Recorded conversations and casual talks between Indians and Europeans may accurately reflect the sentiments expressed in those exchanges, but they rarely constitute a verbatim record of what was said. In these cases, the Indians' words usually were put to paper some time after the conversations. Writers who reconstructed such talks from memory often embellished them by inserting words, phrases, or whole pieces of dialogue. One of the most famous Indian speeches from colonial times was that in which a Mingo chief known as Logan eloquently explained his reasons for going to war against Virginia after frontiersman Michael Cresap murdered his family in 1774. The speech so impressed Thomas Jefferson that he recorded a version of it in his Memorandum Book. Another version appeared in the *Virginia Gazette* in 1775. Jefferson embellished it further in his *Notes on the State of Virginia* in 1782. The final version reads as follows:

> I appeal to any white man to say, if ever he entered Logan's cabin hungry, and he gave him not meat; if ever he came cold and naked, and he clothed him not. During the course of the last long and bloody war, Logan remained idle in his cabin, an advocate for peace. Such was my love for the whites, that my countrymen pointed as they passed, and said, "Logan is the friend of white men." I had even thought to have lived with you, but for the injuries of one man. Col. Cresap, the last spring, in cold blood, and unprovoked, murdered all the relations of Logan, not sparing even my women and children. There runs not a drop of my blood in the veins of any living creature. This called on me for revenge. I have sought it: I have killed many: I have fully glutted my vengeance. For my country, I rejoice at the beams of peace. But do not harbour a thought that mine is the joy of fear. Logan never felt fear. He will not turn on his heel to save his life. Who is there to mourn for Logan?—Not one.[21]

The sentiments convey Logan's tragedy and the breakdown of relations on the Ohio frontier that led to Lord Dunmore's War with the Mingoes and Shawnees in 1774, but the language, style, and obvious biblical parallels suggest that Logan's original words were modified to suit the conventions of non-Indian readers.

In addition, authors commonly employed Indians as a literary convention. Authors would express their views—on society, the church, crime and punishment, contemporary morals—by putting their own words in the mouth of an Indian speaker, who might be real or fictitious. Such speeches often *seem* expressive of Indian views as they contain pointed criticisms of Europeans and their world, but they are accurate only as a record of what a particular European thought Indians *should* think.

Indians who had not learned to write themselves frequently engaged the services of people who could, so that they were able to send letters and what they called "talks." Other Indians, however, did not require the services of translator or scribe. Indian diplomats sometimes spoke to Europeans in the new languages those Europeans had brought to America. Throughout the colonial era, European missionaries and teachers sought out promising Indian youths whom they could educate in their schools, in an effort to instill European skills, European values, and European religion. Indian pupils did not always accept the new teachings, but many did become literate in European languages. Some even learned to read and write in Latin and Greek. Many Indians living in the mission communities or "praying towns" established by Puritan missionaries in seventeenth-century New England could read, and some kept written records of land transfers, births, marriages, deaths, and wills. In the eighteenth century, the Mohegan Indian Samson Occom and other graduates of Eleazar Wheelock's Indian Charity School in Lebanon, Connecticut (which moved to Hanover, New Hampshire, in 1769 and became Dartmouth College), wrote letters, diaries, and even sermons. One student who attended the school was Joseph Brant, a Mohawk Indian who later attained prominence as a war chief during the American Revolution. Brant was able to read and write in both Mohawk and English, and he employed his talent to write letters, petitions, and complaints to colonial governments on behalf of himself and his people. The letters of Occom, Brant, and other literate Indians also give us an opportunity to read words written in private, rather than prepared speeches delivered in public at treaty councils.

Something written, or even published, by an Indian, however, does not necessarily represent a more authentic voice than the words attributed to an Indian by a European writer. The writer may have been Indian, but the reading audience generally was not. The written words might reflect the tastes of the audience rather than the writer's real beliefs and feelings. To our twentieth-century ears, *all* letters written in the seventeenth and eighteenth century can sound stiff and formal, and Indian students at colonial colleges were trained in the conventions of the time. In addition, Indian students often wrote letters with their teachers or missionaries literally or figuratively looking over their shoulders. The letters were often circulated or sent to the college's benefactors to publicize the "progress" of Indian students at the school and to demonstrate the need for continued funding. Native American students and converts who put pen to paper to acknowledge that they had "seen the light" or to confess spiritual or moral "backsliding" may well have done so to impress European readers rather than to inspire or warn fellow Indians.

Indian peoples had their own ways of keeping records, keeping memory alive, and passing on knowledge and wisdom from one generation to the next by oral tradition. They did not use the written word in North America until Europeans introduced them to the power of print. After centuries of contact during which the pen had proven a powerful instrument of conquest and dispossession, Native Americans remained suspicious of the written word and respectful of memory and the spoken word. Four Guns, an Oglala Sioux Indian visiting Washington at the end of the nineteenth century, articulated these feelings: "Whenever white people come together, there is writing. When we go to buy some sugar or tea, we see the white trader busy writing in a book. Even the white doctor, as he sits beside his patient, writes on a piece of paper." The white people, he said, wrote so much that they "must think paper has some mysterious power to help them on in the world." Indians, in contrast, were

> puzzled as to what useful service all this writing serves. . . . The Indian needs no writing. Words that are true sink deep into his heart where they remain. He never forgets them. On the other hand, if the white man loses his paper, he is helpless.[22]

Historians customarily have rejected native oral traditions and stories as "mythology" and have given them little credit as a reliable record of events and experiences. In the last twenty years or so, however, scholars have taken new approaches to broaden our understanding of the Native American past. Ethnohistorians, combining the study of history and anthropology, now try to understand history in the terms of the people who lived through it. They recognize oral traditions as a valuable source, though one that, like the written documents, needs to be used with care: Human memory is fallible, and human beings are prone to remember things differently in the light of experience. This collection includes a few examples of what might be called "mythology" as a way of incorporating Native American traditions and tribal memories of first encounters with Europeans. Unlike the other documents in this collection, these folk traditions often were not written down until several generations after the event they recall. They sometimes reflect a general remembered impression rather than a precise historical occurrence.

Given the tenacity of memory handed down through the years in oral cultures, however, it is likely that they reflect well how Indian people felt about the bearded strangers they met.

In summary, colonial sources are rich in Indian voices. They need to be scrutinized for authenticity and accuracy. Sometimes Indians function as mouthpieces for European words rather than giving full expression to their own thoughts and feelings. Nevertheless, used critically and carefully, these sources offer us an opportunity to look back at early American history and see some occurrences through the words of native people rather than through the rhetoric so often employed by invading Europeans. The Indian voices that have survived from that time, even in muted and distorted form, allow us to question the assumptions of Europeans whose writings for so long monopolized our view of America's early history. They help us to remember that one people's nation building often means another's conquest, that "civilization" is in the eye of the beholder, and that America's colonial and national roots were planted in ground that Indian people had cultivated for thousands of years. Indian voices, however few and however faintly heard across the gulf of time and culture, also offer us something on which to build a fuller appreciation of what life was like in early America. It was a world inhabited not just by European men who had most of the power and did most of the writing, but also by Native Americans, African Americans, women, and children. Only when we include the experiences of all the peoples of early America can we begin to understand our past.

NOTES

[1] George E. Lankford, *Native American Legends* (Little Rock: Harvest House, 1987), 137; reprinted in Barbara Carpenter, ed., *Ethnic Heritage in Mississippi* (Jackson: University Press of Mississippi, 1993), 42.

[2] James H. Merrell, *The Indians' New World: Catawbas and Their Neighbors from European Contact through the Era of Removal* (Chapel Hill: University of North Carolina Press, 1989).

[3] Adriaen Van der Donck, "A Description of the New Netherlands," quoted in Dean R. Snow and Kim M. Lamphear, "European Contact and Indian Depopulation: The Timing of the First Epidemics," *Ethnohistory* 35 (1988): 27.

[4] Henry Whitfield, *The Light appearing more and more towards the perfect Day, or, A farther Discovery of the present state of the Indians in New-England, Concerning the Progresse of the Gospel amongst them* (London, 1651), in *Collections of the Massachusetts Historical Society,* 3rd series, vol. 4 (1834): 112.

[5] Thomas Gage Papers, William L. Clements Library, University of Michigan, Ann Arbor, vol. 137, item 6.

[6] *Archives of Maryland* (Baltimore: Maryland Historical Society, 1884), 2:15.

[7] Barbara Graymont, *The Iroquois in the American Revolution* (Syracuse: Syracuse University Press, 1972), 163.

[8] Carnegie Library, Pittsburgh; George Morgan Letterbook, 2:2.

[9] Kenneth M. Morrison, *The Embattled Northeast* (Berkeley: University of California Press, 1984), 111.

[10] Rev. John Heckewelder, *History, Manners and Customs of the Indian Nations who once inhabited Pennsylvania and the Neighboring States* (Philadelphia: Historical Society of Pennsylvania, 1876), 76.

[11] Cadwallader Colden, *History of the Five Indian Nations,* pt. 1 (London, 1727), xi.

[12] M. Scott Momaday, "The Becoming of the Native: Man in America before Columbus," in Alvin M. Josephy, ed., *America in 1492: The World of the Indian Peoples Before the Arrival of Columbus* (New York: Knopf, 1992), 18.

[13] Paul J. Lindholdt, ed., *Colonial Traveler: A Critical Edition of Two Voyages to New-England by John Josselyn* (Hanover, N.H.: University Press of New England, 1988), 97.

[14] W. Pilkington, ed., *The Journals of Samuel Kirkland* (Clinton, N.Y.: Hamilton College, 1980), 130.

[15] Carl F. Klinck and James J. Talman, eds., *The Journal of Major John Norton, 1816* (Toronto: Champlain Society, 1970), 189.

[16] Colden, *History of the Five Indian Nations,* xx.

[17] Samuel Cole Williams, ed., *Lieutenant Henry Timberlake's Memoirs* (Johnson City, Tenn.: Watauga Press, 1927), 80.

[18] William L. McDowell, ed., *Colonial Records of South Carolina: Documents Relating to Indian Affairs, 1750–1754* (Columbia: South Carolina State Archives, 1958), 180.

[19] Annette Rosentiel, *Red and White: Indian Views of the White Man, 1492–1982* (New York: Universe Books, 1983), 86.

[20] James Sullivan et al., eds. *The Papers of Sir William Johnson,* 14 vols. (Albany: University of the State of New York, 1921–1965), 7:324.

[21] James H. O'Donnell III, "Logan's Oration: A Case Study in Ethnographic Authentication," *Quarterly Journal of Speech* 65 (1979): 150–56.

[22] Quoted in Jerry D. Blanche, ed., *Native American Reader: Stories, Speeches and Poems* (Juneau, Alaska: Denali Press, 1991), 84–85.

1

Voices from the Shore

"We Human Beings are the first, and we are the eldest and the greatest. These parts and countries were inhabited and trod upon by the Human Beings before there were any Axe-Makers [Europeans]."
— Onondaga orator Sadekanaktie,
message to Governor Frontenac, 1694[1]

The things that seldom happen bring astonishment. Think, then, what must be the effect on me and mine, the sight of you and your people, whom we have at no time seen, astride the fierce brutes, your horses, entering with such speed and fury into my country, that we had no tidings of your coming.
— Southeastern Indian chief to Hernando De Soto, 1540[2]

Brothers, these people from the unknown world will cut down our groves, spoil our hunting and planting grounds, and drive us and our children from the graves of our fathers, and our council fires, and enslave our women and children.
— Speech attributed to Metacomet (King Philip) in 1675
by William Apess, a Pequot Indian in 1836[3]

Our history texts tell us much about Europeans' first impressions of America and American Indians. From Christopher Columbus's first meeting with native people in the Caribbean, European travelers penned descriptions of the land and peoples they encountered. But Europeans knew little of what had happened in North America before they arrived, and they often cared even less, dismissing thousands of years of history as a static prelude to European colonization.

Even today, some writers refer to American history before contact with Europeans as *"pre*history." Nevertheless, Europeans did come across pieces of evidence of the world that had existed before their coming. In areas of the Southeast and the Ohio and Mississippi valleys, temple mounds remained as mute testimony to the ancient civilizations that had built them. And, though Indian peoples generally preferred to keep their traditions to themselves, they did occasionally share accounts of tribal history, legends of old times, and memories of how things had been in the days before Europeans changed their world.

Many Indian peoples had, and continue to have, stories of creation and migration that explain how they came to be living in their homelands. Often shrouded in the mists of time, myth, and memory, these legends may strike us as too vague and fanciful to be useful as historical documents, but they convey the peoples' sense of their past and give us a glimpse into the many experiences that shaped American history before Europeans entered the picture.

When Europeans arrived, they tended to judge others according to their own ideas of what constituted "civilization." Consequently, much of what they had to say about Native Americans was couched in negative terms: Their language was unintelligible (they did not speak English or Spanish or French or Dutch); they went naked (did not dress like Europeans); they had no government (Europeans could not understand political systems that often functioned by consensus and kinship); they had no religion (Europeans saw no churches, Bibles, or priests and dismissed Native American beliefs as superstitions); they had no morals (they had *different* standards); they were treacherous (they could not be relied upon to do what Europeans wanted them to do); and their customs were barbarous (different from the customs of Europe and therefore not "civilized").

Judging Native Americans according to their own preconceptions, assuming that their own way of life was superior, and certain that European "civilization" and Christianity must triumph over what they regarded as savagery and paganism, Europeans were ill equipped to value, or to record accurately, the peoples and cultures they encountered in North America. Cultural myopia plagued early relationships and, combined with the Europeans' quest for wealth, land, and converts, ensured that early hospitable relations soon broke down. Many Indian people shared food and knowledge with the first European settlers. Indians and Europeans borrowed and learned from one another and cautiously cooperated, but it was not long before coexistence degenerated into violence.

In some areas of the country, hostilities began almost at first contact. As early as 1524, when Florentine Giovanni da Verrazzano and his crew sailed along the coast of Maine, the Abenaki inhabitants gave evidence of previous unpleasant experiences with Europeans. They wanted to trade for metal goods but refused to let Verrazzano's crew ashore. Finally, in a gesture of contempt that needed no translation, they turned and exposed their buttocks to the Europeans. Ten years later, when Micmacs met Jacques Cartier in the Bay of Chaleur, they held up furs on sticks as an invitation to trade but hid their women in the woods. Hernando De Soto's Spanish invasion of Indian country in the Southeast in the 1540s was particularly brutal and shattered countless Indian lives. Some Indians tried to get rid of the Spaniards by telling them that gold could be found elsewhere; others resorted to ambushes and scorched-earth tactics.

Anglo-Indian relations in Virginia broke down in conflict in 1609; Virginia Indians launched bloody assaults on English colonists in 1622 and again in 1644. Puritan English soldiers slaughtered hundreds of men, women, and children in the Pequot War in 1637; the Dutch fought a vicious war against the Indian tribes of the Hudson River and Long Island in the 1640s. By the late seventeenth century, war between Indians and Europeans was common throughout the country. After King Philip's War (1675–76), the Indian war of resistance against English expansion in New England, Indians and Europeans often expected their relationships to be violent, and so, often, they were.

The selections in Chapter 1 give a sampling of Native American memories of their early history and viewpoints on their early encounters with Europeans. They show how Indian people first met Europeans in dreams and in person. A common thread running through many of their comments is the rapid decline of their world. Native American traditions, whether with foresight or hindsight, often contain predictions of disaster that was sure to follow after Europeans set foot in America.

THE CREATION OF THE WORLD

Many Indian peoples in northeastern North America share a tradition that the world was created on the back of a giant sea turtle. Some people still refer to North America as "turtle island" and revere the turtle. There are many variations of the legend, and the story printed here is just one of several versions among the Iroquois Indians of New York State. Anthropologists in the late nineteenth and early twentieth centuries recorded various accounts of the Iroquois creation story, and those are the ones most commonly related. This account, however, is one of the earliest to be written down, recorded by John Norton around 1816.

John Norton was the son of Scottish and Cherokee parents and an adopted Mohawk. He played a prominent role in his people's affairs in the early nineteenth century, traveled widely among the Indian nations of the eastern woodlands, and also visited England. He had a special interest in the mythology of the Iroquois, and he gave a condensed version of the story told here to an audience at Trinity College, Cambridge, in 1805.

JOHN NORTON

Iroquois Creation Story

ca. 1816

The tradition of the Nottowegui or Five Nations says, "that in the beginning before the formation of the earth; the country above the sky was inhabited by Superior Beings, over whom the Great Spirit presided. His daughter having become pregnant by an illicit connection, he pulled up a great tree by the roots, and threw her through the cavity thereby formed; but, to prevent her utter destruction, he previously ordered the Great Turtle, to get from the bottom of the waters, some slime on its back, and to wait on the surface of the water to receive her on it. When she had fallen on the back of the Turtle, with the mud she found there, she began to form the earth, and by the time of her delivery had encreased it to the extent of a little island. Her child was a daughter, and as she grew up the earth extended under their hands. When the young woman had arrived at the age of discretion, the Spirits who roved about, in human forms, made proposals of marriage for the young woman: the mother always rejected their offers, until a middle aged man, of a dignified appearance, his bow in his hand, and his quiver on his back, paid his addresses. On being accepted, he entered the house, and seated himself on the birth of his intended spouse; the mother was in a birth on the other side of the fire. She observed that her son-in-law did not lie down all night; but taking two arrows out of his quiver, he put them by the side of his bride: at the dawn of day he took them up, and having replaced them in his quiver, he went out.

"After some time, the old woman perceived her daughter to be pregnant, but could not discover where the father had gone, or who he was. At the time of delivery, the twins disputed which way they should go out of the womb; the wicked one said, let us go out of the side; but the other said, not so, lest we kill our mother; then the wicked one pretending to acquiesce, desired his brother to go out first: but as soon as he was delivered, the wicked one, in attempting to go out at her side, caused the death of his mother.

"The twin brothers were nurtured and raised by their Grandmother; the eldest was named Teharonghyawago, or the Holder of Heaven; the youngest was called Tawiskaron, or Flinty rock, from his body being entirely covered

Carl F. Klinck and James J. Talman, eds., *The Journal of Major John Norton, 1816* (Toronto: Champlain Society, 1970), 88–91.

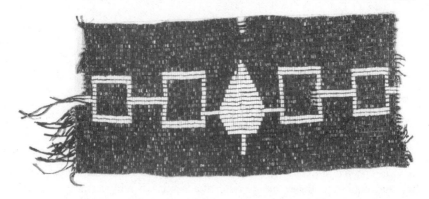

Figure 4.   The Hiawatha Wampum Belt (depicting the Haudenosaunee (the people of the Longhouse), with the central council at Onondaga in the center)
The wampum belt symbolizes the unity provided to the five nations by the Great Tree of Peace, the metaphor for the Haudenosaunee. The Haudenosaunee (sometimes called the Iroquois Confederacy by the French and the League of the Five Nations or the League of the Six Nations by the British) exerted formidable military and political power in eastern North America and was held in high regard by Indian and European nations alike. No one is sure exactly when the Haudenosaunee League was formed, but Haudenosaunee people assert and scholars agree that it predated the arrival of Europeans. There are many versions of the league's formation but the basic story line is consistent: In a time of troubles in which Iroquois people of different tribes were fighting and killing each other, an Onondaga named Hiawatha joined forces with a Huron the people referred to as the Peace Maker to bring an end to the fighting and create a great league of peace. The Onondaga orator Canasatego at the Treaty of Lancaster in 1744 said simply: "Our wise Forefathers established Union and Amity between the *Five Nations*" (see page 104).
     Eventually, five nations agreed to join the league. From east to west they were the Mohawks (the keepers of the eastern door of the confederacy), the Oneidas, the Onondagas (the keepers of the central council fire), the Cayugas, and the Senecas (the keepers of the western door). In 1722, Tuscarora Indians, driven north from the Carolinas by war with the English, took refuge in Haudenosaunee country and were admitted as the sixth nation. The member tribes, which still meet regularly, retain control of their own affairs, but policies concerning the league as a whole are decided by a grand council of fifty chiefs that meet at Onondaga, near Syracuse, New York.

with such a substance. They grew up, and with their bows and arrows, amused themselves throughout the island, which increased in extent, and they were favoured with various animals of Chace. Tawiskaron was the most fortunate hunter, and enjoyed the favour of his Grandmother. Teharonghyawago was not so successful in the Chace, and suffered from their unkindness. When he was a youth, and roaming alone, in melancholy mood, through the island, a human figure, of noble aspect, appearing to him, addressed him thus. 'My son, I have seen your distress, and heard your solitary lamentations; you are unhappy in the loss of a mother, in the unkindness of your Grandmother and brother. I now come to comfort you, I am your father, and will be your Protector; therefore take courage, and suffer not your spirit to sink. Take this (giving him an ear of *maize*) plant it, and attend it in the manner, I shall direct; it will yield you a certain support, independent of the Chace, at the same time that it will render more palatable the viands, which you may thereby obtain. I am the Great Turtle which supports the earth, on which you move. Your brother's ill treatment will increase with his years; bear it with patience till the time appointed, before which you shall hear further.'

"After saying this, and directing him how to plant the corn, he disappeared. Teharonghyawago planted the corn, and returned home. When its verdant sprouts began to flourish above the ground, he spent his time in clearing from it all growth of grass and weeds, which might smother it or retard its advancement while yet in its tender state, before it had acquired sufficient grandeur to shade the ground. He now discovered that his wicked brother caught the timid deer, the stately elk with branching horns, and all the harmless inhabitants of the Forest; and imprisoned them in an extensive cave, for his own particular use, depriving mortals from having the benefit of them that was originally intended by the Great Spirit. Teharonghyawago discovered the direction his brother took in conducting these animals captive to the Cave; but never could trace him quite to the spot, as he eluded his sight with more than common dexterity!

"Teharonghyawago endeavoured to conceal himself on the path that led to the cave, so that he might follow him imperceptibly; but he found it impossible to hide himself from the penetrating Tawiskaron. At length he observed, that altho' his brother saw, with extraordinary acuteness, every surrounding object, yet he never raised his eyes to look above: Teharonghyawago then climbed a lofty tree, which grew near to where he thought the place of confinement was situated: in the meantime, his brother passed, searching with his eyes the thickest recesses of the Forest, but never casting a glance above. He then saw his brother take a straight course, and when he was out of sight, Teharonghyawago descended, and came to the Cave, a short time after he had deposited his charge; and finding there an innumerable number of animals confined, he set them free, and returned home.

"It was not long before Tawiskaron, visiting the Cave, discovered that all his captives, which he had taken so much pains to deprive of their liberty, had been liberated: he knew this to be an act of his brother, but dissembling his anger, he mediated revenge, at some future period.

"Teharonghyawago laboured to people the earth with inhabitants, and to found Villages in happy situations, extending the comforts of men. Tawiskaron was equally active in destroying the works his brother had done; and in accumulating every evil in his power on the heads of ill fated mortals. Teharonghyawago saw, with regret, his brother persevere in every wickedness; but waited with patience the result of what his father had told him.

"At one time, being in conversation with his brother, Tawiskaron said 'Brother, what do you think there is on earth, with which you might be killed?' Teharonghyawago replied, 'I know of nothing that could affect my life, unless it be the foam of the billows of the Lake or the downy topped* reed.' 'What do you think would take your life?' Tawiskaron answered, 'Nothing except horn or flint.' Here their discourse ended.

"Teharonghyawago returning from hunting, heard a voice singing a plaintive air: he listened and heard it name his Mother, who was killed by Tawiskaron; he immediately hastened towards the spot from whence the voice proceeded, crying, 'Who is that, who dares to name my deceased mother in my hearing?' When he came there, he saw the track of a fawn, which he pursued, without overtaking it, till the autumn, when it dropped its first horns; these he took up, and fixed upon the forked branches of a tree.

"He continued the pursuit seven years; and every autumn, when its horns fell, he picked them up, and placed them as he had done the first. At last, he overtook the deer, now grown to be a stately buck: it begged its life, and said, 'Spare me, and I will give you information that may be great service to you.' When he had promised it its life, it spoke as follows, 'It was to give you the necessary information that I have been subjected to your pursuit, and that which I shall now tell you was the intended reward of your perseverance and clemency. Your brother, in coming into the world, caused the death of your Mother; if he was then wicked in his infancy, his malice has grown with his stature; he now premeditates evil against you; be therefore on your guard: as soon as he assaults you, exert yourself, and you will overcome him.'

"He returned home; and not long after this adventure, was attacked by his brother. They fought; the one made use of the horn and flint stone which he had provided: the other sought for froth and the reed, which made little impression on the body of Teharonghyawago. They fought a long time, over the whole of the island, until at last Tawiskaron fell under the conquering hand of his brother. According to the varied tones of their voices in the different places through which they passed during the contest, the people, who afterwards sprung up there, spoke different languages."

*It is called Fox-tail, in America; from the resemblance it bears to it. It is a reed or strong grass that grows in wild, low meadows, — the top containing a down, almost like cotton.

Figure 5. The Iroquois Homeland
After the formation of their league, the Five Nations of the Iroquois or Haudeno-saunee were a dominant power in what is now the northeastern United States. At various times they fought, traded, and negotiated with the French in Canada, the Dutch on the Hudson River, the various English colonies, the United States, and other Indian peoples throughout the eastern woodlands.

THE CREEKS COME TO THEIR HOMELAND

Many Indian peoples throughout North America have ancient traditions explaining how they came to be living in their homelands. In 1735, Chekilli, a Creek head chief, delivered a talk in Savannah in which he described the emergence, migration, and union of various tribes who joined to form the Creek Confederacy. The text of his talk, recorded on a buffalo skin, was apparently sent to the Georgia Trustees in London. In the nineteenth century a legend grew up that the talk was from the Cherokees and that it was sent in the form of a pictograph. In reality, it was a Creek talk and was probably written down in English. Parchment made of animal hide was common in those days. The text of the speech was first printed in Germany in 1739.[4]

CHEKILLI

Origin of the Creek Confederacy

1735

What Chekilli, the head-chief of the upper and lower Creeks said, in a talk held at Savannah, Anno 1735, and which was handed over by the interpreter, written upon a buffalo-skin was, word for word, as follows:

At a certain time the Earth opened in the West, where its mouth is. The Earth opened and the Kasihtas came out of its mouth, and settled nearby. But the Earth became angry and ate up their children; therefore they moved farther West. A part of them, however, turned back, and came again to the same place where they had been, and settled there. The greater number remained behind, because they thought it best to do so. Their children, nevertheless, were eaten by the Earth, so that, full of dissatisfaction, they journeyed toward the sunrise.

They came to a thick, muddy, slimy river—came there, camped there, rested there, and stayed overnight there. The next day they continued their journey and came, in one day, to a red, bloody river. They lived by this river, and ate of its fishes for two years; but there were low springs there; and it did not please them to remain. They went toward the end of this bloody river, and heard a noise as of thunder. They approached to see whence the noise came. At first they perceived a red smoke, and then a mountain which thundered; and on the mountain was a sound as of singing. They sent to see what this was; and it was a great fire which blazed upward, and made this singing noise. This mountain they named the King of Mountains. It thunders to this day; and men are very much afraid of it.

They here met a people of three different Nations. They had taken and

Albert S. Gatschet, *A Migration Legend of the Creek Indians* (Philadelphia: D. G. Brinton, 1884), 1:244–51.

saved some of the fire from the mountain; and, at this place, they also obtained a knowledge of herbs and of other things.

From the East, a white fire came to them; which, however, they would not use. From the South came a fire which was [blue?]; neither did they use it. From the West, came a fire which was black; nor would they use it. At last, came a fire from the North, which was red and yellow. This they mingled with the fire they had taken from the mountain; and this is the fire they use today; and this, too, sometimes sings. On the mountain was a pole which was very restless and made a noise, nor could any one say how it could be quieted. At length they took a motherless child, and struck it against the pole; and thus killed the child. They then took the pole, and carry it with them when they go to war. It was like a wooden tomahawk, such as they now use, and of the same wood.

Here they also found four herbs or roots, which sang and disclosed their virtues: first, Pasaw, the rattlesnake root; second Micoweanochaw, red-root; third Sowatchko, which grows like wild fennel; and fourth, Eschalapootchke, little tobacco. These herbs, especially the first and third, they use as the best medicine to purify themselves at their Busk.[5] At this Busk, which is held yearly, they fast, and make offerings of the first fruits. Since they have learned the virtues of these herbs, their women, at certain times, have a separate fire, and remain apart from the men five, six, and seven days, for the sake of purification. If they neglected this, the power of the herbs would depart; and the women would not be healthy.[6]

About this time a dispute arose, as to which was the oldest, and which should rule; and they agreed, as they were four Nations, they would set up four poles, and make them red with clay which is yellow at first, but becomes red by burning. They would go to war; and whichever Nation should first cover its pole, from top to bottom, with the scalps of their enemies, should be oldest.

They all tried, but the Kasihtas covered their pole first, and so thickly that it was hidden from sight. Therefore, they were looked upon, by the whole Nation, as the oldest. The Chickasaws covered their pole next; then the Alabamas; but the Abihkas did not cover their pole higher than to the knee.[7]

At that time there was a bird of large size, blue in color, with a long tail, and swifter than an eagle, which came every day and killed and ate their people. They made an image in the shape of a woman, and placed it in the way of this bird. The bird carried it off, and kept it a long time, and then brought it back. They left it alone, hoping it would bring something forth. After a long time, a red rat came forth from it, and they believed the bird was the father of the rat. They took council with the rat how to destroy its father. Now the bird had a bow and arrows; and the rat gnawed the bowstring, so that the bird could not defend itself, and the people killed it. They called this bird the King of Birds. They think the eagle is a great King; and they carry its feathers when they go to War or make Peace; the red mean War; the white, Peace. If an enemy approaches with white feathers and a white mouth, and cries like an eagle, they dare not kill him.

After this they left that place, and came to a white footpath. The grass and everything around were white; and they plainly perceived that people had been there. They crossed the path, and slept near there. Afterward they turned back to see what sort of path that was, and who the people were who had been there, in the belief that it might be better for them to follow that path. They went along it to a creek called Coloose-hutche, that is, Coloose-creek, because it was rocky there and smoked.[8]

They crossed it, going toward the sunrise, and came to a people and a town named Coosa.[9] Here they remained four years. The Coosas complained that they were preyed upon by a wild beast, which they called man-eater or lion, which lived in a rock.

The Kasihtas said they would try to kill the beast. They dug a pit and stretched over it a net made of hickory-bark. They then laid a number of branches, crosswise, so that the lion could not follow them, and, going to the place where he lay, they threw a rattle into his den. The lion rushed forth in great anger, and pursued them through the branches. Then they thought it better that one should die rather than all; so they took a motherless child, and threw it before the lion as he came near the pit. The lion rushed at it, and fell in the pit, over which they threw the net, and killed him with blazing pine-wood. His bones, however, they keep to this day; on one side, they are red, on the other blue.

The lion used to come every seventh day to kill the people; therefore, they remained there seven days after they had killed him. In remembrance of him, when they prepare for War, they fast six days and start on the seventh. If they take his bones with them, they have good fortune.

After four years they left the Coosas, and came to a river which they called Nowphawpe, now Callasi-hutche. There they tarried two years; and, as they had no corn, they lived on roots and fishes, and made bows, pointing the arrows with beaver teeth and flint-stones, and for knives they used split canes.

They left this place, and came to a creek, called Wattoola-hawka-hutche, Whooping-creek, so called from the whooping of cranes, a great many being there; they slept there one night. They next came to a river, in which there was a waterfall; this they named the Owatunka-river. The next day they reached another river, which they called the Aphoosa pheeskaw.

The following day they crossed it, and came to a high mountain, where were people who, they believed, were the same who made the white path. They, therefore, made white arrows and shot at them, to see if they were good people. But the people took their white arrows, painted them red, and shot them back. When they showed these to their chief, he said that it was not a good sign; if the arrows returned had been white, they could have gone there and brought food for their children, but as they were red they must not go. Nevertheless, some of them went to see what sort of people they were; and found their houses deserted. They also saw a trail which led into the river; and, as they could not see the trail on the opposite bank, they believed that the people had gone into the river, and would not again come forth.

At that place is a mountain, called Moterelo, which makes a noise like beating on a drum; and they think this people live there. They hear this noise on all sides when they go to war.

They went along the river, till they came to a waterfall, where they saw great rocks, and on the rocks were bows lying; and they believed the people who made the white path had been there.

They always have, on their journeys, two scouts who go before the main body. These scouts ascended a high mountain and saw a town. They shot white arrows into the town; but the people of the town shot back red arrows. Then the Kasihtas became angry, and determined to attack the town, and each one have a house when it was captured.

They threw stones into the river until they could cross it, and took the town (the people had flattened heads)[10] and killed all but two persons. In pursuing these they found a white dog, which they slew. They followed the two who escaped, until they came again to the white path, and saw the smoke of a town, and thought that this must be the people they had so long been seeking. This is the place where now the tribe of Apalachicolas live, from whom Tomochichi is descended.[11]

The Kasihtas continued bloody-minded; but the Apalachicolas gave them black drink, as a sign of friendship,[12] and said to them: "Our hearts are white, and yours must be white, and you must lay down the bloody tomahawk, and show your bodies as a proof that they shall be white." Nevertheless, they were for the tomahawk; but the Apalachicolas got it by persuasion, and buried it under their beds. The Apalachicolas likewise gave them white feathers, and asked to have a chief in common. Since then they have always lived together.

Some settled on one side of the river, some on the other. Those on one side are called Kasihtas, those on the other, Cowetas; yet they are one people, and the principal towns of the Upper and Lower Creeks. Nevertheless, as the Kasihtas first saw the red smoke and the red fire, and make bloody towns, they cannot yet leave their red hearts, which, though white on one side, are

Figure 6.   Governor James Oglethorpe of Georgia Presenting Tomochichi and Other Creek Indians to the Lords Trustees of the Colony of Georgia

In 1734, Governor James Oglethorpe of Georgia traveled to England with a party of Creek Indians, led by Tomochichi from the Yamacraw village near Savannah. Tomochichi had established trading relations with Oglethorpe and expressed an interest in receiving Christian teachers. Tomochichi's wife, Senaukey, and his nephew and successor, Toonahowi, accompanied him. The Indians met King George II, the Archbishop of Canterbury, and, as shown in this painting by William Verelst, the Lords Trustees of the Colony of Georgia. Tomochichi died five years after returning from England; Toonahowi was killed fighting the Spaniards in 1753.

red on the other. They now know that the white path was the best for them: for, although Tomochichi was a stranger, they see he has done them good; because he went to see the great King with Esquire Oglethorpe, and hear his talk, and had related it to them, and they had listened to it, and believed it. [See Figure 6.]

A DREAM OF STRANGERS

Native American oral traditions frequently recall the astonishment people felt when they first saw European sailing ships. In 1633 a Montagnais Indian in eastern Canada related to French Jesuit priests a story his grandmother had told him of his ancestors' reaction at seeing a French ship for the first time. The Montagnais thought it was a floating island; and, when the French offered them ship's biscuits and wine, they threw the biscuits overboard, thinking "the Frenchmen drank blood and ate wood."[13]

In this account, the coming of strange new people is foreseen in a traditional way, revealed in a dream to a young Micmac woman. Dreams played a crucial role in the lives of many Indian peoples, putting them in touch with the spirit world and allowing them glimpses of the future. Dreams provided guidance in their lives in the same way that the Bible offered direction to many Christians.

This account was related in 1869 by a Micmac named Josiah Jeremy. The Micmac Indians lived in the area of present-day Nova Scotia, Prince Edward Island, Cape Breton, and northern Maine. Living along the Gulf of St. Lawrence and the Atlantic Ocean, they were among the first of the original inhabitants of North America to encounter seagoing Europeans, and they traded with the French explorer Jacques Cartier in 1534.

JOSIAH JEREMY

The Floating Island

1869

When there were no people in this country but Indians, and before any others were known, a young woman had a singular dream. She dreamed that a small island came floating in towards the land, with tall trees on it, and living beings,—among whom was a man dressed in rabbit-skin garments. The next day she related her dream, and sought for an interpretation. It was the custom in those days, when any one had a remarkable dream, to consult the wise men, and especially the magicians and soothsayers. These pondered over the girl's dream, but could make nothing of it. The next day an event

Silas Rand, *Legends of the Micmacs* (New York: Longmans, Green, 1894).

occurred that explained all. Getting up in the morning, what should they see but a singular little island, as they supposed, which had drifted near to the land and become stationary there! There were trees on it, and branches to the trees, on which a number of bears, as they supposed, were crawling about. They all seized their bows, arrows, and spears, and rushed down to the shore, intending to shoot the bears; what was their surprise to find that these supposed bears were men, and that some of them were lowering down into the water a very singularly constructed canoe, into which several of them jumped and paddled ashore. Among them was a man dressed in white,—a priest with his white stole on,—who came towards them making signs of friendship, raising his hand towards heaven, and addressing them in an earnest manner, but in a language which they could not understand.

The girl was now questioned respecting her dream. Was it such an island as this that she had seen. Was this the man? She affirmed that they were indeed the same. Some of them, especially the necromancers, were displeased, they did not like it that the coming of these foreigners should have been intimated to this young girl, and not to them. Had an enemy of the Indian tribes with whom they were at war been about to make a descent upon them, they could have foreseen and foretold it by the power of their magic; but of the coming of this teacher of a new religion they could know nothing.

The new teacher was gradually received into favor, though the magicians opposed him. The people received his instructions, and submitted to the rites of baptism; the priest learned their tongue, and gave them the Prayer Book written in what they call *abootŭloeëgăsĭk'* (ornamental mark-writing); a mark standing for a word, and rendering it so difficult to learn that it may be said to be impossible.

MEETING THE DUTCH AT MANHATTAN

The Reverend John Heckewelder, a Moravian missionary who worked among Indian people in the Ohio Valley, recorded the following account of the first encounter between Indians and the Dutch at what is today Manhattan Island. Heckewelder took down the story "verbatim as it was related to me by aged and respected" Delawares and Mahicans in the 1760s. The Delawares, Mahicans, and their neighbors had been living in the coastal region of New Jersey and the Hudson River when the Dutch first arrived in 1609, but they were driven steadily westward by the pressure of European settlement.

JOHN HECKEWELDER

The Arrival of the Dutch

ca. 1765

A long time ago, when there was no such thing known to the Indians as people with a *white skin,* (their expression,) some Indians who had been out a-fishing, and where the sea widens, espied at a great distance something remarkably large swimming, or floating on the water, and such as they had never seen before. They immediately returning to the shore apprised their countrymen of what they had seen, and pressed them to go out with them and discover what it might be. These together hurried out, and saw to their great surprise the phenomenon, but could not agree what it might be; some concluding it either to be an uncommon large fish, or other animai, while others were of opinion it must be some very large house. It was at length agreed among those who were spectators, that as this phenomenon moved towards the land, whether or not it was an animal, or anything that had life in it, it would be well to inform all the Indians on the inhabited islands of what they had seen, and put them on their guard. Accordingly, they sent runners and watermen off to carry the news to their scattered chiefs, that these might send off in every direction for the warriors to come in. These arriving in numbers, and themselves viewing the strange appearance, and that it was actually moving towards them, (the entrance of the river or bay,) concluded it to be a large canoe or house, in which the great Mannitto (great or Supreme Being) *himself* was, and that he probably was coming to visit them. By this time the chiefs of the different tribes were assembled on York Island, and were counselling (or deliberating) on the manner they should receive their Mannitto on his arrival. Every step had been taken to be well provided with a plenty of meat for a sacrifice; the women were required to prepare the best of victuals; idols or images were examined and put in order; and a grand dance was supposed not only to be an agreeable entertainment for the Mannitto, but might, with the addition of a sacrifice, contribute towards appeasing him, in case he was angry with them. The conjurors were also set to work, to determine what the meaning of this phenomenon was, and what the result would be. Both to these, and to the chiefs and wise men of the nation, men, women, and children were looking up for advice and

New-York Historical Society Collections, 2nd ser., 1:71–74.

35

protection. Between hope and fear, and in confusion, a dance commenced.
While in this situation fresh runners arrive declaring it a house of various
colours, and crowded with living creatures. It now appears to be certain that
it is the great Mannitto bringing them some kind of game, such as they had
not before; but other runners soon after arriving, declare it a large house of
various colours, full of people, yet of quite a different colour than they (the
Indians) are of; that they were also dressed in a different manner frcm them,
and that one in particular appeared altogether red, which must be the
Mannitto himself. They are soon hailed from the vessel, though in a language they do not understand; yet they shout (or yell) in their way. Many
are for running off to the woods, but are pressed by others to stay, in order
not to give offence to their visiters, who could find them out, and might
destroy them. The house (or large canoe, as some will have it,) stops, and a
smaller canoe comes ashore with the red man and some others in it; some
stay by this canoe to guard it. The chiefs and wise men (or councillors) had
composed a large circle, unto which the red-clothed man with two others
approach. He salutes them with friendly countenance, and they return the
salute after their manner. They are lost in admiration, both as to the colour
of the skin (or these whites) as also to their manner of dress, yet most as to
the habit of him who wore the red clothes, which shone with something they
could not account for. He *must* be the great Mannitto (Supreme Being,) they
think, but why should he have a *white skin?* A large hockhack [Their word
for gourd, bottle, decanter] is brought forward by one of the (supposed)
Mannitto's servants, and from this a substance is poured out into a small cup
(or glass) and handed to the Mannitto. The (expected) Mannitto drinks; has
the glass filled again, and hands it to the chief next to him to drink. The chief
receives the glass, but only smelleth at it, and passes it on to the next chief,
who does the same. The glass thus passes through the circle without the
contents being tasted by any one; and is upon the point of being returned
again to the red-clothed man, when one of their number, a spirited man and
great warrior jumps up—harangues the assembly on the impropriety of
returning the glass with the contents in it; that the same was handed them
by the Mannitto in order that they should drink it, as he himself had done
before them; that this would please him; but to return what he had given to
them might provoke him, and be the cause of their being destroyed by him.
And that, since he believed it for the good of the nation that the contents
offered them *should* be drank, and as no one was willing to drink it *he would,*
let the consequence be what it would; and that it was better for one man to
die, than a whole nation to be destroyed. He then took the glass and bidding
the assembly a farewell, *drank it off.* Every eye was fixed on their resolute
companion to see what an effect this would have upon him, and he soon

beginning to stagger about, and at last dropping to the ground, they bemoan him. He falls into a sleep, and they view him as expiring. He awakes again, jumps up, and declares that he never felt himself before so happy as after he had drank the cup. Wishes for more. His wish is granted; and the whole assembly soon join him, and become intoxicated. [The Delawares call this place (New-York Island) *Mannahattanink* or *Mannahachtanink* to this day. They have frequently told me that it derived its name from this general *intoxication,* and that the word comprehended the same as to say, *the island or place of general intoxication.* The Mahicanni, (otherwise called Mohiggans by the English, and Mahicanders by the Low Dutch,) call this place by the same name as the Delawares do; yet think it is owing or given in consequence of a kind of wood which grew there, and of which the Indians used to make their bows and arrows. This wood the latter (Mohiccani) call *"gawaak."* The universal name the Monseys have for New-York, is *Laaphawachking,* which is interpreted, *the place of stringing beads (wampum).* They say this name was given in consequence of beads being here distributed among them by the Europeans; and that after the European vessel had returned, wherever one looked, one would see the Indians employed in stringing the beads or wampum the whites had given them.]

After this general intoxication had ceased, (during which time the whites had confined themselves to their vessel,) the man with the red clothes returned again to them, and distributed presents among them, to wit, beads, axes, hoes, stockings, &c. They say that they had become familiar to each other, and were made to understand by signs; that they now would return home, but would visit them next year again, when they would bring them more presents, and stay with them awhile; but that, as they could not live without eating, they should then want a little land of them to sow some seeds in order to raise herbs to put in their broth. That the vessel arrived the season following, and they were much rejoiced at seeing each other; but that the whites laughed at them (the Indians,) seeing they knew not the use of the axes, hoes, &c., they had given them, they having had these hanging to their breasts as ornaments; and the stockings they had made use of as tobacco pouches. The whites now put handles (or helves) in the former, and cut trees down before their eyes, and dug the ground, and showed them the use of the stockings. Here (say they) a general laughter ensued among them (the Indians), that they had remained for so long a time ignorant of the use of so valuable implements; and had borne with the weight of such heavy metal hanging to their necks for such a length of time. They took every white man they saw for a Mannitto, yet inferior and attendant to the *supreme Mannitto,* to wit, to the one which wore the red and laced clothes. Familiarity daily increasing between them and the whites, the latter now proposed to stay with them, asking them only for so much land as the hide of a bullock would cover (or encompass,) which hide was brought forward and spread on the ground before them. That they readily granted this request; whereupon the whites took a knife, and beginning at one place on this hide, cut it up into a rope not thicker than the finger of a little child, so that by the time this hide was cut up there was a great heap. That this rope was drawn out to a great distance, and then brought round again, so that both ends might mcet. That they carefully avoided its breaking, and that upon the whole it encompassed a large piece of ground. That they (the Indians) were surprised at the superior wit of the whites, but did not wish to contend with them about a little land, as they had enough. That they and the whites lived for a long time contentedly together, although these asked from time to time more land of them; and proceeding higher up the Mahicanittuk (Hudson river), they believed they would soon want all their country, and which at this time was already the case.

"WHAT CAN YOU GET BY WARRE . . . ?"

The English settlers at Jamestown, Virginia, were ill prepared for life in what to them was a new world and a strange land. Half of the colonists died during the first winter of 1607. The survivors depended heavily on the Powhatan Indians of the coastal plain to feed and assist them. The Indians exchanged corn for merchandise, but aggressive English behavior alienated them. Moreover, many Indians believed that the English "were a people come from under the world to take their world from them." One chief told Captain John Smith, "We perceive and well know that you intend to destroy us, that are here to intreat and desire your friendship."[14] Knowing the English could not survive without the Indians' corn harvest, he threatened to abandon the country and leave them to starve if they chose to wage war. Growing tensions between the English and Indians broke down in hostilities in 1609.

In "The Proceedings of the English Colonie in Virginia," which he published first in 1612, John Smith recounted an exchange with the Indian leader Powhatan. Powhatan had heard rumors from Indians at Nansemond on the lower James River that a nation would arise from Chesapeake Bay to destroy his empire, and Smith's policy of instilling respect by the threat of force did nothing to calm his fears. Powhatan's opening comments may indicate that he was so old he had outlived most of his people or, more likely, that the Powhatans already had suffered three epidemics, of which no record survives.

POWHATAN

Speech to Captain John Smith

1609

Captaine Smith, you may understand that I having seene the death of all my people thrice, and not any one living of these three generations but my selfe; I know the difference of Peace and Warre better than any in my Country. But now I am old and ere long must die, my brethren, namely Opitchapam, Opechancanough, and Kekataugh,[15] my two sisters, and their two daughters, are distinctly each others successors. I wish their experience no lesse then mine, and your love to them no lesse then mine to you. But this bruit from Nandsamund, that you are come to destroy my Country, so much affrighteth all my people as they dare not visit you. What will it availe you to take that by force you may quickly have by love, or to destroy them that provide you food. What can you get by warre, when we can hide our provisions and fly to the woods? whereby you must famish by wronging us your friends. And why are you thus jealous of our loves seeing us unarmed, and both doe, and are willing still to feede you, with that you cannot get but by our labours? Thinke you I am so simple, not to know it is better to eate good meate, lye well, and sleepe quietly with my women and children, laugh and be merry with you, have copper, hatchets, or what I want being your friend: then be forced to flie from all, to lie cold in the woods, feede upon Acornes, rootes, and such trash, and be so hunted by you, that I can neither rest, eate, nor sleepe; but my tyred men must watch, and if a twig but breake, every one cryeth there commeth Captaine Smith: then must I fly I know not whether: and thus with miserable feare, end my miserable life, leaving my pleasures to such youths as you, which through your rash unadvisednesse may quickly as miserably end, for want of that, you never know where to finde. Let this therefore assure you of our loves, and every yeare our friendly trade shall furnish you with Corne; and now also, if you would come in friendly manner to see us, and not thus with your guns and swords as to invade your foes.

Philip L. Barbour, ed., *The Complete Works of Captain John Smith* (Chapel Hill: University of North Carolina Press, 1986), 1:247.

"THE COMING OF A STRANGE RACE"

In 1854, a Mahican Indian named Josiah Quinney gave a speech at a July 4 celebration in New York State. The Mahicans originally lived on the Hudson River, but in the 1730s many of them took up residence with neighboring tribes at the mission village of Stockbridge in Massachusetts. The Stockbridge Indians fought for the British in the French and Indian War and for the Americans during the Revolution, but that did not prevent them from being edged off their lands. They moved to New York after the Revolution and then on to Wisconsin early in the nineteenth century. Quinney told of the origins and early migrations of his people and then related this tradition of the coming of Europeans and added his own comments on almost 250 years of history.

JOSIAH QUINNEY

July 4 Speech

1854

The tribe, to which your speaker belongs, and of which there were many bands, occupied and possessed the country from the sea-shore, at Manhattan, to Lake Champlain. Having found an ebb and flow of the tide, they said: "This is Muh-he-con-new,"—"like our waters, which are never still." From this expression, and by this name, they were afterwards known, until their removal to Stockbridge, in the year 1730. Housatonic River Indians, Mohegan, Manhattas, were all names of bands in different localities, but bound together, as one family, by blood, marriage and descent.

At a remote period, before the advent of the Europeans, their wise men foretold the coming of a strange race, from the sunrise, as numerous as the leaves upon the trees, who would eventually crowd them from their fair possessions. But apprehension was mitigated by the knowledge and belief, at that time entertained, that their original home was not there, and after a period of years, they would return to the West, from whence they had come; and, moreover, said they, "all the red men are sprung from a common ancestor, made by the Great Spirit from red clay, who will unite their strength to avert a common calamity." This tradition is confirmed by the common belief, which prevails in our day with all the Indian tribes; for they recognize one another by their color, as brothers, and acknowledge one Great Creator.

Two hundred and fifty winters ago, this prophecy was verified, and the Muh-he-con-new, for the first time, beheld the "pale-face." Their number was small, but their canoes were big. In the select and exclusive circles of your rich men, of the present day, I should encounter the gaze of curiosity, but not such as overwhelmed the senses of the Aborigines, my ancestors. "Our visitors were white, and must be sick. They asked for rest and kindness, we gave them both. They were strangers, and we took them in—naked, and we clothed them." The first impression of astonishment and pity, was succeeded by awe and admiration of superior art, intelligence and address. A passion for information and improvement possessed the Indian—a residence was freely offered—territory given—and covenants of friendship exchanged.

Your written accounts of events at this period are familiar to you, my friends. Your children read them every day in their school books; but they do not read—no mind at this time can conceive, and no pen record, the terrible story of recompense for kindness, which for two hundred years has been paid the simple, trusting, guileless Muh-he-con-new. I have seen much myself—have been connected with more, and, I tell you, I know all. The tradition of the wise men is figuratively true, "that our home, at last, will be found in the West;" for, another tradition informs us, that "far beyond the setting sun, upon the smiling, happy lands, we shall be gathered with our Fathers, and be at rest."

NOTES

[1] Daniel K. Richter, *The Ordeal of the Longhouse: The Peoples of the Iroquois League in the Era of European Colonization* (Chapel Hill: University of North Carolina Press, 1992), 184.

[2] Edward G. Bourne, ed., *Narrative of De Soto* (New York: Allerton Book Co., 1904), 1:55.

[3] Barry O'Connell, ed., *On Our Own Ground: The Complete Writings of William Apess, a Pequot* (Amherst: University of Massachusetts Press, 1992), 295.

[4] Rodney M. Baine, "The Myth of the Creek Pictograph," *Atlanta History* (Summer 1988): 43–45.

[5] The Busk or Green Corn Festival was the major ritual of the year among southeastern Indian peoples.

[6] In many Indian societies, women withdrew during their menstrual periods to avoid contaminating the medicine power of their menfolk or of the community as a whole. The custom may have stemmed from a belief in the special power of women at these times rather than from fear of "pollution."

[7]The Chickasaws were not members of the Creek Confederacy, although they appear in the migration legend.

[8]Probably Okaloosa Creek.

[9]Coosa was the "mother town" of the Upper Creeks.

[10]A number of southeastern peoples practiced the custom of skull deformation.

[11]On Tomochichi, see Figure 6 on page 32.

[12]Black drink was a strong tea used to induce vomiting in rituals of purification.

[13]Reuben G. Thwaites, ed., *The Jesuit Relations and Allied Documents* (Cleveland: Burrows Brothers, 1896–1901), 5:119–21. For similar traditions see William S. Simmons, *Spirit of the New England Tribes: Indian History and Folklore, 1620–1984* (Hanover, N.H.: University Press of New England, 1986), chap. 4.

[14]Philip L. Barbour, ed., *The Complete Works of Captain John Smith,* 3 vols. (Chapel Hill: University of North Carolina Press, 1986), 1:247, 2:175.

[15]Opechancanough, Opitchapam, and Kekataugh ruled the populous chiefdom of Pamunkey, near the mouth of the Pamunkey River. Helen C. Rountree, *The Powhatan Indians of Virginia* (Norman: University of Oklahoma Press, 1988), 117. Opechancanough was taken prisoner by Smith in 1608 and led the later wars of resistance against the English in Virginia.

2

Cultural Conflicts, Contests, and Confluences

Since that you are heere strangers and come into our Countrey, you should rather confine yourselves to the Customes of our Countrey, than impose yours upon us.
——Wicomesse Indian to the governor of Maryland, 1633[1]

You tell us fine stories, and there is nothing in what you say that may not be true; but that is good for you who come across the seas. Do you not see that, as we inhabit a world so different from yours, there must be another heaven for us, and another road to reach it?
——Huron Indian to Jesuit missionary Jean de Brébeuf, 1635[2]

We love you more than you love us; for when we take any prisoners from you, we treat them as our own children.
——Delaware Indians to Moravian ambassador Christian Frederick Post, 1758[3]

The European invasion of America produced a collision of worldviews. Indians and Europeans endeavored to deal with each other across gulfs of misunderstanding, and Europeans sought to achieve cultural and religious dominance, as well as military, political, and economic control in their "new world." Missionaries, teachers, and others labored to convert American Indians into "civilized" Christians, but conversion proved to be not a simple task.

Some Indian people embraced the new ways of life that Europeans offered them. Bombarded by lethal new diseases, wrenching changes, and the loss of loved ones to smallpox, alcohol, and violence, many looked for new answers, and there is no doubt that for some people conversion to Christianity was a profound and life-changing experience.

Mittark, the first Christian Indian at Gay Head on the west end of the island of Martha's Vineyard, endured painful separation from his people after his conversion but returned to them as a minister. On his deathbed in 1683, he apparently looked forward to the Christian promise of an escape from the troubles of the world: "Here I'm in pain, there I shall be freed from all Pain, and enjoy the Rest that never endeth." Sixteen-year-old Abigail Kemp, an Indian from Martha's Vineyard who died about 1710, was reported to have similar faith "that I shall when I die leave all my Pain and Affliction behind me, and enter into everlasting Rest and Happiness."[4]

Many others borrowed selectively from the Europeans, incorporating new merchandise and new beliefs into traditional patterns of life and thought. Still others demanded proof of European claims to superiority, ridiculed their pretensions, and rejected their way of life and religion. Often, they responded to European demands to accept their "civilization" by declaring, "You have your ways, we have ours."

Such cultural relativism exasperated missionaries who were convinced that theirs was the one true religion. At other times, Indians cited the example set by Christians as the best reason for rejecting Christianity. Early in the eighteenth century, a Susquehannock Indian listened as a Swedish missionary preached to his people about original sin and their need for Christianity. He then responded with a logical, point-by-point refutation of the missionary's arguments and concluded: "In a word, we find the Christians much more depraved in their morals than we are; and we judge from their doctrine by the badness of their lives."[5]

The exchange of cultures was a two-way street. As Indian populations plummeted and non-Indian neighbors proliferated, Indians intermarried with Europeans and Africans and sought to bolster population losses by adopting captives. Marrying and adopting outsiders were long-established practices, but now the outsiders were more often from a different world, and the ethnic composition of some Indian communities began to change. Many Indians in northern New England and eastern Canada bore French names by the seventeenth century; by the eighteenth century, it was common for Indian leaders in the Southeast to have the names of Scottish or English fathers. Intermarriage between Indians and Europeans produced new peoples whom the French called *métis,* children of mixed parentage who often came to function as intermediaries and culture brokers in dealings between Indians and Europeans. Some Indians intermarried so extensively with Africans that southern whites in the nineteenth century consigned both groups to the same racial category.

Indian people, Indian ways of life, and Indian country often exerted seductive influences on European colonists. Some captives were adopted into Indian societies and stayed there. Other people went willingly to live in Indian country with the Indians. European immigrants sometimes copied Native American ways of speaking, eating, dressing, hunting, farming, trading, traveling, fighting, and even organizing their societies.

In addition, competition developed between Europeans as to which particular European culture should emerge triumphant in North America. The Protestant English hoped to establish their version of Christianity in America at a time when it looked as if the Catholicism of their French and Spanish rivals was destined to take hold. Protestant and Catholic missionaries competed with one another for Indian converts, just as the shamans, the traditional Indian spiritual leaders, tried to fend them off. For the English, more than for French Jesuits, conversion to Christianity required conversion to the English way of life. Missionaries and teachers often formed the spearhead of a sustained assault on Native American culture. Some Indian students who attended colonial colleges went on to become missionaries and teachers themselves; others returned home to play valuable roles as intermediaries and interpreters; some dropped out or simply ran away. Indian parents sometimes complained that their children were good for nothing when they came home from school, and on occasion, with tongue in cheek, they offered to return the favor and educate the offspring of prominent English families in the ways of the forest.

In the end, what emerged in early America was often a mix of peoples and cultures. European ways changed Native American societies, sometimes dramatically, but in the process Indian cultures left their own subtle imprints on the new American societies that emerged.

A NATIVE AMERICAN THEOLOGICAL DEBATE

The English were relative latecomers to the contest for Native American souls, and they never enjoyed the success of their French rivals in the North or of Spanish missionaries in the South. The earliest sustained English missionary effort in New England was begun by Thomas Mayhew, Jr., among the Indians of Martha's Vineyard in the 1640s, and the Mayhew family continued the work for generations.

The most famous New England missionary, however, was John Eliot, who came to America in 1631 and devoted his life to converting the Indians of Massachusetts. He learned their language, compiled a dictionary, and even translated the Bible into the language of his Massachusett converts. Despite such efforts, Indians did not easily accept the new teachings, which not only threatened their traditional ways of life but also introduced alien concepts such as the existence of hell as a punishment for wrongdoers.

Eliot settled his Indian converts into mission communities called "praying towns," where he hoped they would be quarantined from the influence of the unconverted. Beginning in 1671, he also published a series of contrived dialogues between "praying Indians" and their unconverted relatives. These dialogues were intended to serve as a kind of training manual for Indian missionaries going to work among their own people where they could expect to encounter opposition and skepticism from those who saw no reason to abandon their traditional beliefs. Not all of the words attributed to the Indians in the dialogue are a factual record. However, based on Eliot's experiences, they do represent a paraphrasing of some of the issues that concerned Indian people as they confronted the new religion and the demands of the missionaries. The following exchange was supposed to have occurred in the course of a discussion between an Indian convert named Piumbukhou and his kinsfolk, to whom he had returned to teach about the Bible.[6]

JOHN ELIOT

A Dialogue between Piumbukhou and His Unconverted Relatives

ca. 1671

KINSMAN: I had rather that my actions of love should testify how welcome you are, and how glad I am of this your kind visitation, than that I should say it in a multitude of words. But in one word, you are very welcome into my heart, and I account it among the best of the joys of this day, that I see your face, and enjoy your company in my habitation.

KINSWOMAN: It is an addition to the joys of this day, to see the face of my loving kinsman. And I wish you had come a little earlier, that you might have taken part with us in the joys of this day, wherein we have had all the delights that could be desired, in our merry meeting, and dancing.

And I pray cousin, how doth your wife, my loving kinswoman, is she yet living? And is she not yet weary of your new way of praying to God? And what pleasure have you in those ways?

Henry W. Bowden and James P. Ronda, eds., *John Eliot's Indian Dialogues* (Westport, Conn.: Greenwood Press, 1980), 71.

PIUMBUKHOU: My wife doth remember her love to you. She is in good health of body, and her soul is in a good condition. She is entered into the light of the knowledge of God, and of Christ. She is entered into the narrow way of heavenly joys, and she doth greatly desire that you would turn from these ways of darkness in which you so much delight, and come taste and see how good the Lord is.

And whereas you wish I had come sooner, to have shared with you in your delights of this day. Alas, they are no delights, but griefs to me, to see that you do still delight in them. I am like a man that have tasted of sweet wine and honey, which have so altered the taste of my mouth, that I abhor to taste of your sinful and foolish pleasures, as the mouth doth abhor to taste the most filthy and stinking dung, the most sour grapes, or most bitter gall. Our joys in the knowledge of God, and of Jesus Christ, which we are taught in the Book of God, and feel in our heart, is sweeter to our soul, than honey is unto the mouth and taste.

KINSWOMAN: We have all the delights that the flesh and blood of man can devise and delight in, and we taste and feel the delights of them, and would you make us believe that you have found out new joys and delights, in comparison of which all our delights do stink like dung? Would you make us believe that we have neither eyes to see, nor ears to hear, nor mouth to taste? Ha, ha, he! I appeal to the sense and sight and feeling of the company present, whether this be so.

ALL. You say very true. Ha, ha, he!

PIUMBUKHOU. Hearken to me, my friends, and see if I do not give a clear answer unto this seeming difficulty. Your dogs take as much delight in these meetings, and the same kinds of delight as you do. They delight in each others company. They provoke each other to lust, and enjoy the pleasures of lust as you do. They eat and play and sleep as you do. What joys have you more than dogs have to delight the body of flesh and blood?

But all mankind have an higher and better part than the body. We have a soul, and that soul shall never die. Our soul is to converse with God, and to converse in such things as do concern God, and heaven, and an eternal estate, either in happiness with God, if we walk with him and serve him in this life, or in misery and torment with the Devil, if we serve him in this life. The service of God doth consist in virtue, and wisdom, and delights of the soul, which will reach to heaven, and abide forever.

But the service of the Devil is in committing sins of the flesh, which defile both body and soul, and reach to hell, and will turn all to fire and flame to torment your souls and bodies in all eternity.

Now consider, all your pleasures and delights are such as defile you with sin, and will turn to flame, to burn and torment you. They provoke

God to wrath, who hath created the prison of hell to torment you, and the more you have took pleasure in sin, the greater are your offences against God, and the greater shall be your torments.

But we that pray to God repent of our old sins, and by faith in Christ we seek for, and find a pardon for what is past, and grace and strength to reform for time to come. So that our joys are soul joys in godliness, and virtue, and hope of glory in another world when we die.

Your joys are bodily, fleshly, such as dogs have, and will all turn to flames in hell to torment you.

KINSMAN. If these things be so, we had need to cease laughing, and fall to weeping, and see if we can draw water from our mournful eyes to quench these tormenting flames. My heart trembles to hear these things. I never heard so much before, nor have I any thing to say to the contrary, but that these things may be so. But how shall I know that you say true? Our forefathers were (many of them) wise men, and we have wise men now living. They all delight in these our delights. They have taught us nothing about our soul, and God, and heaven, and hell, and joy and torment in the life to come. Are you wiser than our fathers? May not we rather think that *English* men have invented these stories to amaze us and fear us out of our old customs, and bring us to stand in awe of them, that they might wipe us of our lands, and drive us into corners, to seek new ways of living, and new places too? And be beholding to them for that which is our own, and was ours, before we knew them.

ALL. You say right.

PIUMBUKHOU. The Book of God is no invention of Englishmen. It is the holy law of God himself, which was given unto man by God, before Englishmen had any knowledge of God; and all the knowledge which they have, they have it out of the Book of God. And this book is given to us as well as to them, and it is as free for us to search the scriptures as for them. So that we have our instruction from a higher hand, than the hand of man. It is the great Lord God of heaven and earth, who teacheth us these great things of which we speak. Yet this is also true, that we have great cause to be thankful to the English, and to thank God for them. For they had a good country of their own, but by ships sailing into these parts of the world, they heard of us, and of our country, and of our nakedness, ignorance of God, and wild condition. God put it into their hearts to desire to come hither, and teach us the good knowledge of God; and their King gave them leave so to do, and in our country to have their liberty to serve God according to the word of God. And being come hither, we gave them leave freely to live among us. They have purchased of us a great part of those lands which they possess. They love us, they do us right, and no wrong willingly. If any do us wrong, it is without the consent of their rulers, and upon our complaints our wrongs are righted. They are (many of them, especially the ruling part) good men, and desire to do us good. God put it into the heart of one of their ministers (as you all know) to teach us the knowledge of God, by the word of God, and hath translated the holy Book of God into our language, so that we can perfectly know the mind and counsel of God. And out of this book have I learned all that I say unto you, and therefore you need no more doubt of the truth of it, then you have cause to doubt that the heaven is over our head, the sun shineth, the earth is under our feet, we walk and live upon it, and breathe in the air. For as we see with our eyes these things to be so, so we read with our own eyes these things which I speak of, to be written in God's own book, and we feel the truth thereof in our own hearts.

KINSWOMAN. Cousin, you have wearied your legs this day with a long journey to come and visit us, and you weary your tongue with long discourses. I am willing to comfort and refresh you with a short supper.

ALL. Ha, ha, he. Though short, if sweet that has good favor to a man that is weary. Ha, ha, he.

KINSWOMAN. You make long and learned discourses to us which we do not well understand. I think our best answer is to stop your mouth, and fill your belly with a good supper, and when your belly is full you will be content to take rest yourself, and give us leave to be at rest from these gastering and heart-trembling discourses. We are well as we are, and desire not to be troubled with these new wise sayings.

A MICMAC QUESTIONS
FRENCH "CIVILIZATION"

The French in eastern Canada may have found traveling in the woods and living in the Indians' encampments "mean and miserable," but they learned that the Indians preferred their lodgings to "the most superb and commodious of our houses." They also found that their assumptions about the superiority of French civilization over the Indian way of life meant little in Indian country. Chrestien LeClerq, a Recollet missionary to the Micmacs of the Gaspé Peninsula, who composed a dictionary for future missionaries to the area, interpreted and recorded the following speech given by a Micmac elder to a group of French settlers. The cultural relativism displayed in the Micmac's response is typical of many statements by American Indians when confronted with European demands that they embrace the European "civilization."

CHRESTIEN LeCLERQ

A Micmac Responds
to the French

ca. 1677

I am greatly astonished that the French have so little cleverness, as they seem to exhibit in the matter of which thou hast just told me on their behalf, in the effort to persuade us to convert our poles, our barks, and our wigwams into those houses of stone and of wood which are tall and lofty, according to their account, as these trees. Very well! But why now, . . . do men of five to six feet in height need houses which are sixty to eighty? For, in fact, as thou knowest very well thyself, Patriarch—do we not find in our own all the conveniences and the advantages that you have with yours, such as reposing, drinking, sleeping, eating, and amusing ourselves with our friends when we wish? This is not all, . . . my brother, hast thou as much ingenuity and cleverness as the Indians, who carry their houses and their wigwams with them so that they may lodge wheresoever they please, independently of any seignior whatsoever? Thou art not as bold nor as stout as we, because when thou goest on a voyage thou canst not carry upon thy shoulders thy buildings and thy edifices. Therefore it is necessary that thou preparest as many lodgings as thou makest changes of residence, or else thou lodgest in a hired house which does not belong to thee. As for us, we find ourselves secure from all these inconveniences, and we can always say, more truly than thou, that we are at home everywhere, because we set up our wigwams with ease wheresoever we go, and without asking permission of anybody. Thou reproachest us, very inappropriately, that our country is a little hell in contrast with France, which thou comparest to a terrestrial paradise, inasmuch as it yields thee, so thou sayest, every kind of provision in abundance. Thou sayest of us also that we are the most miserable and most unhappy of all men, living without religion, without manners, without honour, without social order, and, in a word, without any rules, like the beasts in our woods and our forests, lacking bread, wine, and a thousand other comforts which thou hast in superfluity in Europe. Well, my brother, if thou dost not yet know the real feelings which our Indians have towards thy country and

William F. Ganong, trans. and ed., *New Relation of Gaspesia, with the Customs and Religion of the Gaspesian Indians,* by Chrestien LeClerq (Toronto: Champlain Society, 1910), 104–06.

towards all thy nation, it is proper that I inform thee at once. I beg thee now
to believe that, all miserable as we seem in thine eyes, we consider ourselves
nevertheless much happier than thou in this, that we are very content with
the little that we have; and believe also once for all, I pray, that thou
deceivest thyself greatly if thou thinkest to persuade us that thy country is
better than ours. For if France, as thou sayest, is a little terrestrial paradise,
art thou sensible to leave it? And why abandon wives, children, relatives,
and friends? Why risk thy life and thy property every year, and why venture
thyself with such risk, in any season whatsoever, to the storms and tempests
of the sea in order to come to a strange and barbarous country which thou
considerest the poorest and least fortunate of the world? Besides, since we
are wholly convinced of the contrary, we scarcely take the trouble to go to
France, because we fear, with good reason, lest we find little satisfaction
there, seeing, in our own experience, that those who are natives thereof leave
it every year in order to enrich themselves on our shores. We believe, further,
that you are also incomparably poorer than we, and that you are only simple
journeymen, valets, servants, and slaves, all masters and grand captains
though you may appear, seeing that you glory in our old rags and in our
miserable suits of beaver which can no longer be of use to us, and that you
find among us, in the fishery for cod which you make in these parts, the
wherewithal to comfort your misery and the poverty which oppresses you.
As to us, we find all our riches and all our conveniences among ourselves,
without trouble and without exposing our lives to the dangers in which you
find yourselves constantly through your long voyages. And, whilst feeling
compassion for you in the sweetness of our repose, we wonder at the
anxieties and cares which you give yourselves night and day in order to load
your ship. We see also that all your people live, as a rule, only upon cod
which you catch among us. It is everlastingly nothing but cod—cod in the
morning, cod at midday, cod at evening, and always cod, until things come
to such a pass that if you wish some good morsels, it is at our expense; and
you are obliged to have recourse to the Indians, whom you despise so much,
and to beg them to go a-hunting that you may be regaled. Now tell me this
one little thing, if thou hast any sense: Which of these two is the wisest and
happiest—he who labours without ceasing and only obtains, and that with
great trouble, enough to live on, or he who rests in comfort and finds all that
he needs in the pleasure of hunting and fishing? It is true, . . . that we have
not always had the use of bread and of wine which your France produces;
but, in fact, before the arrival of the French in these parts, did not the
Gaspesians live much longer than now? And if we have not any longer
among us any of those old men of a hundred and thirty to forty years, it is

only because we are gradually adopting your manner of living, for experience is making it very plain that those of us live longest who, despising your bread, your wine, and your brandy, are content with their natural food of beaver, of moose, of waterfowl, and fish, in accord with the custom of our ancestors and of all the Gaspesian nation. Learn now, my brother, once for all, because I must open to thee my heart: there is no Indian who does not consider himself infinitely more happy and more powerful than the French.

AN INDIAN WOMAN
BEQUEATHS HER PROPERTY

The Massachusetts Bay Colony required that wills be signed and sealed in the presence of witnesses to be considered legal documents. The will of Naomai Omaush, a Wampanoag woman from Gay Head on Martha's Vineyard, demonstrates that she had embraced Christianity and acquired some European goods. It also suggests that she had adopted some of the forms of "doing business" in colonial society and with them, perhaps, some new notions about property and its transfer. The document was originally written in the Massachusett dialect of the Algonkian language.

NAOMAI OMAUSH

Will

1749

Know ye this all Christian people of God. I Naomai Ommaush of Gayhead know that very soon I go the way of all the earth, whence I shall not be able to return again. And now I hope, if I should die this year, I would have my sins be forgiven by the blood of my Lord, the Lord Jesus Christ.

And again I know that although my body dies and has rotted (?), it shall

Clements Library, University of Michigan, Ann Arbor. Translated and published in Ives Goddard and Kathleen J. Bragdon, eds., *Native Writings in Massachusett,* 2 vols. (Philadelphia: American Philosophical Society, 1988), 1:55.

rise again on the last day, and also my soul shall also enter where he is, on the great day of resurrection, to go to meet the Lord in heaven. And then we shall dwell with the lord forever.

And I Naomai Omaush say this before God: I willingly bequeath this property of mine to my kin. Each one shall take, after I die, what I have not yet used.

To Zachary Hossueit, the minister, I bequeath one *ohquoh*—it is straight-looking (?) (and) large—and also six pewter dishes, and also seventeen pewter spoons. [[And this]]* And also to his wife Butthiah Hossueit I bequeath one of my dresses—whichever one she pleases she shall choose when I have died. And I say at this time, no one shall have the authority to defraud them out of the things I bequeath to them. And, witnesses, see [[m[y m]ark (and) m[y sea]l]] my mark and also my seal.

Naomai Omaush, her (X) mark and Seal (S)

Witnesses:
Jude Hossueit, his mark (X).
Buthiah Accomus, her mark (X). On July 8, 1749.

On July 8, 1749, on that date (?) I also say I bequeath to [[my broth]] my kinsman *(nuttauwatueonk)* Calab Elisha one blanket.

On July 8, 1749, on that date (?) I say that I bequeath to my kinswoman *(nuttauwatueonk)* Jeanohumun one *ohquohkoome kaskepessue* and also one of my dresses.

On July 8, 1749, on that date (?) also I bequeath to my kinsman *(nuttauwam)* Henry Amos (some of) that cloth of mine that I may then have; of the red he shall have one *penchens* because of how kind he has been to me.

On July 8, 1749, on that date (?) I bequeath to my kinswoman *(nuttauwaeh)* Ezther Henry one dress of mine of blue (?) calico; I bought it from her late mother, and she shall have it.

On July 8, 1749, on that day I bequeath to my kinswoman *(nuttauwam)* Marcy Noah one petticoat. And those other things more that I have of household goods, those I shall use as long as I live. And then if I do not use them all, you shall divide them up when I have died.

My bequeathing of all this to my kin *(nuttauwamoog)* was done; I willingly do it on this date (?) before my G[o]d, the Lord Jesus Christ.
[Se]e my mark and also my seal.

Naomai Omaush, her (X) mark and seal (S)

*Letters in brackets indicate deletions by the writer of the document; words in parentheses are the original Massachuset terms.—ED.

[Wi]tnesses:
[Jude] Hossueit, his mark (X).
[Buth]i[a]h Accomus, her mark (X).

AUTOBIOGRAPHY OF AN
INDIAN MINISTER

The Mohegan Indians of Connecticut had lost huge tracts of land to English colonists by the early eighteenth century, and it had become increasingly difficult to practice their traditional economy of hunting, fishing, and gathering. Confronted with apparently insurmountable pressures on their old ways and beliefs, many sought escape from their new world by turning to alcohol. Others turned to Christianity and education as offering hope for survival. Mohegan Samson Occom (1723–1792) converted to Christianity at age sixteen, studied with Reverend Eleazar Wheelock in the 1740s, and went on to become well known as a schoolteacher and an Indian minister. He traveled to England in 1764–65, preaching sermons to raise money for Wheelock's school. Occom's brief autobiographical sketch contains an account of his conversion during the era of the Great Awakening, the emotionally intense religious revival that swept colonial America in the 1740s. It also reveals the various occupations Occom tried in colonial society and gives vent to his complaints against what he came to see as the church's exploitation of Indian missionaries.

SAMSON OCCOM

A Short Narrative of My Life

1768

From my Birth till I received the Christian Religion

I was Born a Heathen and Brought up In Heathenism, till I was between 16
& 17 years of age, at a Place Calld Mohegan, in New London, Connecticut,
in New England. My Parents Livd a wandering life, for did all the Indians
at Mohegan, they Chiefly Depended upon Hunting, Fishing, & Fowling for
their Living and had no Connection with the English, excepting to Traffic
with them in their small Trifles; and they Strictly maintained and followed
their Heathenish Ways, Customs & Religion, though there was Some Preaching among them. Once a Fortnight, in ye Summer Season, a Minister from
New London used to come up, and the Indians to attend; not that they
regarded the Christian Religion, but they had Blankets given to them every
Fall of the Year and for these things they would attend and there was a Sort
of School kept, when I was quite young, but I believe there never was one
that ever Learnt to read any thing,—and when I was about 10 Years of age
there was a man who went about among the Indian Wigwams, and wherever
he Could find the Indian Children, would make them read; but the Children
Used to take Care to keep out of his way;—and he used to Catch me Some
times and make me Say over my Letters; and I believe I learnt Some of them.
But this was Soon over too; and all this Time there was not one amongst us,
that made a Profession of Christianity— —Neither did we Cultivate our
Land, nor kept any Sort of Creatures except Dogs, which we used in Hunting;
and we Dwelt in Wigwams. These are a Sort of Tents, Covered with Matts,
made of Flags. And to this Time we were unaquainted with the English
Tongue in general though there were a few, who understood a little of it.

Typescript in Baker Library Special Collections, Dartmouth College, Hanover, N.H.

Figure 7.   The Reverend Samson Occom (1723–1792)
Painted by Nathaniel Smibert (1735–1756).

From the Time of our Reformation till I left Mr. Wheelocks

When I was 16 years of age, we heard a Strange Rumor among the English,
that there were Extraordinary Ministers Preaching from Place to Place and
a Strange Concern among the White People. This was in the Spring of the
Year. But we Saw nothing of these things, till Some Time in the Summer,
when Some Ministers began to visit us and Preach the Word of God; and the
Common People all Came frequently and exhorted us to the things of God,
which it pleased the Lord, as I humbly hope, to Bless and accompany with
Divine Influence to the Conviction and Saving Conversion of a Number of us;
amongst whom I was one that was Imprest with the things we had heard.
These Preachers did not only come to us, but we frequently went to their
meetings and Churches. After I was awakened & converted, I went to all the
meetings, I could come at; & Continued under Trouble of Mind about 6

months; at which time I began to Learn the English Letters; got me a Primer, and used to go to my English Neighbours frequently for Assistance in Reading, but went to no School. And when I was 17 years of age, I had, as I trust, a Discovery of the way of Salvation through Jesus Christ, and was enabl'd to put my trust in him alone for Life & Salvation. From this Time the Distress and Burden of my mind was removed, and I found Serenity and Pleasure of Soul, in Serving God. By this time I just began to Read in the New Testament without Spelling,—and I had a Stronger Desire Still to Learn to read the Word of God, and at the Same Time had an uncommon Pity and Compassion to my Poor Brethren According to the Flesh. I used to wish I was capable of Instructing my poor Kindred. I used to think, if I Could once Learn to Read I would Instruct the poor Children in Reading,—and used frequently to talk with our Indians Concerning Religion. This continued till I was in my 19th year: by this Time I Could Read a little in the Bible. At this Time my Poor Mother was going to Lebanon, and having had Some Knowledge of Mr. Wheelock and hearing he had a Number of English youth under his Tuition, I had a great Inclination to go to him and be with him a week or a Fortnight, and Desired my Mother to Ask Mr. Wheelock whether he would take me a little while to Instruct me in Reading. Mother did so; and when She Came Back, She Said Mr. Wheelock wanted to See me as Soon as possible. So I went up, thinking I Should be back again in a few Days; when I got up there, he received me With kindness and Compassion and in Stead of Staying a Fortnight or 3 Weeks, I Spent 4 Years with him.—After I had been with him Some Time, he began to acquaint his Friends of my being with him, and of his Intentions of Educating me, and my Circumstances. And the good People began to give Some Assistance to Mr. Wheelock, and gave me Some old and Some New Clothes. Then he represented the Case to the Honorable Commissioners at Boston, who were Commission'd by the Honorable Society in London for Propagating the gospel among the Indians in New England and parts adjacent, and they allowed him 60 £ in old Tender, which was about 6 £ Sterling, and they Continu'd it 2 or 3 years, I can't tell exactly.—While I was at Mr. Wheelock's, I was very weakly and my Health much impaired, and at the End of 4 Years, I over Strained my Eyes to such a Degree, I Could not persue my Studies any Longer; and out of these 4 years I Lost Just about one year;—And was obliged to quit my Studies.

From the Time I left Mr. Wheelock till I went to Europe

As soon as I left Mr. Wheelock, I endeavored to find Some Employ among the Indians; went to Nahantuck,[7] thinking they may want a School Master, but they had one; then went to Narraganset, and they were Indifferent about a School, and went back to Mohegan, and heard a number of our Indians were going to Montauk, on Long Island, and I went with them, and the Indians there were very desirous to have me keep a School amongst them, and I Consented, and went back a while to Mohegan and Some time in November I went on the Island, I think it is 17 years ago last November. I agreed to keep School with them Half a Year, and left it with them to give me what they Pleased; and they took turns to Provide Food for me. I had near 30 Scholars this winter; I had an evening School too for those that could not attend the Day School—and began to Carry on their meetings, they had a Minister, one Mr. Horton,[8] the Scotch Society's Missionary; but he Spent, I think two thirds of his Time at Sheenecock, 30 Miles from Montauk. We met together 3 times for Divine Worship every Sabbath and once on every Wednesday evening. I (used) to read the Scriptures to them and used to expound upon Some particular Passages in my own Tongue. Visited the Sick and attended their Burials.—When the half year expired, they Desired me to Continue with them, which I complied with, for another half year, when I had fulfilled that, they were urgent to have me Stay Longer, So I continued amongst them till I was Married, which was about 2 years after I went there. And Continued to Instruct them in the Same manner as I did before. After I was married a while, I found there was need of a Support more than I needed while I was Single,—and made my Case Known to Mr. Buell[9] and to Mr. Wheelock, and also the Needy Circumstances and the Desires of these Indians of my Continuing amongst them, and the Commissioners were so good as to grant £ 15 a year Sterling— —And I kept on in my Service as usual, yea I had additional Service; I kept School as I did before and Carried on the Religious Meetings as often as ever, and attended the Sick and their Funerals, and did what Writings they wanted, and often Sat as a Judge to reconcile and Decide their Matters Between them, and had visitors of Indians from all Quarters; and, as our Custom is, we freely Entertain all Visitors. And was fetched often from my Tribe and from others to see into their Affairs Both Religious, Temporal,—Besides my Domestic Concerns. And it Pleased the Lord to Increase my Family fast—and Soon after I was Married, Mr. Horton left these Indians and the Shenecock & after this I was (alone) and then I had the whole care of these Indians at Montauk, and visited the Shenecock Indians often. Used to set out Saturdays towards Night and come back again Mondays. I have been obliged to Set out from Home after Sun Set, and Ride 30 Miles in the Night, to Preach to these Indians. And Some Indians at Shenecock Sent their Children to my School at Montauk, I kept one of them Some Time, and had a Young Man a half year from Mohegan, a Lad from Nahantuck, who was with me almost a year; and had little or nothing for keeping them.

My Method in the School was, as Soon as the Children got together, and took their proper Seats, I Prayed with them, then began to hear them. I generally began (after some of them Could Spell and Read,) With those that were yet in their Alphabets, So around, as they were properly Seated till I got through and I obliged them to Study their Books, and to help one another. When they could not make out a hard word they Brought it to me—and I usually heard them, in the Summer Season 8 Times a Day 4 in the morning, and in ye after Noon.—In the Winter Season 6 Times a Day, As Soon as they could Spell, they were obliged to Spell when ever they wanted to go out. I concluded with Prayer; I generally heard my Evening Scholars 3 Times Round, And as they go out the School, every one, that Can Spell, is obliged to Spell a Word, and to go out Leisurely one after another. I Catechised 3 or 4 Times a Week according to the Assembly's Shout or Catechism, and many Times Proposed Questions of my own, and in my own Tongue. I found Difficulty with Some Children, who were Some what Dull, most of these can soon learn to Say over their Letters, they Distinguish the Sounds by the Ear, but their Eyes can't Distinguish the Letters, and the way I took to cure them was by making an Alphabet on Small bits of paper, and glued them on Small Chips of Cedar after this manner A B & C. I put these on Letters in order on a Bench then point to one Letter and bid a Child to take notice of it, and then I order the Child to fetch me the Letter from the Bench; if he Brings the Letter, it is well, if not he must go again and again till he brings ye right Letter. When they can bring any Letters this way, then I just Jumble them together, and bid them to set them in Alphabetical order, and it is a Pleasure to them; and they soon Learn their Letters this way.—I frequently Discussed or Exhorted my Scholars, in Religious matters.—My Method in our Religious Meetings was this; Sabbath Morning we Assemble together about 10 o'C and begin with Singing; we generally Sung Dr. Watt's[10] Psalms or Hymns. I distinctly read the Psalm or Hymn first, and then gave the meaning of it to them, and after that Sing, then Pray, and Sing again after Prayer. Then proceed to Read from Suitable portion of Scripture, and so Just give the plain Sense of it in Familiar Discourse and apply it to them. So continued with Prayer and Singing. In the after Noon and Evening we Proceed in the Same Manner, and so in Wednesday Evening. Some Time after Mr. Horton left these Indians, there was a remarkable revival of religion among these Indians and many were hopefully converted to the Saving knowledge of God in Jesus. It is to be observed before Mr. Horton left these Indians they had Some Prejudices infused in their minds, by Some Enthusiastical Exhorters from New England, against Mr. Horton, and many of them had left him; by this means he was Discouraged, and was disposed from these Indians. And being acquainted with the Enthusiasts in New

England & the make and the Disposition of the Indians I took a mild way to reclaim them. I opposed them not openly but let them go on in their way, and whenever I had an opportunity, I would read Such pages of the Scriptures, and I thought would confound their Notions, and I would come to them with all Authority, Saying "these Saith the Lord"; and by this means, the Lord was pleased to Bless my poor Endeavours, and they were reclaimed, and Brought to hear almost any of the ministers.— —I am now to give an Account of my Circumstances and manner of Living. I Dwelt in a Wigwam, a Small Hut with Small Poles and Covered with Matts made of Flags, and I was obligd to remove twice a Year, about 2 miles Distance, by reason of the Scarcity of wood, for in one Neck of Land they Planted their Corn, and in another, they had their wood, and I was obligd to have my Corn carted and my Hay also,—and I got my Ground Plow'd every year, which Cost me about 12 shillings an acre; and I kept a Cow and a Horse, for which I paid 21 shillings every year York currency, and went 18 miles to Mill for every Dust of meal we used in my family. I Hired or Joined with my Neighbours to go to Mill, with a Horse or ox Cart, or on Horse Back, and Some time went myself. My Family Increasing fast, and my Visitors also. I was obligd to contrive every way to Support my Family; I took all opportunities, to get Some thing to feed my Family Daily. I Planted my own Corn, Potatoes, and Beans; I used to be out hoeing my Corn Some times before Sun Rise and after my School is Dismist, and by this means I was able to raise my own Pork, for I was allowed to keep 5 Swine. Some mornings & Evenings I would be out with my Hook and Line to Catch fish, and in the Fall of Year and in the Spring, I used my gun, and fed my Family with Fowls. I Could more than pay for my Powder & Shot with Feathers. At other Times I Bound old Books for Easthampton People, made wooden Spoons and Ladles, Stocked Guns, & worked on Cedar to make Pails, (Piggins), and Churns & C. Besides all these Difficulties I met with advers Providence, I bought a Mare, had it but a little while, and she fell into the Quick Sand and Died, After a while Bought another, I kept her about half year, and she was gone, and I never have heard of nor Seen her from that Day to this; it was Supposed Some Rogue Stole her. I got another and Died with a Distemper, and last of all I Bought a Young Mare, and kept her till She had one Colt, and She broke her Leg and Died, and Presently after the Cold [Colt] Died also. In the whole I Lost 5 Horse Kind; all these Losses helped to pull me down; and by this Time I got greatly in Debt, and acquainted my Circumstances to Some of my Friends, and they Represented my Case to the Commissioners of Boston, and Interceded with them for me, and they were pleased to vote 15 £ for my Help, and Soon after Sent a Letter to my good Friend at New London, acquainting him that they had Superseded their Vote; and my Friends were so good as to represent my Needy Circumstances Still to them, and they were so good at Last, as to Vote £ 15 and Sent it, for which I am very thankful; and the Revd Mr. Buell was so kind as to write in my behalf to the gentlemen of Boston; and he told me they were much Displeased with him, and heard also once again that they blamed me for being Extravagant; I Can't Conceive how these gentlemen would have me Live. I am ready to (forgive) their Ignorance, and I would wish they had Changed Circumstances with me but one month, that they may know, by experience what my Case really was; but I am now fully convinced, that it was not Ignorance, For I believe it can be proved to the world that these Same Gentlemen gave a young Missionary a Single man, *one Hundred Pounds* for one year, and fifty Pounds for an Interpreter, and thirty Pounds for an Introducer; so it Cost them one Hundred & Eighty Pounds in one Single Year, and they Sent too where there was no Need of a Missionary.

Now you See what difference they made between me and other missionaries; they gave me 180 Pounds for 12 years Service, which they gave for one years Services in another Mission.—In my Service (I speak like a fool, but I am Constrained) I was my own Interpreter. I was both a School master and Minister to the Indians, yea I was their Ear, Eye & Hand, as Well as Mouth. I leave it with the World, as wicked as it is, to Judge, whether I ought not to have had half as much, they gave a young man Just mentioned which would have been but £ 50 a year; and if they ought to have given me that, I am not under obligations to them, I owe them nothing at all; what can be the Reason that they used me after this manner? I can't think of any thing, but this as a Poor Indian Boy Said, Who was Bound out to an English Family, and he used to Drive Plow for a young man, and he whipt and Beat him allmost every Day, and the young man found fault with him, and Complained of him to his master and the poor Boy was Called to answer for himself before his master, and he was asked, what it was he did, that he was So Complained of and beat almost every Day. He Said, he did not know, but he Supposed it was because he could not drive any better; but says he, I Drive as well as I know how; and at other Times he Beats me, because he is of a mind to beat me; but says he believes he Beats me for the most of the Time "because I am an Indian".

So I am *ready* to Say, they have used me thus, because I Can't Influence the Indians so well as other missionaries; but I can assure them I have endeavoured to teach them as well as I know how;—but I *must Say,* "I believe it is because I am a poor Indian". I Can't help that God has made me So; I did not make my self so.—

LETTERS OF A NARRAGANSETT FAMILY

Formerly one of the major powers in southern New England, the Narragansett Indians of Rhode Island were devastated by King Philip's War (1675–76), during which an English army destroyed their main village. Reduced in numbers and surrounded by more and more English neighbors, they struggled to survive in the eighteenth century. The emotional intensity of the religious revival known as the Great Awakening appealed strongly to the poor and powerless Indians of Rhode Island and southern Connecticut, and most Narragansetts converted to Christianity in 1743. They established their own Narragansett Church on their reservation, with their own minister.

Several Narragansetts attended Moor's Indian Charity School, established by Eleazar Wheelock in Lebanon, Connecticut, in 1754. In 1769, the school was moved to Hanover, New Hampshire, and became Dartmouth College. Wheelock hoped to produce more students like Samson Occom who would serve as missionaries to their people, but the school's record in Indian education was mixed at best, and much of Wheelock's energy was diverted into fundraising. Nonetheless, a trickle of Indian students attended the college, and many learned to read and write.

Wheelock and other teacher-missionaries often used their students' letters to promote funding. As Daniel Simon's letter illustrates, however, Indians did not write only what their teachers wanted to read. Nor were students the only Indians to write letters to teachers. Parents and relatives were very concerned about the experience of Indian youth in colonial colleges, as the first letter, written (or dictated) by the elder Sarah Simon, attests. That letter, together with the younger Sarah Simon's letter, illustrates the importance of family ties as well as the pain of separation that was the common experience of Indian students in white schools from the seventeenth to the twentieth century.

Colonial colleges aimed to give Indian students an education as well as to instill in them skills and a work ethic that would prepare them to participate in white society *and* help with the school's upkeep. Daniel Simon was one of five children sent to Wheelock's school by the widowed Sarah Simon. He entered the school in 1768 or 1769 and was the first Native American to graduate with a degree from Dartmouth College. He was licensed to preach in 1778, taught in the mission school in Stockbridge, and later served as missionary to the Indians at Cranbury, New Jersey. He found some fault with the allocation of energies to the various agendas at Wheelock's school, which required more work than studying.

SARAH SIMON

Letter to Eleazar Wheelock

1767

Charlestown ye 9th of October AD 1767

Dear S^r

I've great satisfaction, in the account my daughter Sarah has given me of Your pious care of those Children which are under Your tuition. In perticular, do express most harty Thanks, for the education of my Daughter. I've a little Son that I want You shou'd receive into Your School. if You wou'd, I shou'd except it as an Inesteemable Favour. and wholy give him up to You, to be altogether under Your wise Instruction, 'till he arrives to ye age of twentyone years: beging this favour only, that You wou'd at proper seasons, allow him ye privelidge of visiting me.

from y^r very humbl^e Servt

Sarah Simon

James Dow McCallum, ed., *The Letters of Eleazar Wheelock's Indians* (Hanover, N.H.: Dartmouth College Publications, 1932), 220–21, 227, 229.

SARAH SIMON (THE DAUGHTER)

Letter to Eleazar Wheelock

1769

Lebanon April 4th 1769

Revend and Honrd Sir

as I have Receved many kind favours I desire to bag one homble requast ond that is whether the Doctor would be willing to let me go to my home if I would not be gone no longer then if I only want to Mohegin. for I wont very much to See my Mother I understand She has mate with trouble latly and She wants see me and she is not able to come to See me. and tharfore I think it my gret Duty to go and See hir.

for I donot think that she is long for this world I have no Reson to thing so. for She is very weekly and always Sick. my Parant is very near and Dear to me: and being I do not desine to Ever to go home and live with hir again, I Desire to beg that favour to go and see hir as ofen as the Doctor is willing I should for I dont want to ofand the Doc^{tr} in the least. but I feel willing to do any thing Sir that you think is bast for me.

Oh how I orto Blease and adore that grat and kind God that put it in the hands some of his Pepple to take so much Care of the poor indions nee above all the rast. it Seems to me I could go any where or do any thing if it would do any good to my poor Parishing Brethren.

So I desire to Subscrib mysilfe your

Ever Dutyfull Sarvent

Sarah Simon

DANIEL SIMON

Letter to Eleazar Wheelock

1771

Sept 1771

I now make bould to write to the most Reverend Doctor, when I Came frist to this School I understood that this School was for to bring up Such Indians, as was not able to bring up themselves, but the doctor is to learn them to work, but I have been to work Ever Since I have been able; and therefore if the doctor will let me follow my Studys, I Shall be thinkful, as I understood the doctor when I talked with him, that we must work as much as to pay our way; and if we Should, what good will the Charity money do the Indians; which was given to them, if we poor Indians Shall work as much as to pay for our learning, we Can go Some other pace [place] as good as here for learning, if we are ablie to work and pay for our learning and I Say now, wo unto that poor Indian; or white man that Should Ever Com to this School, with out he is rich; I write as I think, and the doctor must not get mad with me, as I am a going to tell the doctor, what I think, I intend to deal with the Doctor as honnest is Ever the doctor had a Indian, and if the doctor dont let me follow my Studys more then I have don; I must leave the School, I Cannot Speand my time here, I am old, and I must improve all the time I Can if I undertake to get learning, and if I Cannot get learning here as I understood I might; I have no business here, and I must leave the School and if the doctor will let me go home to Charles town this fall I will Strive to get Sum body to pay the doctor his money for my learning, and if I Cannot I will Com back and pay the doctor for the jorney; and I will go to Studing arithmetic this winter, and in the Spring I will go a mong the Indians if the doctor and I Can agree, and if so be I can get any body to pay for my learning I shall follow my Studes, and if I Cannot I must leave the School, and if I have a Rong understaning of this School, I am willing to acknowledge but I belive I have not and so I writ no more but your most Dutiful pupil

Daniel Simon

I Should be glad if the doctor will give an answer to this

THE IROQUOIS REJECT
WHEELOCK'S "BENEVOLENCE"

In 1772, Eleazar Wheelock sent an emissary to the Oneida country in northern New York State to learn, among other things, the Indians' attitude toward his missionaries and toward sending their children to Dartmouth College. In June 1772, Oneida headmen at the village of Kanowalohale at the site of present-day Vernon, New York, gave their answer, which was duly reported to Wheelock. That same year, Wheelock sent his son Ralph to the Onondaga council in a final effort to get the central Iroquois council to agree to the education of their youth. In both cases, the Indians' frank response reveals the widely different attitudes held by Iroquois and English societies about the teaching and treatment of children. Henceforward, Wheelock concentrated his recruiting efforts among the Indians in Canada.

Speech of the Oneida Headmen
1772

Kanawarohare June 5th 1772

The headmen met at Mr Kirkland's[11] house, & delivered the following answer to [Eleazar Wheelock]. . . .

Father, attend, & hear for our father the less. The occasion of our entering your house this morning is, to answer the speech delivered us the other day-evening from our great father, which was this (here repeated over the speech *verbatim*)

Father now attend; hear the result of our council—as you desired us to speak plainly & deal faithfully, so we shall do.

Our minds do not advance with the great minister's proposal: indeed they are at a perfect stand. We see no way open for prosecuting his purposes.

English schools we do not approve of here, as serviceable to our spiritual interest: & almost all those who have been instructed in English are a

---

James Dow McCallum, ed., *The Letters of Eleazar Wheelock's Indians* (Hanover, N.H.: Dartmouth College Publications, 1932), 281–88.

Figure 8. Founding of Dartmouth College
In 1769, Eleazar Wheelock moved his "Indian school" from Lebanon, Connecticut, to Hanover, New Hampshire, where the school became Dartmouth College. As this 1839 engraving by Samuel E. Brown suggests, the avowed mission of the college was to bring Christianity and education to the "wilderness." In reality, funding often took precedence over learning, and the number of Indian students dwindled steadily until Dartmouth recommitted itself to providing education for Native Americans in the 1970s.

reproach to us. This we supposed our father was long ago sufficiently appraised of.

And as to our neighbouring towns, there is not, at present, the least gleam of light—even no appearance at all which embraces such a proposal.

Our father does not know the mind of Indians: their minds are invincible: they are strongly attached to other things. We don't say to what their minds are most strongly inclined; but of this we are confident, that they are not disposed to embrace the Gospel: for here we are upon the spot, with open ears, ready to receive such intelligence.

Moreover; we are dispised by our brethren, on account of our christian profession. Time was when we were esteemed as honorable & important in the confederacy: but now we are looked upon as small things; or rather nothing at all. Now may we not well conclude that they don't favor your designs? or would they not speak well of us, instead of reproaching us for embracing this religion you are endeavoring to publish among them?

As to your expectations of a favorable answer from the Onondagas, we must desire you to cut off your hope, & not protract it to any farther length; for we know by experience that hope defered is very painful.

Father we must tell you, Your former speech there, by your son, made so little impression, & left so few marks, that we have never been able since to find any traces of it; tho' we have often discoursed with one & another upon the subject. We never conceived that the least expectation should be at all excited in our great father's mind of their acceptance of his proposal, from what past there, if he has been rightly informed.

(Then turning to Mr Kirkland they proceeded—And you father, well knew, having often heard, the result of that meeting, & we took it for granted you had rightly informed our great father, *long ago*.)

Our great father the great minister is at great trouble & expence to gospelise us Indians—& must be grieved, even pained in heart, that so many of his designs are frustrated; & so many of his attempts prove utterly abortive! To remedy this, we advise our father to consider well, & take good heed in his future endeavors—yea, let him take very good heed. Let him move slowly; very slowly.—Let him examine thoroughly & critically in the minds & state of the Indians, in whatever place he may design any future mission. We pity him on account of his great distance from the Indian country.—

How often has he sent, this great distance, with high expectations of success, when there has not been the least encouraging appearance among us! And so his missions have turned out a mere sham, & all in vain! Why, father, we are here upon the spot, within hearing of what passes through the whole house of our confederacy; if we had ever heard anything encourageing, from any quarter of our neighbourhood, with respect to the gospel's moveing forward, we should have instantly informed you. And here are those who are commissioned more immediately for that purpose.

As to what we understand of your son's mission to Onondaga, & their answer, we lords beg to refer you to those who have attended your son in his journey there; as they undoubtedly may be more perfectly acquainted with the whole transactions, on both sides; & also inform what past there. Here sits one, *Thomas* by name, who well knows the whole affair from first to last.

Whenever we hear of any place in our neighbourhood, we shall readily inform our father the great minister, that he may not send any more in vain at this great distance.

We would again desire that our father's long deferd expectations from Onondaga may pain him no more—& hope he will take good heed & well digest his future missions. Let him not send again without sufficient information & good encouragement: because some Indians are not wise, & have thought they must too hastily become religious, before they have time to make their choice, & duly considered the nature of the offers made them.

Father, agreeable to your desire we have thus spoke our minds freely & with fidelity.—

Speech of the Onondaga Council
1772

Brother, we heartily thank you that we now understand the whole of your message, as you are come with the word of God.

You have spoke exceeding well! Very *sweet* words indeed, as comeing from the tongue, from when we perceive you have spoke!

But brother, do you think we are altogether ignorant of your methods of instruction? (Then takeing & shakeing him by the shoulder said) Why, brother, you are deceiveing yourself! We understand not only your speech, but your *manner* of teaching Indian. We understand affairs that are transacted at a great distance to the westward—they are all brought here; this is our centering council-house: just so well am I acquainted with your deportment. I view all your conduct as just by, under my eyes. Take care brother!—In the first place, correct yourself. Learn yourself to understand the word of God, before you undertake to teach & govern others: for when you have come to understand it yourself, perhaps some of our children will like to make trial of your instructions. For the present brother, I shall watch your future conduct. You have spoke *exceeding* well, even to our *surprise,* that our children should become *wise in all things* by your instructions, & treated as *children* at your house, & not *servants!*

Brother, take care—you were too hasty, & strong in your manner of speaking, before the children & boys have any knowledge of your language.

Why, brother, if another hears my dog barking, or having hold of a creature, & bids him get out, & perhaps he don't obey him immediately, not understanding the voice; upon which the stranger catches up a club & malls my dog—I shall resent it because he is my dog. Brother, I love my dog. What do you think of children then in the like case? . . .

Brother, you must learn of the French ministers if you would understand, & know how to treat Indians. They don't speak roughly; nor do they for every little mistake take up a club & flog them. It seems to us that they teach the word of God—they are very charitable—& can't see those they instruct *naked* or *hungry.* . . .

Brother, possess your mind in peace. We will take into consideration the message you have brought us:—But our people must assemble first.

As the word of God is of such vast importance, our brethern the *outward* door, the *Senecas,* must be informed. When they speak their minds, you shall hear ours; if *they* embrace your message, *we* shall undoubtedly.

Neither our brethren the *Mohawks,* nor the *Onoidas* did tell us when they began to embrace your religion. But we are the central-council-house, & can't determine without the voice of all our distant brethren.

A DELAWARE "MOUTHPIECE"

Joseph Pepee, a Christian Delaware from New Jersey, served as interpreter for missionary David McClure during the latter's travels to the Delaware towns in the Ohio country in 1772. He not only translated for McClure but acted as the medium through which McClure responded to doubting Indians. One of the Delawares objected to conversion because the Christians he knew were not good role models. They were, he said, "worse, or more wicked than we are, and we think it better to be such as we are than such as they are." McClure gave Pepee instructions about how he should answer, "knowing him capable of it," and Pepee "enlarged with great zeal and ability." McClure recorded the gist of the talk, but how much of it was Pepee and how much McClure is hard to say. McClure's words give an accurate account of the decline in Indian fortunes as Europeans increased in number, but it is questionable how many of the Indian listeners shared the McClure/Pepee interpretation of the cause of that decline.

JOSEPH PEPEE

Response to the
Unconverted Delawares
1772

The white people, whom you are acquainted with, (meaning the traders) are no Christians; they do not know or do the things which God has told them in the Bible. No, Christians will not receive them into their society. If you want to see christians you must go to Philadelphia. There you will see good people, who love the word of the Great God, and mind it. . . .

We remember, . . . that our fathers told us, how numerous the Indians were in their days, & in the days of their fathers. Great towns of Indians were all along the sea shore, and on the Rivers, and now, if you travel through that country, you will scarcely see an Indian; but you will see great and flourishing towns of white people, who possess the land of our fathers. And we are cut off, and fall back upon these distant rivers, and are reduced to a small number. The white people increase, and we Indians decrease. I can tell you, my countrymen, the reason of this. The white people worship the true God, and please him, and God blesses and prospers them. We and our fathers worshiped Devils, or them that are no Gods, and therefore God frowns upon us. And if you continue ignorant of him, when you have opportunity to know God and worship him, he will cut you off, & give this good country to a people that shall serve him. And if it shall be asked what has become of the Indians that lived here? none will be able to tell. You will be cut off, and your children as a great many powerful Indian nations have been, and none of them are left.

"THE WHITE WOMAN OF THE GENESEE"

Accurate information about and viewpoints from Native American women in colonial times are extremely scarce, and historians usually have tried to reconstruct the experiences of Indian women through words written by European men. One of the few exceptions is the life story of Mary Jemison, a white woman who was captured and adopted by the Senecas at about age

---

Franklin B. Dexter, ed., *Diary of David McClure* (New York: Knickerbocker Press, 1899), 81–82.

---

fifteen in 1758. The Iroquois traditionally adopted captives into their society to fill the place of deceased relatives. Mary Jemison married an Indian husband and raised a family. In time and in cultural allegiance she became a Seneca, sharing fully the lives of eighteenth-century Seneca women. She lived most of her life in the Genesee country of western New York, the Seneca heartland, and became known as the "white woman of the Genesee." In her old age, she dictated her story. Though the narrative of her life is flawed by the intrusive influence of her nineteenth-century writer, it nevertheless provides us with a rare opportunity to read the words of a woman who was living in Indian country in times of dramatic change.

Indian warriors took hundreds of colonists captive during the early wars in North America. Some of the captives were killed, some were ritually tortured, some were ransomed, and some escaped or were otherwise liberated. Many, however, lived the rest of their lives in Indian villages. Captive children sometimes grew up thinking they were Indians. Older captives often built new lives, marrying into Indian society and raising children as the memories of their former life faded. Contrary to English colonial propaganda and Hollywood stereotypes, Indians did not always subject their captives to cruel treatment. Indeed, Indian war parties regularly treated with kindness prisoners whom they expected to adopt, especially women and children. Once adopted and accepted into Indian society, many captives refused the opportunity to return home, preferring life with their new families. Many women appear to have found life in an Indian community more rewarding than the isolation and hard work that was the common lot of a wife on the colonial frontier.

These extracts from the autobiography of Mary Jemison give insights into the ways in which—by adoption, acceptance, kind treatment, and family ties—one woman came to be a "white Indian." After the American Revolution, Mary Jemison had the chance to return to white society but refused. By the time she died, she had had two husbands (one a Delaware, the other a Seneca), she had borne eight children (only three of whom survived her), and she had thirty-nine grandchildren and fourteen great-grandchildren. Jemison is still a prominent name among the Senecas.

MARY JEMISON

A Narrative of Her Life

1824

At night we arrived at a small Seneca Indian town, at the mouth of a small river, that was called by the Indians, in the Seneca language, She-nan-jee, where the two Squaws to whom I belonged resided. There we landed, and the Indians went on; which was the last I ever saw of them.

Having made fast to the shore, the Squaws left me in the canoe while they went to their wigwam or house in the town, and returned with a suit of Indian clothing, all new, and very clean and nice. My clothes, though whole and good when I was taken, were now torn in pieces, so that I was almost naked. They first undressed me and threw my rags into the river; then washed me clean and dressed me in the new suit they had just brought, in complete Indian style; and then led me home and seated me in the center of their wigwam.

I had been in that situation but a few minutes, before all the Squaws in the town came in to see me. I was soon surrounded by them, and they immediately set up a most dismal howling, crying bitterly, and wringing their hands in all the agonies of grief for a deceased relative.

Their tears flowed freely, and they exhibited all the signs of real mourning. At the commencement of this scene, one of their number began, in a voice somewhat between speaking and singing, to recite some words to the following purport, and continued the recitation till the ceremony was ended; the company at the same time varying the appearance of their countenances, gestures and tone of voice, so as to correspond with the sentiments expressed by their leader:

"Oh our brother! Alas! He is dead—he has gone; he will never return! Friendless he died on the field of the slain, where his bones are yet lying unburied! Oh, who will not mourn his sad fate? No tears dropped around him; oh, no! No tears of his sisters were there! He fell in his prime, when his arm was most needed to keep us from danger! Alas! he has gone! and left us in sorrow, his loss to bewail: Oh where is his spirit? His spirit went naked, and hungry it wanders, and thirsty and wounded it groans to return! Oh helpless and wretched, our brother has gone! No blanket nor food to nourish and warm him; nor candles to light him, nor weapons of war:—Oh, none of

James E. Seaver, *A Narrative of the Life of Mrs. Mary Jemison* (1824 and various editions).

those comforts had he! But well we remember his deeds!—The deer he could take on the chase! The panther shrunk back at the sight of his strength! His enemies fell at his feet! He was brave and courageous in war! As the fawn he was harmless: his friendship was ardent: his temper was gentle: his pity was great! Oh! our friend, our companion is dead! Our brother, our brother, alas! he is gone! But why do we grieve for his loss? In the strength of a warrior, undaunted he left us, to fight by the side of the Chiefs! His war-whoop was shrill! His rifle well aimed laid his enemies low: his tomahawk drank of their blood: and his knife flayed their scalps while yet covered with gore! And why do we mourn? Though he fell on the field of the slain, with glory he fell, and his spirit went up to the land of his fathers in war! Then why do we mourn? With transports of joy they received him, and fed him, and clothed him, and welcomed him there! Oh friends, he is happy; then dry up your tears! His spirit has seen our distress, and sent us a helper whom with pleasure we greet. Dickewamis has come: then let us receive her with joy! She is handsome and pleasant! Oh! she is our sister, and gladly we welcome her here. In the place of our brother she stands in our tribe. With care we will guard her from trouble; and may she be happy till her spirit shall leave us."

In the course of that ceremony, from mourning they became serene—joy sparkled in their countenances, and they seemed to rejoice over me as over a long lost child. I was made welcome amongst them as a sister to the two Squaws before mentioned, and was called Dickewamis; which being inter-preted, signifies a pretty girl, a handsome girl, or a pleasant, good thing. That is the name by which I have ever since been called by the Indians.

I afterwards learned that the ceremony I at that time passed through, was that of adoption. The two squaws had lost a brother in Washington's war, sometime in the year before, and in consequence of his death went up to Fort Pitt, on the day on which I arrived there, in order to receive a prisoner or an enemy's scalp, to supply their loss.

It is a custom of the Indians, when one of their number is slain or taken prisoner in battle, to give to the nearest relative to the dead or absent, a prisoner, if they have chanced to take one, and if not, to give him the scalp of an enemy. On the return of the Indians from conquest, which is always announced by peculiar shoutings, demonstrations of joy, and the exhibition of some trophy of victory, the mourners come forward and make their claims. If they receive a prisoner, it is at their option either to satiate their vengeance by taking his life in the most cruel manner they can conceive of; or, to receive and adopt him into the family, in the place of him whom they have lost. All the prisoners that are taken in battle and carried to the encampment or town by the Indians, are given to the bereaved families, till their number is made good. And unless the mourners have but just received the news of their bereavement, and are under the operation of a paroxysm of grief, anger and revenge; or, unless the prisoner is very old, sickly, or homely, they generally save him, and treat him kindly. But if their mental wound is fresh, their loss so great that they deem it irreparable, or if their prisoner or prisoners do not meet their approbation, no torture, let it be ever so cruel, seems sufficient to make them satisfaction. It is family, and not national, sacrifices amongst the Indians, that has given them an indelible stamp as barbarians, and identified their character with the idea which is generally formed of unfeeling ferocity, and the most abandoned cruelty.

It was my happy lot to be accepted for adoption; and at the time of the ceremony I was received by the two squaws, to supply the place of their brother in the family; and I was ever considered and treated by them as a real sister, the same as though I had been born of their mother.

During my adoption, I sat motionless, nearly terrified to death at the appearance and actions of the company, expecting every moment to feel their vengeance, and suffer death on the spot. I was, however, happily disappointed, when at the close of the ceremony the company retired, and my sisters went about employing every means for my consolation and comfort.

Being now settled and provided with a home, I was employed in nursing the children, and doing light work about the house. Occasionally I was sent out with the Indian hunters, when they went but a short distance, to help them carry their game. My situation was easy; I had no particular hardships to endure. But still, the recollection of my parents, my brothers and sisters, my home, and my own captivity, destroyed my happiness, and made me constantly solitary, lonesome and gloomy.

My sisters would not allow me to speak English in their hearing; but remembering the charge that my dear mother gave me at the time I left her, whenever I chanced to be alone I made a business of repeating my prayer, catechism, or something I had learned in order that I might not forget my own language. By practising in that way I retained it till I came to Genesee flats, where I soon became acquainted with English people with whom I have been almost daily in the habit of conversing.

My sisters were diligent in teaching me their language; and to their great satisfaction I soon learned so that I could understand it readily, and speak it fluently. I was very fortunate in falling into their hands; for they were kind good natured women; peaceable and mild in their dispositions; temperate and decent in their habits, and very tender and gentle towards me. I have great reason to respect them, though they have been dead a great number of years.

The town where they lived was pleasantly situated on the Ohio, at the mouth of the Shenanjee: the land produced good corn; the woods furnished a plenty of game, and the waters abounded with fish. Another river emptied itself into the Ohio, directly opposite the mouth of the Shenanjee. We spent the summer at that place, where we planted, hoed, and harvested a large crop of corn, of an excellent quality.

I had then been with the Indians four summers and four winters, and had become so far accustomed to their mode of living, habits and dispositions, that my anxiety to get away, to be set at liberty, and leave them, had almost subsided. With them was my home; my family was there, and there I had many friends to whom I was warmly attached in consideration of the favors, affection and friendship with which they had uniformly treated me, from the time of my adoption. Our labor was not severe; and that of one year was exactly similar, in almost every respect, to that of the others, without that endless variety that is to be observed in the common labor of the white people. Notwithstanding the Indian women have all the fuel and bread to procure, and the cooking to perform, their task is probably not harder than that of white women, who have those articles provided for them; and their cares certainly are not half as numerous, nor as great. In the summer season, we planted, tended and harvested our corn, and generally had all our children with us; but had no master to oversee or drive us, so that we could work as leisurely as we pleased. We had no ploughs on the Ohio; but performed the whole process of planting and hoeing with a small tool that resembled, in some respects, a hoe with a very short handle.

Our cooking consisted in pounding our corn into samp or hommany, boiling the hommany, making now and then a cake and baking it in the ashes, and in boiling or roasting our venison. As our cooking and eating utensils consisted of a hommany block and pestle, a small kettle, a knife or two, and a few vessels of bark or wood, it required but little time to keep them in order for use.

Spinning, weaving, sewing, stocking knitting, and the like, are arts which have never been practised in the Indian tribes generally. After the revolutionary war, I learned to sew, so that I could make my own clothing after a poor fashion; but the other domestic arts I have been wholly ignorant of the application of, since my captivity. In the season of hunting, it was our business, in addition to our cooking, to bring home the game that was taken by the Indians, dress it, and carefully preserve the eatable meat, and prepare or dress the skins. Our clothing was fastened together with strings of deer skin, and tied on with the same.

In that manner we lived, without any of those jealousies, quarrels, and revengeful battles between families and individuals, which have been common in the Indian tribes since the introduction of ardent spirits amongst them.

The use of ardent spirits amongst the Indians, and the attempts which have been made to civilize and christianize them by the white people, has constantly made them worse and worse; increased their vices, and robbed them of many of their virtues; and will ultimately produce their extermination. I have seen, in a number of instances, the effects of education upon some of our Indians, who were taken when young, from their families, and placed at school before they had had an opportunity to contract many Indian habits, and there kept till they arrived to manhood; but I have never seen one of those but what was an Indian in every respect after he returned. Indians must and will be Indians, in spite of all the means that can be used for their cultivation in the sciences and arts.

One thing only marred my happiness, while I lived with them on the Ohio; and that was the recollection that I had once had tender parents, and a home that I loved. Aside from that consideration, or, if I had been taken in infancy, I should have been contented in my situation. Notwithstanding all that has been said against the Indians, in consequence of their cruelties to their enemies—cruelties that I have witnessed, and had abundant proof of—it is a fact that they are naturally kind, tender and peaceable towards their friends, and strictly honest; and that those cruelties have been practised, only upon their enemies, according to their idea of justice.

NOTES

[1] Clayton Coleman Hall, ed., *Narratives of Early Maryland* (New York: Scribner's, 1910), 89–90.

[2] John Gilmeary Shea, ed., *History and General Description of New France,* by P. F. X. Charlevoix, S.J. 6 vols. (New York, 1870), 2:79.

[3] See page 133.

[4] Experience Mayhew, *Indian Converts: Or, Some Account of the Lives and Dying Speeches of a considerable Number of the Christianized Indians of Martha's Vineyard* (London, 1727), 22, 237.

[5] Helen Hunt Jackson, *A Century of Dishonor* (New York, 1881), 299–300.

[6] For additional discussion of these and other Native American responses to Christianity, see James P. Ronda, " 'We Are Well as We Are': An Indian Critique of Seventeenth-Century Christian Missions," *William and Mary Quarterly* 34 (1977): 66–82.

[7] Niantic. In the seventeenth century, the western Niantics of southern Connecticut had been allies of the Pequots; the eastern Niantics in Rhode Island had been allies of the Narragansetts.

[8] Reverend Azariah Horton (1715–1777), a missionary to the Shinnecock Indians on Long Island.

[9] Reverend Samuel Buell (1716–1798), a minister at Easthampton, Long Island.

[10] Isaac Watts, the famous eighteenth-century hymn writer.

[11] Reverend Samuel Kirkland (1741–1808), Presbyterian missionary to the Oneidas and founder of Hamilton College in Clinton, New York.

3

Land, Trade, and Treaties

---

*We know our Lands are now become more valuable. The white People think
we do not know their Value; but we are sensible that the Land is everlasting,
and the few Goods we receive for it are soon worn out and Gone.*
—Canasatego to the governor of Pennsylvania, 1742[1]

*These wicked Whiskey Sellers, when they have once got the Indians in
Liquor, make them sell the very Clothes from their Backs. In short, if this
Practice be continued, we must be inevitably ruined.*
—Oneida sachem Scarouady to Pennsylvania treaty commissioners, 1753[2]

Frontier diplomacy involved a lot of talk. Indians and colonists met in formal
council to discuss issues of concern, make peace, prevent war, and renew
friendships. Very often the talks were conducted on equal terms, with Europeans following much of the protocol of Indian diplomacy. In general, however, discussion focused on the two things Europeans wanted most from
Indian people: their land and their trade. The issue of land was never far
from the surface in negotiations. Europeans used a broad repertoire of
devices to obtain land, one of which was to encourage Indians to run up large
debts in trade. The tribe's accumulated bill then could be settled only by the
cession of territory. Indian leaders sometimes used land sales as a strategy
for trying to keep colonists at bay, hoping that this time their land hunger
would be satisfied, but the pressure on Indian lands was unrelenting, a
constant source of friction.

Indians waged a continuing struggle against fraudulent treaties and
trespass. Treaties between government agents and Indian delegates and
illegal transactions between land speculators and compliant chiefs deprived
Native Americans of millions of acres of land. When tensions exploded in
open conflict and Indians were defeated, treaties often contained stipulations
that they cede yet more land as atonement for their "war guilt." In 1790, the
new United States Congress passed the Indian Trade and Non-Intercourse
Act, declaring that sales of Indian land were invalid unless they had congres-
sional approval. This did not stop the loss of Indian lands, however. Many
modern lawsuits by Indian tribes in the eastern United States hinge on
violations of the Trade and Non-Intercourse Act.

Trade was often a key ingredient in establishing political and military alliances. In Indian societies, trade traditionally took the form of ritual exchanges that cemented relationships. But with the coming of the European fur and deerskin trades, Indian people became increasingly dependent on European trade to provide the necessities of life. Many Indians became commercial hunters, exchanging animal pelts for new merchandise, especially firearms. Europeans competed for Indian trade and Indians sometimes played the competitors against each other. Dekanissore, or Decanesora, an Onondaga orator who took a prominent role in negotiations with the French and English around 1700, threatened to "speake no more of praying or Christianity." French and British trade goods were too expensive; he would, he said, listen to the religion of whoever offered the best trade.[3]

European trade goods and European alcohol contributed to the destabilization of Indian societies. Each created its own form of dependency and undermined the ability of Indian communities to resist encroachment on their lands. Indian leaders, seeing the devastating impact of alcohol on their people and concerned about their declining economic independence, complained about the effects of trade with Europeans even as they realized that they could no longer do without it. "My people ... cannot ... live independent of the English," said Skiagunsta, head warrior of the Lower Cherokees. "The clothes we wear we cannot make ourselves. They are made for us. We use their ammunition with which to kill deer. We cannot make our guns. Every necessary of life we must have from the white people."[4]

Whether they traded lands or furs, Indian people found they were exchanging a nonreplenishable resource for the merchandise of Europe and a future of increasing dependency. With their lands and game gone, Indians often were reduced to taking jobs in the colonial economy or pursuing a precarious subsistence on the margins of colonial society. The inequitable nature of their dealings with Europeans did not escape Indians. The records of early America are full of complaints by Indian people that they have been cheated out of their lands and furs.

SUBMISSION TO "OLD ENGLAND"

As their numbers dwindled and their independence diminished before their eyes, Native Americans often felt their best chance of survival lay in accepting the inevitable and putting themselves under the protection of colonial powers. The following "act of submission," however, illustrates Native American statecraft, not Native American impotence.

The Narragansett Indians of Rhode Island acted as allies to the English in the destruction of the Pequots in 1637. The Narragansett sachem Miantonomi had played an important role in the Pequot War, but in 1642 he called for drastic and united action on the part of the Indians before it was too late to stop the English from ruining the Indian world. "You know our fathers had plenty of deer and skins, our plains were full of deer, as also our woods, and of turkies, and our coves full of fish and fowl," he reminded the Montauk Indians of Long Island. "But these English have gotten our land, they with scythes cut down the grass, and with axes fell the trees; their cows and horses eat the grass, and their hogs spoil our clam banks, and we shall all be starved."[5] The next year, war broke out between the Narragansetts and the Mohegan Indians of Connecticut. Miantonomi was captured and executed by Mohegans, who were urged on by the English.

The Narragansetts were still a power in the region, but they sensed their growing isolation as other tribes were decimated by war and disease and the Puritan English increased in strength. They therefore placed themselves under English protection in a "voluntary and free submission" in 1644. But notice that the Narragansetts make their submission to King Charles I and the government of "Old England," not to the Puritan authorities in New England. The Puritans regarded the Narragansetts as "going over their heads" to a higher authority, but the Narragansetts astutely asserted their equality with the New England Puritans; they and the colonists were both subjects of the king. The Narragansetts looked to Old England, not to New England, for justice and protection.

NARRAGANSETT INDIANS

Act of Submission

1644

The Act and Deed of the voluntary and free submission of the chiefe Sachem, and the rest of the Princes, with the whole people of the Nanhigansets, unto the Government and protection of that Honorable State of Old-England; set downe, here. verbatim.

Know all Men, Colonies, Peoples, and Nations, unto whom the fame hereof shall come; that wee, the chiefe Sachems, Princes or Governours of the Nanhigansets (in that part of America, now called New-England), together with the joynt and unanimous consent of all our people and subjects, inhabitants thereof, do upon serious consideration, mature and deliberate advise and counsell, great and weighty grounds and reasons moving us thereunto, whereof one most effectual unto us, is, that noble fame we have heard of that Great and mighty Prince, Charles,[6] King of Great Britaine, in that honorable and princely care he hath of all his servants, and true and loyall subjects, the consideration whereof moveth and bendeth our hearts with one consent, freely, voluntarily, and most humbly to submit, subject, and give over ourselves, peoples, lands, rights, inheritances, and possessions whatsoever, in ourselves and our heires successively for ever, unto the protection, care and government of that worthy and royal Prince, Charles, King of Great Britaine and Ireland, his heires and successors forever, to be ruled and governed according to the ancient and honorable lawes and customes, established in that so renowned realme and kingdome of Old England; we do, therefore, by these presents, confesse, and most willingly and submissively acknowledge ourselves to be the humble, loving and obedient servants and subjects of his Majestie; to be ruled, ordered, and disposed of, in ourselves and ours, according to his princely wisdome, counsell and lawes of that honorable State of Old England; *upon condition of His Majesties' royal protection,* and wrighting us of what wrong is, or may be done unto us, according to his honorable lawes and customes, exercised amongst his subjects, in their preservation and safety, and in the defeating and overthrow of his, and their enemies; not that we find ourselves necessitated hereunto,

---

Records of the Colony of Rhode Island (Providence, 1856), 1:134–36.

---

in respect of our relation, or occasion we have, or may have, with any of the natives in these parts, knowing ourselves sufficient defence, and able to judge in any matter or cause in that respect; but have just cause of jealousy and suspicion of some of His Majesty's pretended subjects. Therefore our desire is, to have our matters and causes heard and tried according to his just and equall lawes, in that way and order His Highness shall please to appoint: *Nor can we yield over ourselves unto any, that are subjects themselves in any case;* having ourselves been the chief Sachems, or Princes successively, of the country, time out of mind; and for our present and lawfull enacting hereof, being so farre remote from His Majestie, wee have, by joynt consent, made choice of foure of his loyall and loving subjects, our trusty and well-beloved friends, Samuel Gorton, John Wickes, Randall Houlden and John Warner,[7] whom we have deputed, and made our lawfull Attornies or Commissioners, not only for the acting and performing of this our Deed, in the behalfe of his Highnesse, but also for the safe custody, carefull conveyance, and declaration hereof unto his grace: being done upon the lands of the Nanhigansett, at a Court or Generall Assembly called and assembled together, of purpose, for the publick enacting, and manifestation hereof.

And for the further confirmation, and establising of this our Act and Deed, wee, the abovesaid Sachems or Princes, have, according to that commendable custome of Englishmen, subscribed our names and sett our seals hereunto, as so many testimonies of our fayth and truth, our love and loyalty to that our dread Soveraighne, and that according to the Englishmen's account. Dated the nineteenth day of April, one thousand six hundred and forty-four.

Pessicus, his marke, Chief Sachem, and successor of that late deceased Miantonomy.

The marke of that ancient Canonicus, Protector of that late deceased Miantonomy, during the time of his nonage[8]

The marke of Mixan, son and heire of that abovesaid Conanicus.

Witnessed by two of the chiefe counsellors to Sachem Pessicus.

Indians.
Awashoosse, his marke,

Tomanick,
his marke.

Sealed and delivered, in the presence of these persons:

English.
Christopher Helme,
Robert Potter,
Richard Carder.

TWO LAND DEEDS FROM MAINE

Deeds in which Indian people agreed to sell lands are common in colonial records. Some are no doubt forgeries; some were written, if not dictated, by the colonists. Often the latter documents were executed under dubious circumstances, with Indians acting under threat of violence, the influence of alcohol, or misapprehension about just what they were signing away. Different concepts of land tenure complicated the issue. Viewing land as a resource to be shared rather than as a commodity to be bought and sold, Indians often believed that they were conveying only the right to occupy the land, not exclusive ownership. Abenaki sachem Nanuddemance, in his deed to John Parker of lands on the Kennebec River, specifically reserved to himself the right to hunt and fish on those lands.

However, not all land sales were fraudulent; some were legitimate transactions between parties who understood the terms of the agreements and the implications of their actions. Land deeds can therefore shed light on native patterns of land tenure and tribal boundaries: Land was held in common by the entire tribe, but it seems clear that some members of the tribe had more rights to some lands than others. It also seems clear that Native Americans quite quickly came to grasp English notions of property and to understand the pitfalls in what one historian has called "the deed game." Deeds suggest some of the motives Indian people had for selling: They may have needed less land in the wake of population loss to new diseases, they may have needed to obtain money to buy goods or pay debts in the wake of the disruption of their traditional economy, or they may have believed they were not losing much since they specifically retained hunting and fishing rights. Deeds also provide the actual names of Indian people who might otherwise remain anonymous. The intriguingly named Robin (or Robert) Hood, or Rawmegin, was an influential sachem who signed seventeen deeds between 1639 and 1675. We know little or nothing about Uphannu, alias "Jane the Indian of Scarborough," but the fact that she sold a tract of land at Blue Point with her mother and brother in 1659 reveals something about the role of women in seventeenth-century Abenaki society.

Many deeds are long and detailed; the two reprinted here are short, but they are nonetheless valuable records of cross-cultural encounters. It was not uncommon for land grantees to wait several years before recording their deeds, doing so only when they themselves were preparing to sell their lands.

NANUDDEMANCE

Deed to John Parker

June 14, 1659

This Instrument Witnesseth this 14th of June 1659 : that I Nanuddemance Proprietor of these Lands hereafter mentioned, have lett sett & sould all my right title of the sayd Lands & Tymber, with the appurtenances of Marsh, & Upland Meddow, unto John Parker now dwelling upon the sd Land. unto him his heyres executors & administrators for ever, for one beaver skine received, & the yearly rent of one bushell of Corne, & a quart of Lyquor to bee payd unto the sd Nanuddemance & his heyres for ever at or before every five & Twenteth day of Decemb[r] being Christmas day at the dwelling house of the sd Parker, reserveing out of the aforesd Land, Lyberty unto mee my heyres to fish fowle & hunt. alsoe to sett otter Trapps with out Molestation/ The aforesd Land being bounded as followeth/

Begining at the first high head. upon the South West side of Sagadahoe River. & soe running up the sd River unto Winnigans Cricke being by estimation six Miles. or there abouts. & all that Tract of Land South Westward unto the Eastern part of Cascoe Bay/ To confirme the treuth hereof, I have hereunto sett my hand the day & yeare above written/

York Deeds (Portland, Maine, 1887), vol. 2, fols. 13, 113–14.

Witnesses/
  Henery Jocelyn/
  Richard Foxwell/
  Roger Spencer/

of   The Marke
             Nanuddemance

The marke of *ᏚᏉ*
Mr Robert Hoode Sagamore/

    A true Coppy of this grant or deed above written, transcribed out of the originall & their with compared this 22nd day of May : 1667 : p Edw: Rishworth Re : Cor :

JANE OF SCARBOROUGH

Deed to Andrew and Arthur Alger

September 19, 1659

The 19th of Septemb^r 1659 :
The declaration of Jane the Indean of Scarbrough concerneing Land/
    This aforesayd Jane alias uphañum doth declare that her mother namely Naguasqua the wife of Wickwarrawaske Sagamore, & her brother namely ugagoyuskitt & her selfe namely uphannu ⁓ coæqually hath sould unto Andrew Alger, & to his brother Arther Alger a Tract of Land, beginning att the Mouth of ye River Called blew Poynt River, where the River doth part, & soe bounded up along with the River Called Oawascoage in Indean, & soe up three scoore poole above the falls, on the one side, & on the other side bounded up along with the Northermost River, that Treaneth by the great hill of Abram Jocelyns & goeth Northward, bounding from the head of ye River South West & soe to the aforesd bounds, namely three scoore pooles, above the Falls; This aforesayd Uphanum doth declare, that her mother & brother & shee hath already in hand received full satisfaction of the aforesayd Algers for the aforesd the Land from the begining of the world to this day provided on conditions that for tyme to come from yeare to yeare yearly, the aforesd Algers shall peaceably suffer uphannum to plant In Andrew Algers fejld, soe long as uphannu ⁓ & her mother Neguasqua doe both live/

& alsoe one busll of corne for acknowledgm^t every yeare soe long as they both shall Live/ Uphannu ˜ doth declare that ye bargan was made In the yeare 1651 : unto which shee doth subscribe/

the marke of uphannum/

In ye Prsence of Robert Cooke/ the day & date above written/

Jane an Indean Woman, did appeare before mee the 21th of June 1672 : & did acknowledg this Instrum^t was the deed of her mother & her selfe, before mee Bryan Pendleton

Assõte/

A true Coppy of this Instrument, with the acknowledgment y^{r}of, transcribed out of the originall & y^{r}with compared, this 25th of June 1672 : p Edw : Rishworth ReCor :

INDIAN LAND CLAIMS DISPUTED

The sachem Mittark of Gay Head on Martha's Vineyard died in 1683 and was succeeded by his son, Joseph or Josiah Mittark, who apparently sold Gay Head lands to Governor Thomas Dongan of New York. The Gay Head Indians protested the sale and produced the following document, originally written in the Massachusett language, to support their case before an Indian commission. Subsequent inquiry suggested that the document may have been written long after Mittark's death, and the Indians' claims were refused. Nevertheless, the document clearly conveys the Indians' beliefs about the nature of landholding and the obligations of the sachemship, which in southern New England seems usually to have passed through the male line.

MITTARK

Agreement of Gay Head Indians
Not to Sell Land to the English

1681

I am Muttaak, sachem of Gay Head and Nashaquitsa as far as Wanemessit. Know this all people. I Muttaak and my chief men and my children and my people, these are our lands. Forever we own them, and our posterity forever shall own them. I Muttaak and we the chief men, and with our children and all our (common) people (present), have agreed that no one (shall) sell land. But if anyone larcenously sells land, you shall take (back) your land, because it is forever your possession. But if anyone does not keep this agreement, he shall fall (and) have nothing more of this land at Gay Head and Nashaquitsa at all forever. I Muttaak and we the chief men, and our posterity, (say): And it shall be so forever. I Ummuttaak say this, and my chief men: if any of these sons of mine protects my sachemship, he shall forever be a sachem. But if [any of]* my sons does not protect my sachemship and sells it, he shall fall forever. And we chief men say this, and our sachem: if any of these sons of ours protects our chieftainship, he shall forever be a chief man. But if any of our sons does not protect our chieftainship and sells it, he shall fall forever. I Umuttaag, sachem, say this and my chief men; [this is] our agreement. We say it before God. It shall be so forever. I Ummuttaak, this is my hand (X), on the date September 11, 1681.

We chief men say this [and] our sachem; this is our agreement. [We say it] before God. It shall be so forever. These are our hands (X — X — X).

I John Keeps am a witness and this is my hand concerning the agreement of Ummuttaak and his chief men of Gay Head and Nashaquitsa, all (and) both. I Puttukquannan am a witness. I witnessed this agreement of Ummuttaak and his chief men of Gay Head and Nashaquitsa, both. No one forever (shall) sell it; they (shall) keep it. I Puttakquannan, this is my hand (X).

I Sasauwapinnoo am a witness. I witnessed the agreement of Ummuttaak and his chief men of Gay Head and Nashaquitsa, all (and) both. I Sasauwapinnoo, my hand.

*The brackets signify small omissions in the original copy, presumably copying errors by the English clerk who recorded it.

Ives Goddard and Kathleen J. Bragdon, eds., *Native Writings in Massachusett*, 2 vols. (Philadelphia: American Philosophical Society, 1988), 1:96–97.

THE "RIVER INDIANS"
ANSWER GOVERNOR BURNET

In late August 1722, William Burnet, governor of New York, met with Mahican Indians from the Hudson River (the English called all Indians on the lower Hudson "River Indians") to renew the Covenant Chain, the metaphor of friendship between the king of England and the Indians. In his opening remarks, the governor admonished the Mahicans for squandering their pelts and corn to buy rum and advised them to be more sober in the future. The Indians' reply was first translated from Mahican into Dutch and then from Dutch into English. Indians sometimes punctuated their speeches with presentations of beaver pelts rather than wampum, and such gifts represented an important ingredient of Indian diplomacy. Twenty years later the Onondaga orator Canasatego gave the governor of Pennsylvania a bundle of furs at a conference in Philadelphia, remarking, "It is customary with us to make a Present of Skins whenever we renew our Treaties."[9]

MAHICAN INDIANS

Reply to William Burnet,
Governor of New York

1722

Father

We are sensible that you are much in the right, that Rum does a great deal of Harm, we approve of all that you said on that Point, but the matter is this, When our people come from Hunting to the Town or Plantations and acquaint the Traders & People that we want Powder and Shot & Clothing, they first give us a large cup of Rum, and after we get the Taste of it crave for more so that in fine all the Beaver & Peltry we have hunted goes for drink, and we are left destitute either of Clothing or Ammunition, Therefore we desire our father to order the Tap or Crane to be shut & to prohibit y^e selling

E. B. O'Callaghan, ed., *Documents Relative to the Colonial History of the State of New York,* 15 vols. (Albany: Weed, Parsons, 1855), 5:662–63.

Figure 9. Etow Oh Koam, Mahican Chief
The Mahican Indians of the Hudson River first met Europeans when the Dutch
entered their homeland in 1609. They soon became involved in trade and, as the
document suggests, had a long and troubled history of dealing with the inroads of
European influences. In this portrait by John Verelst, Etow Oh Koam wears facial
tattoos and moccasins and holds a war club, but he also wears a European-style tunic,
a sword, and a scarlet cloak presented to him during his visit to London in 1710.

of Rum, for as long as the Christians will sell Rum, our People will drink it,   do give 3 Beavers

Father

We acknowledge that our Father is very much in the right to tell us that we squander away our Indian Corn which should subsist our Wives & Children but one great cause of it is y^t many of our People are obliged to hire Land of the Christians at a very dear Rate, to give half the Corn for Rent & the other half they are tempted by Rum to sell, & so the Corn goes, y^t ye Poor women & children are left to shift as well as the can   do give 3 Beavers

Father

We have no more Land the Christians when they buy a small spot of Land of us, ask us if we have no more Land & when we say yes they enquire the name of the Land & take in a greater Bounds than was intended to be sold them & the Indians not understanding what is writ in the Deed or Bill of Sale sign it and are so deprived of Part of their Lands — Give 3 Beavers

Father

In former days when the Christians came to settle this Country they came with a ship & desired to fasten their Cable to the Hills near Hosak above Albany, which we readily granted & ever since we have lived in Friendship & Amity together, which we hope will continue so long as Sun & Moon endure   Gave 3 Beavers

THE ALIENATION OF THE NATCHEZ

In 1723, the Natchez Indians of what is today southern Mississippi went to war with the French. Antoine Simon Le Page du Pratz, a French traveler who spent five years among the Natchez, sensed the growing tension when the Stung Serpent, a high-ranking noble he had counted as his friend, passed him by with barely a word. When du Pratz demanded to know the reason for his coldness, the Stung Serpent, "brother to the Great Sun, and Chief of the Warriors of the Natchez," gave a reply, reprinted here, to which the Frenchman could not find an answer.

The French virtually destroyed the Natchez in the ensuing conflict. Natchez survivors fled for refuge to the Chickasaws, who also waged bitter war against the French in the first half of the eighteenth century.

ANTOINE Le PAGE du PRATZ

Reply of the Stung Serpent

1723

Why did the French come into our country? We did not go to seek them. They asked land of us, because their country was too little for all the men that were in it. We told them they might take land where they pleased, there was enough for them and for us; that it was good the same sun should enlighten us both, and that we should walk as friends, in the same path, and that we would give them of our provisions, assist them to build, and to labor in their fields. We have done so; is not this true? What occasion, then, had we for Frenchmen? Before they came, did we not live better than we do, seeing we deprive ourselves of a part of our corn, our game, and fish, to give a part to them? In what respect, then, had we occasion for them? Was it for their guns? The bows and arrows, which we used, were sufficient to make us live well. Was it for their white, blue, and red blankets? We can do well enough with buffalo skins which are warmer; our women wrought feather blankets for the winter, and mulberry mantles for the summer; which indeed were not so beautiful, but our women were more laborious and less vain than they are now. In fine, before the arrival of the French we lived like men who can be satisfied with what they have; whereas at this day we are like slaves, who are not suffered to do as they please.

THE CASCO BAY TREATY

Treaty documents drawn up by Europeans constituted only the summary of lengthy proceedings with Indian delegates in formal councils. Misunderstandings, mistranslations, and even deliberate distortions and deceptions sometimes crept into the final text. In 1727, the English finalized a treaty with several bands of Abenaki Indians at Casco Bay in what is now Maine. (The treaty is reproduced in Appendix I.) As was usual in English treaties with Eastern Indians, the language and the terms of the treaty placed blame for past hostilities squarely on the shoulders of the Indians and depicted the Indians as rebellious subjects begging peace from their sovereign King

Antoine Le Page du Pratz, *The History of Louisiana,* trans. from the French (London, 1774), 41. Reprinted by J. S. W. Harmanson, New Orleans, 1947.

George. This testimony by a Penobscot who participated in the Casco Bay negotiations is extremely valuable in that it gives a detailed account of the deliberations from the Indians' perspective and points to the gulf that could exist between what Indian delegates remembered saying and what English treaty makers recorded. Loron, alias Sauguaarum or Sagourrab, Alexis, François Xavier, Meganumbee, and others were delegates from the Penobscot, Norridgewock, Passamaquoddy, Maliseet, and other tribes that the English called "Eastern Indians."

LORON SAUGUAARUM

An Account of Negotiations Leading to the Casco Bay Treaty

1727

I Panaouamskeyen, do inform ye—ye who are scattered all over the earth take notice—of what has passed between me and the English in negotiating the peace that I have just concluded with them. It is from the bottom of my heart that I inform you; and, as a proof that I tell you nothing but the truth, I wish to speak to you in my own tongue.

My reason for informing you, myself, is the diversity and contrariety of the interpretations I receive of the English writing in which the articles of peace are drawn up that we have just mutually agreed to. These writings appear to contain things that are not, so that the Englishman himself disavows them in my presence, when he reads and interprets them to me himself.

I begin then by informing you; and shall speak to you only of the principal and most important matter.

First, that I did not commence the negotiation for a peace, or settlement, but he, it was, who first spoke to me on the subject, and I did not give him any answer until he addressed me a third time. I first went to Fort St. George to hear his propositions, and afterwards to Boston, whither he invited me on the same business.

We were two that went Boston: I, Laurance Sagourrab, and John Ehen-

---

nekouit. On arriving there I did indeed salute him in the usual mode at the first interview, but I was not the first to speak to him. I only answered what he said to me, and such was the course I observed throughout the whole of our interview.

He began by asking me, what brought me hither? I did not give him for answer—I am come to ask your pardon; nor, I come to acknowledge you as my conqueror; nor, I come to make my submission to you; nor, I come to receive your commands. All the answer I made was that I was come on his invitation to me to hear the propositions for a settlement that he wished to submit to me.

Wherefore do we kill one another? he again asked me. 'Tis true that, in reply, I said to him—You are right. But I did not say to him, I acknowledge myself the cause of it, nor I condemn myself for having made war on him.

He next said to me—Propose what must be done to make us friends. 'Tis true that thereupon I answered him—It is rather for you to do that. And my reason for giving him that answer is, that having himself spoken to me of an arrangement, I did not doubt but he would make me some advantageous proposals. But I did not tell him that I would submit in every respect to his orders.

Thereupon, he said to me—Let us observe the treaties concluded by our Fathers, and renew the ancient friendship which existed between us. I made him no answer thereunto. Much less, I repeat, did I, become his subject, or give him my land, or acknowledge his King as my King. This I never did, and he never proposed it to me. I say, he never said to me—Give thyself and thy land to me, nor acknowledge my King for thy King, as thy ancestors formerly did.

He again said to me—But do you not recognize the King of England as King over all his states? To which I answered—Yes, I recognize him King of all his lands; but I rejoined, do not hence infer that I acknowledge thy King as my King, and King of my lands. Here lies my distinction—my Indian distinction. God hath willed that I have no King, and that I be master of my lands in common.

He again asked me—Do you not admit that I am at least master of the lands I have purchased? I answered him thereupon, that I admit nothing, and that I knew not what he had reference to.

He again said to me—If, hereafter, any one desire to disturb the negotiation of the peace we are at present engaged about, we will join together to arrest him. I again consented to that. But I did not say to him, and do not understand that he said to me, that we should go in company to attack such person, or that we should form a joint league, offensive and defensive, or that I should unite my brethren to his. I said to him only, and I understand him to say to me, that if any one wished to disturb our negotiation of peace, we would both endeavor to pacify him by fair words, and to that end would direct all our efforts.

He again said to me—In order that the peace we would negotiate be permanent, should any private quarrel arise hereafter between Indians and Englishmen, they must not take justice into their own hands, nor do any thing, the one to the other. It shall be the business of us chiefs to decide. I again agreed with him on that article, but I did not understand that he alone should be judge. I understood only that he should judge his people, and that I would judge mine.

Finally he said to me—There's our peace concluded; we have regulated every thing.

I replied that nothing had been yet concluded, and that it was necessary that our acts should be approved in a general assembly. For the present, an armistice is sufficient. I again said to him—I now go to inform all my relatives of what has passed between us, and will afterwards come and report to you what they'll say to me. Then he agreed in opinion with me.

Such was my negotiation on my first visit to Boston.

As for any act of grace, or amnesty, accorded to me by the Englishman, on the part of his King, it is what I have no knowledge of, and what the Englishman never spoke to me about, and what I never asked him for.

On my second visit to Boston we were four: I, Laurence Sagourrab, Alexis, Francois Xavier and Migounambe. I went there merely to tell the English that all my nation approved the cessation of hostilities, and the negotiation of peace, and even then we agreed on the time and place of meeting to discuss it. That place was Caskebay, and the time after Corpus Christi.[10]

Two conferences were held at Caskebay. Nothing was done at these two conferences except to read the articles above reported. Every thing I agreed to was approved and ratified, and on these conditions was the peace concluded.

One point only did I regulate at Caskebay. This was to permit the Englishman to keep a store at St. Georges; but a store only, and not to build any other house, nor erect a fort there, and I did not give him the land.

These are the principal matters that I wished to communicate to you who are spread all over the earth. What I tell you now is the truth. If, then, any one should produce any writing that makes me speak otherwise, pay no attention to it, for I know not what I am made to say in another language, but I know well what I say in my own. And in testimony that I say things as they are, I have signed the present minute which I wish to be authentic and to remain for ever.

THE "WALKING PURCHASE":
A DELAWARE COMPLAINT
AND AN IROQUOIS RESPONSE

Between 1630 and 1767, the Delaware or Lenni Lenape Indians of New Jersey and Pennsylvania signed nearly eight hundred deeds of land to colonists. In 1734, Thomas Penn, the son of William Penn, first governor and proprietor of Pennsylvania, claimed to have found a copy of a deed made in 1686 in which certain Delaware chiefs agreed to grant his father and his heirs lands "as far as a man can go in a day and a half," and from there to the Delaware River and down its course. Thomas Penn and the colonial authorities were eager to measure out the lands, and a number of Delaware chiefs reluctantly agreed. The Pennsylvanians violated the spirit of the agreement, however, by clearing a path and, on the day appointed for the "walk" in September 1737, they produced not a single person to walk the distance but a team of three runners. The point at which the third man collapsed exhausted at noon on the second day, about sixty-five miles from the starting point, was taken as the distance a man could walk in the time allotted.

The infamous "Walking Purchase" deprived the Delawares of the last of their lands in the upper Delaware and Lehigh valleys in Pennsylvania. The Indians made many complaints to the colonial authorities, but to little avail. In the petition of November 21, 1740, Delaware chiefs admitted selling certain tracts of land but denied ever having sold any land to William Penn or his sons. The governor of Pennsylvania complained against the Delawares' "Rudeness & ill Manners" on the issue and solicited the support of the Iroquois during a council in Philadelphia in the summer of 1742. After due deliberation of the evidence, the Onondaga Canasatego delivered a stinging rebuke to the Delawares, in which he asserted Iroquois dominance over the Delawares and their lands and ordered them to move to where the Six Nations could keep an eye on them. In 1756, the Delaware chief Teedyuscung was still fuming over the fraud, and in the early years of the American Revolution the Delaware chief White Eyes openly and defiantly rejected Iroquois claims to hegemony over his people or their lands.

The main interpreter at the 1742 conference in Philadelphia, as in many between the Iroquois and Pennsylvania in the mid-eighteenth century, was Conrad Weiser (1696–1760). Weiser had lived with the Mohawks in his youth and had learned their language. He had a long career on the frontier as a farmer, magistrate, soldier, and Indian agent.

Figure 10.   Lapowinsa, Delaware Chief
Lapowinsa was one of the Delaware chiefs who signed the "Walking Purchase"
treaty. His portrait was painted in 1735 by Gustavus Hesselius, a Swede who settled
in Philadelphia in 1711 and worked as a professional portrait painter.

DELAWARE INDIANS

Complaint against the "Walking Purchase"

November 21, 1740

To Mr. Jeremiah Langhorne[11] & all Magistrates of Pennsilvania

We pray that You You would take Notice of the Great Wrong We Receive in Our Lands, here are about 100 families Settled On it for what Reason they Cant tell. They tell them *that Thomas Penn has sold them the Land Which We think must be Very Strange that T. Penn Should Sell him that which was never his for We never Sold him this land.* The Case was this. That When We Were With Penn to treat as usual with his Father, He keep begging & plagueing us to Give him some Land & Never gives us leave to treat upon any thing till he Wearies us Out of Our Lives but What should We give Penn any Land for We never had any thing from him but honest Dealings & Civility. If he lets us alone We will let him alone. The Lands we do Own to be Ours, Begin, at the Mouth of Tohickon Runs up along the said Branch to the Head Springs thence up With a strait line [*to*] Patquating thence with a strait Line to the Blew Mountain thence to a Place called Mohaining thence along a Mountain called Neshameek thence along the Great Swamp to a Branch of Delaware River So along Delaware River to the Place where it first began.[12] All this is Our own Land Except Some tracts We have disposed off. The Tract of Durham The tract of Nicholas Depuis The Tract of Old Weiser[13] We have Sold *But for the Rest We have Never sold & We Desire Thomas Penn Would take these People off from their Land in Peace that we May not be at the trouble to drive them off for the Land We Will hold fast With both Our hands not in privately but in Open View of all the Countrey & all Our Friends & Relations That is the Eastern Indians & Our Uncles the five Nations & the Mohikkons & the twitways Shawanahs Shawekelou Tuskeroroes & the Takkesaw[14] the last. These all shall be by & hear us Speak & We Shall Stand at Our Uncles Breast When We Shall Speak.* Now Gentlemen & all others We Desire some of Your Assistance in this Affair for We have lived in Brotherly Friend Ship So We Desire to Continue the same if So be We can be Righted any Manner of Ways So We Remainz

Your Friends

Donald H. Kent, ed., *Pennsylvania Indian Treaties, 1737–1756* (Frederick, Md.: University Publications of America, 1984), 24, 45–46.

Wrote in the Margent of the Letters: The Indians Acknowledges this to be done by their Direction.

[*Forwarding note*] This is a Copy of a Petition Sent by the Indians Sometime ago so hoping his Excellency May look Over it & take it into Consideration.

CANASATEGO

Response to the Delawares' Complaint
July 12, 1742

At a Council held at the Proprietor's, July 12. 1742
Cousins,

Let this Belt of Wampum serve to chastise you. You ought to be taken by the Hair of the Head and shaked severely, till you recover your Senses and become sober. You don't know what Ground you stand on, nor what you are doing. Our Brother *Onas's*[15] Cause is very just and plain, and his Intentions to preserve Friendship. On the other Hand, Your Cause is bad; your Heart far from being upright; and you are maliciously bent to break the Chain of Friendship with our Brother *Onas* and his People. We have seen with our Eyes a Deed sign'd by nine of your Ancestors above *Fifty* Years ago for this very Land, and a Release sign'd, not many Years since, by some of your-selves and Chiefs now living, to the Number of fifteen or upwards.—But how come you to take upon you to sell Land at all: We conquered you; we made Women of you; you know you are Women, and can no more sell Land than Women; nor is it fit you should have the Power of selling Lands, since you would abuse it. This Land that you claim is gone through your Guts; you have been furnish'd with Cloaths, Meat and Drink, by the Goods paid you for it, and now you want it again, like Children as you are.—But what makes you sell Land in the Dark. Did you ever tell us that you had sold this Land. Did we ever receive any Part, even the Value of a Pipe-Shank, from you for it. You have told us a blind Story, that you sent a Messenger to us to inform us of the Sale, but he never came amongst us, nor we never heard any thing about it.—This is acting in the Dark, and very different from the Conduct our *Six* Nations observe in their Sales of Land; on such Occasions they give publick Notice, and invite all the *Indians* of their united Nations, and give them all a Share of the Present they receive for their Lands.—This is the

Behaviour of the wise united Nations.—But we find you are none of our Blood: You act a dishonest Part, not only in this but in other Matters; Your Ears are ever open to slanderous Reports about our Brethren; you receive them with as much Greediness as lewd Women receive the Embraces of bad Men. And for all these Reasons we charge you to remove instantly; we don't give you the Liberty to think about it. You are Women. Take the Advice of a wise Man, and remove immediately. You may return to the other Side of *Delaware* where you came from: But we do not know whether, considering how you have demean'd yourselves, you will be permitted to live there; or whether you have not swallowed that Land down your Throats as well as the Land on this Side. We therefore assign you two Places to go, either to *Wyomen* or *Shamokin*.[16] You may go to either of these Places, and then we shall have you more under our Eye, and shall see how you behave. Don't deliberate; but remove away, and take this Belt of Wampum.

This being interpreted by *Conrad Weiser* into *English,* and by *Cornelius Spring* into the *Delaware* Language, *Canassatego* taking a String of Wampum, added further.

After our just Reproof, and absolute Order to depart from the Land, you are now to take Notice of what we have further to say to you. This String of Wampum serves to forbid you, your Children and Grand-Children, to the latest Posterity forever, medling in Land-Affairs; neither you nor any who shall descend from you, are ever hereafter to presume to sell any Land: For which Purpose, you are to preserve this String, in Memory of what your Uncles have this Day given you in Charge.—We have some other Business to transact with our Brethren, and therefore depart the Council, and consider what has been said to you.

THE TREATY OF LANCASTER

The Treaty of Lancaster, Pennsylvania, was one of the most important Indian treaties of colonial times. Arranged to settle disputes between the Iroquois and various colonies, the treaty council that produced it lasted a fortnight in 1744 and brought together two dozen deputies from the Six Nations, more than two hundred other Indians, Governor George Thomas of Pennsylvania, and commissioners from Virginia and Maryland. The talks were held in the Lancaster courthouse, with Conrad Weiser acting as interpreter. With Britain and France on the verge of renewed war, the Six Nations promised to remain neutral.

The Onondaga spokesman, Canasatego, dominated the conference. Richard Peters, an Anglican clergyman and provincial secretary active in Indian affairs, described him as "a tall well-made man" with "a very full chest and brawny limbs. He had a manly countenance, mixed with a good-natured smile. He was about sixty years of age, very active, and had a surprising liveliness in his speech." Peters was favorably impressed by the Indians' diplomacy and said they were "superior to the commissioners in point of sense and argument."[17]

When the governor of Maryland disputed Iroquois land claims on the basis that Maryland had possessed the land for more than a century, Canasatego gave a lengthy speech in which he reviewed the history of contact between Indians and Europeans in North America. On the final day of the conference, Canasatego responded to the Virginia commissioners' invitation to send six Iroquois youths to be educated at the College of William and Mary in Williamsburg. Colonial governments regularly invited Indian chiefs to send their children to English schools, where they would receive a formal education, but Canasatego politely declined the invitation. Finally, in a speech delivered on July 4, the Onondaga orator offered the colonists some advice on the need to unite, citing the example of the ancient League of the Iroquois. Some people interpret Canasatego's words as evidence that, forty-five years later, the Founding Fathers based the United States Constitution on that of the Iroquois.

When Canasatego left Lancaster, he was wearing a scarlet coat and a gold-laced hat presented to him by the commissioners of Virginia and Maryland. Despite his impressive performance at the conference, the Treaty of Lancaster resulted in a massive loss of Indian land between the Susquehanna River and the Allegheny Mountains.

CANASATEGO

Speech at the Treaty of Lancaster
July 4, 1744

Brother, the Governor of Maryland,

When you mentioned the Affair of the Land Yesterday, you went back to old Times, and told us, you had been in Possession of the Province of *Maryland* above One Hundred Years; but what is One Hundred Years in Comparison of the Length of Time since our Claim began? since we came out of this Ground? For we must tell you, that long before One Hundred Years our Ancestors came out of this very Ground, and their Children have remained here ever since. You came out of the Ground in a Country that lies beyond the Seas, there you may have a just Claim, but here you must allow us to be your elder Brethren, and the Lands to belong to us long before you knew any thing of them. It is true, that above One Hundred Years ago the *Dutch* came here in a Ship, and brought with them several Goods; such as Awls, Knives, Hatchets, Guns, and many other Particulars, which they gave us; and when they had taught us how to use their Things, and we saw what sort of People they were, we were so well pleased with them, that we tied their Ship to the Bushes on the Shore; and afterwards, liking them still better the longer they staid with us, and thinking the Bushes too slender, we removed the Rope, and tied it to the Trees; and as the Trees were liable to be blown down by high winds, or to decay of themselves, we, from the Affection we bore them, again removed the Rope, and tied it to a strong and big Rock *(here the Interpreter said, They mean the* Oneido *Country)* and not content with this, for its further Security we removed the Rope to the big Mountain *(here the Interpreter says they mean the* Onandago *Country)* and there we tied it very fast, and rowlled Wampum about it; and, to make it still more secure, we stood upon the Wampum, and sat down upon it, to defend it, and to prevent any Hurt coming to it, and did our best Endeavours that it might remain uninjured for ever. During all this Time the New-comers, the *Dutch,* acknowledged our Right to the Lands, and sollicited us, from Time to Time, to grant them Parts of our Country, and enter into League and Covenant with us, and to become one People with us.

After this the *English* came into the Country, and, as we were told, became

Pennsylvania Colonial Records 4:698–734.

one People with the *Dutch.* About two Years after the Arrival of the *English,* an *English* Governor came to *Albany* and finding what great Friendship subsisted between us and the *Dutch,* he approved it mightily, and desired to make as strong a League, and to be upon as good Terms with us as the *Dutch* were, with whom he was united, and to become one People with us: And by his further Care in looking into what had passed between us, he found that the Rope which tied the Ship to the great Mountain was only fastened with Wampum, which was liable to break and rot, and to perish in a Course of Years; he therefore told us, he would give us a Silver Chain, which would be much stronger, and would last for ever. This we accepted, and fastened the Ship with it, and it has lasted ever since. Indeed we have had some small Differences with the *English,* and, during these Misunderstanding, some of their young Men would, by way of Reproach, be every now and then telling us, that we should have perished if they had not come into the Country and furnished us with Strowds[18] and Hatchets, and Guns, and other Things necessary for the Support of Life; but we always gave them to understand that they were mistaken, that we lived before they came amongst us, and as well, or better, if we may believe what our Forefathers have told us. We had then Room enough, and Plenty of Deer, which was easily caught; and tho' we had not Knives, Hatchets, or Guns, such as we have now, yet we had Knives of Stone, and Hatchets of Stone, and Bows and Arrows, and those served our Uses as well then as the *English* ones do now. We are now straitened, and sometimes in want of Deer, and liable to many other inconveniencies since the *English* came among us, and particularly from that Pen-and-Ink Work that is going on at the Table *(pointing to the Secretary)* and we will give you an Instance of this. Our Brother *Onas,* a great while ago, came to *Albany* to buy the *Sasquahannah* Lands of us, but our Brother, the Governor of *New York,* who, as we suppose, had not a good Understanding with our Brother *Onas,* advised us not to sell him any Land, for he would make an ill Use of it; and, pretending to be our good Friend, he advised us, in order to prevent *Onas's,* or any other Person's imposing upon us, and that we might always have our Land when we should want it, to put it into his Hands; and told us, he would keep it for our Use, and never open his Hands, but keep them close shut, and not part with any of it, but at our Request. Accordingly we trusted him, and put our Land into his Hands, and charged him to keep it safe for our Use; but, some Time after, he went to *England,* and carried our Land with him, and there sold it to our Brother *Onas,* for a large Sum of Money; and when, at the Instance of our Brother *Onas,* we were minded to sell him some Lands, he told us, we had sold the *Sasquahannah* Lands already to the Governor of *New-York,* and that he had bought them from him in *England;* tho', when he came to understand how the Governor of *New-York* had deceived us, he very generously paid us for our Lands over again.

Tho' we mention this Instance of an Imposition put upon us by the Governor of *New-York,* yet we must do the *English* the Justice to say, we have had their hearty Assistances in our Wars with the *French,* who were no sooner arrived amongst us than they began to render us uneasy, and to provoke us to War, and we have had several Wars with them; during all which we constantly received Assistance from the *English,* and, by their Means, we have always been able to keep up our Heads against their Attacks.

We now come nearer home. We have had your Deeds interpreted to us, and we acknowledge them to be good and valid, and that the *Conestogoe* or *Sasquahannah Indians* had a Right to sell those Lands to you, for they were then theirs; but since that Time we have conquered them, and their Country now belongs to us, and the Lands we demanded Satisfaction for are no Part of the Lands comprized in those Deeds; they are the *Cohongoroutas*[19] Lands; those, we are sure, you have not possessed One Hundred Years, no, nor above Ten Years, and we made our Demands so soon as we knew your People were settled in those Parts. These have never been sold, but remain still to be disposed of; and we are well pleased to hear you are provided with Goods, and do assure you of our Willingness to treat with you for those unpurchased Lands; in Confirmation whereof, we present you with this Belt of Wampum. . . .

Brother Assaragoa;[20]

You told us Yesterday, that all Disputes with you being now at an End; you desired to confirm all former Treaties between *Virginia* and us, and to make our Chain of Union as bright as the Sun.

We agree very heartily with you in these Propositions; we thank you for your good Inclinations; we desire you will pay no Regard to any idle Stories that may be told to our Prejudice. And, as the Dispute about the Land is now intirely over, and we perfectly reconciled, we hope, for the future, we shall not act towards each other but as becomes Brethren and hearty Friends.

We are very willing to renew the Friendship with you, and to make it as firm as possible, for us and our Children with you and your Children to the latest Generation, and we desire you will imprint these Engagements on your Hearts in the Strongest Manner; and, in Confirmation that we shall do the same, we give you this Belt of Wampum. . . .

Brother Assaragoa;

You told us likewise, you had a great House provided for the Education of Youth, and that there were several white People and *Indians* Children there to learn Languages, and to write and read, and invited us to send some of our Children amongst you, &c.

We must let you know we love our Children too well to send them so great a Way, and the *Indians* are not inclined to give their Children Learning. We allow it to be good, and we thank you for your Invitation; but our Customs differing from yours, you will be so good as to excuse us. . . .

Brother Onas, Assaragoa, and Tocarry-hogan,[21]

At the Close of your respective Speeches Yesterday, you made us very handsome Presents, and we should return you something suitable to your Generosity; but, alas, we are poor, and shall ever remain so, as long as there are so many *Indian* Traders among us. Theirs and the white Peoples Cattle have eat up all the Grass, and made Deer scarce. However, we have provided a small Present for you, and tho' some of you gave us more than others, yet, as you are all equally our Brethren, we shall leave it to you to divide it as you please.—And then presented three Bundles of Skins, which were received with the usual Ceremony from the three Governments.

We have one Thing further to say, and that is, We heartily recommend Union and a good Agreement between you our Brethren. Never disagree, but preserve a strict Friendship for one another, and thereby you, as well as we, will become the stronger.

Our wise Forefathers established Union and Amity between the *Five Nations;* this has made us formidable; this has given us great Weight and Authority with our neighbouring Nations.

We are a powerful Confederacy; and, by your observing the same Methods our wise Forefathers have taken, you will acquire fresh Strength and Power; therefore whatever befals you, never fall out one with another.

A GUARDIAN SYSTEM
FOR INDIAN LANDS

When Christian Indian communities were first established in the Massachusetts Bay Colony, the legislature provided that they should choose their own officials. Native self-rule became increasingly circumscribed, however.

In 1746, Massachusetts passed a law providing that three guardians be appointed for each Indian settlement. The guardians had the power "to take into their hands" the Indians' lands and then allot them to the various Indian inhabitants as they saw fit. Surplus lands could be leased to settlers, and the guardians were supposed to use the income for the support of the Indians.

The following document, written by Indians from Mashpee on Cape Cod, shows that the guardian system was open to abuse. It also shows that Indian people recognized that literacy, besides being a vehicle for the conveyance of land, could be a means of voicing discontent and lodging formal protest against encroachments on their land. The Mashpee Indians complained several times to the Massachusetts General Court. Obtaining no relief, they took their appeal to the king of England. The Crown ordered an investigation and colonial policy was changed: In 1763 Massachusetts incorporated Mashpee as a self-governing district, in effect organizing the tribe as a town. After the Revolution, however, in which men from Mashpee fought and died in the American cause, Massachusetts took away Mashpee's right of self-government and reinstituted the guardian system.

INDIANS AT MASHPEE

Petition to the
Massachusetts General Court
June 11, 1752

Barnstable, June 11, 1752

Oh! Our honorable gentlemen and kind gentlemen in Boston in Massachusetts Bay, here in New England, the great ones who oversee the colony in Boston, gentlemen. Oh!, Oh!, gentlemen, hear us now, Oh! ye, us poor Indians. We do not clearly have thorough understanding and wisdom. Therefore we now beseech you, Oh!, Boston gentlemen. Oh! Hear our weeping, and hear our beseeching of you, Oh!, and answer this beseeching of you by us, Oh!, gentlemen of Boston, us poor Indians in Mashpee *in Barnstable County*.

Now we beseech you, what can we do with regard to our land, which was conveyed to you by these former sachems of ours. What they conveyed to

Ives Goddard and Kathleen Bragdon, eds., *Native Writings in Massachusett* (Philadelphia: American Philosophical Society, 1988), 373.

you(?) was this piece of land. This was conveyed to us by Indian sachems. Our former Indian sachems were called Sachem Wuttammohkin and Sachem Quettatsett, in Barnstable County, the Mashpee Indian place. This Indian land, this was conveyed to us by these former sachems of ours. We shall not give it away, nor shall it be sold, nor shall it be lent, but we shall always use it as long as we live, we together with all our children, and our children's children, and our descendants, and together with all their descendants. They shall always use it as long as Christian Indians live. We shall use it forever and ever. Unless we all peacefully agree to give it away or to sell it. But as of now not one of all of us Indians has yet agreed to give away, or sell, or lend this Indian land, or marsh, or wood. Fairly, then, it is this: we state frankly we have never conveyed them away.

But now clearly we Indians say this to all you gentlemen of ours in Boston: We poor Indians in Mashpee, *in Barnstable County,* we truly are much troubled by these English neighbors of ours being on this land of ours, and in our marsh and trees. Against our will these Englishmen take away from us [these] what was our land. They parcel it out to each other, and the marsh along with it, against our will. And as for our streams, they do not allow us peacefully to be when we peacefully go fishing. They beat us greatly, and they have houses on our land against our will. Truly we think it is this: We poor Indians soon shall not have any place to reside, together with our poor children, because these Englishmen trouble us very much in this place of ours in Mashpee, Barnstable County.

Therefore now, Oh! you kind gentlemen in Boston, in Massachusetts Bay, now we beseech you: defend us, and they would not trouble us any more on our land.

RESOLVING CONFLICTS
WITH COLONIAL NEIGHBORS

By the 1750s, the Catawba Indians of South Carolina were facing a crisis that threatened their very existence. Their numbers had been drastically reduced by war and disease; their hunting and the deerskin trade on which they had come to rely were in sharp decline; they were virtually surrounded by English colonists and their farms, and a drought devastated their crops. In such circumstances, tensions between hungry Indians and their colonial neighbors often ran high, even in peacetime.

In August 1754, the Catawba chief Nopkehe, known to the English as King Hagler, was called to a meeting at the home of a colonist named Matthew Toole in an attempt to resolve disputes that had arisen. A number of settlers came forward and accused the Catawbas of engaging in insulting and threatening behavior. Hagler answered their charges one by one. The episode shows Indians and colonists trying to settle their problems without resorting to war, but it also reveals the extent of their differences and the areas of conflict between them.

KING HAGLER (NOPKEHE)

Reply to Colonists' Complaints
1754

Brothers and Wariors

I am Exceeding glad to meet you here this day, and to have the oppertunity of haveing a talk one with an Other in a Brotherly and Loveing manner, and to Brighten, and Strengthen, that Chain of Friendship which has so long remained between us and the people of those three Provinces, and I am Very Sorry to hear those Complaints that are Laid to our People's Charge, But now will Open our Ears to here those Grievances & Complaints that shall be made by you against our Young men and Others, and we do Heartily Thank our Good Brother the President of North Carolina for his good Talk in his Letter to us, and also for his appointing You to meet us here, to have this Discourse. . . .

Brothers as You are Wariors Yourselves, You well know that we oftentimes goe to War against our Enemies and Many Times we are Either makeing our Escape from our Enemies or in pursuit of them, which prevents us from hunting for meat to Eat when we are in Danger, least our Enemy should Discover us; and as this is our Case many times we are forced to go to Your houses when Hungry, and no sooner we do appear but your Dogs bark and as soon as You Discover Our Comeing You Imediately hide Your Bread Meal and Meat or any Other thing that is fit to Eat about your houses, and we being sensible that this is the Case, it is True we serch, and if we finde any Eatables in the house we Take some, and Especially from those who behave so Churlish and ungreatfull to us, as they are very well assured, of our great need many times for the Reasons we now give, If we ask a little

Victuals you Refuse us & then we Owne we Take a Loaf of bread a little meal or meat to Eat, and then You Complain and say those are Transgressions, it is True there are many in those Settlements that are very kind and Curtious to us when or as often as we come they give us Bread and milk meat or Butter very freely if they have any ready and never Do refuse whether we do ask or no, and if it should happen that they have nothing we goe away Contented with them, for we well know that if they had any thing ready we would have it freely &c not Refused by them. . . .

You I Remember Brothers accuse our People with attempting To take away a Child from one of Your People, but I hope you will not harbour this Thought of us so as to Imagine it was done in Earnest, for I am Informed it was Only done by way of a joke by one of our wild Young men in Order to Surprize the People, that were the parents of the Child, to have a Laugh at the Joke

But as to their Takeing other things such as knives Cloaths or Such Things we own it is not right to do but there are some of our young fellows will do those tricks altho' by us they are oftentimes Cautioned from such ill Doings altho' to no purpose for we Cannot be present at all times to Look after them, and when they goe to war or hunting Among the Inhabitants we generally warn them from being any ways offencive to any white person upon any Consideration whatever,

Brothers here is One thing You Yourselves are to Blame very much in. That is You Rot Your grain in Tubs, out of which you take and make Strong Spirits You sell it to our young men and give it them, many times; they get very Drunk with it this is the Very Cause that they oftentimes Commit those Crimes that is offencive to You and us and all thro' the Effect of that Drink it is also very bad for our people, for it Rots their guts and Causes our men to get very sick and many of our people has Lately Died by the Effects of that strong Drink, and I heartily wish You would do something to prevent Your People from Dareing to Sell or give them any of that Strong Drink, upon any Consideration whatever for that will be a great means of our being free from being accused of those Crimes that is Committed by our young men and will prevent many of the abuses that is done by them thro' the Effects of that Strong Drink . . .

Brothers and Warriors You Talk very well, and as to your talk about our people takeing your Horses and Mares, it is very True there are a great many of our Creatures that Runs amongst the white peoples and there are also many stole from us by these people for it is not Long ago since we caught a white man with some of our Horses and sent him to Justice, but was not punished as Represented to us while agoe . . .

As to our Liveing on those Lands we Expect to live on those Lands we now possess During our Time here for when the Great man above made us he also made this Island he also made our forefathers and of this Colour and Hue (Showing his hands & Breast) he also fixed our forefathers and us here and to Inherit this Land and Ever since we Lived after our manner and fashion we in those Days, had no Instruments To support our living but Bows which we Compleated with stones, knives we had none, and as it was our Custom in those days to Cut our hair, which we Did by Burning it of our heads and Bodies with Coals of Fire, our Axes we made of stone we bled our selves with fish Teeth our Cloathing were Skins and Furr, instead of which we Enjoy those Cloaths which we got from the white people and Ever since they first Came among us we have Enjoyed all those things that we were then destitute of for which we thank the white people, and to this Day we have Lived in a Brotherly Love & peace with them and more Especially with these Three Governments and it is our Earnest Desire that Love and Friendship which has so Long remain'd should Ever Continue.

Our Brother the Governor of Virginia sent for us not Long agoe, we gladly answered his Call, and he Entertained us and shook hands with us very kindly, and had he Indulged us we would have Gone with the white people to war against their Enemies the French, but arms and ammunition being not sufficient to supply the white people who were then going out, we were forced to Return Back to our Nation again untill further Instructions from him

We understand that our Brothers and the french has had a battle and that several of our friends were kill'd I am heartily sorry for it

We Never had the pleasure of seeing our Good Brother the President of North Carolina as yet, but this Let our Brother know that we want to be brothers and Friends with him & all his people, and with the great king over the water, and all his Children, and to Confirm the same I shall as soon as get home I will Call all our nation Together and charge the young men and Wariors Not to Misbehave on any Consideration whatever to the white people and as we do Expect an Everlasting Friendship between you and us, we Expect your kinds to us for ever as you may depend upon our Friendship and kindness to you.

And Tell our Brother the President of North Carolina that if this war Continues between the white people and the french that I and my people are ready and Willing to Obey his Orders in giveing all possible assistance in my power to him when called by him or the Governor of Virginia and as a pledge of the same Take our Brother this letter as a token of Everlasting Friendship and return him Thanks for our good Talk this, Day with Each other.

Then they shook Hands all round.

COLONISTS ENCROACH
ON THE STANWIX LINE

In 1763 the British government issued a proclamation to restrict colonial encroachments on Indian land. The Appalachian Mountains were to be the boundary of English settlement; west of the mountains was to be an Indian reserve, and Indian lands there could be bought only by the Crown's representatives in formal and open council. But the British government was far from the scene, and the proclamation did not stop the loss of Indian lands.

At the Treaty of Fort Stanwix in 1768, British Indian superintendent Sir William Johnson secured a large cession of lands from Iroquois delegates. The parties agreed that the Ohio River henceforth should constitute the boundary between Indian territory and colonial settlement. The Shawnees and other tribes objected that the lands given up so readily by the Iroquois belonged to *them*. Even the Stanwix line was penetrated as settlers trespassed on Indian lands and threatened to spark renewed hostilities.

John Killbuck, a Delaware chief, described the colonists' encroachment in December 1771 at a meeting between Delawares, Munsies, and Mahicans and the governors of Pennsylvania, Maryland, and Virginia.

JOHN KILLBUCK

Speech to the Governors
of Pennsylvania, Maryland,
and Virginia

December 4, 1771

Brethren, in former times our forefathers and yours lived in great friendship together and often met to strengthen the chain of their friendship. As your people grew numerous we made room for them and came over the Great Mountains to Ohio. And some time ago when you were at war with the French your soldiers came into this country, drove the French away and built forts. Soon after a number of your people came over the Great Mountains and settled on our lands. We complained of their encroachments into our country, and, brethren, you either could not or would not remove them. As we did not choose to have any disputes with our brethren, the English, we agreed to make a line and the Six Nations at Fort Stanwix three years ago sold the King all the lands on the east side of the Ohio down to the Cherokee[22] River, which lands were the property of our confederacy, and gave a deed to Sir William Johnson as he desired. Since that time great numbers more of your people have come over the Great Mountains and settled throughout this country. And we are sorry to tell you that several quarrels have happened between your people and ours, in which people have been killed on both sides, and that we now see the nations round us and your people ready to embroil in a quarrel, which gives our nation great concern, as we on our parts want to live in friendship with you, as you have always told us you have laws to govern your people by (but we do not see that you have). Therefore, brethren, unless you can fall upon some method of governing your people who live between the Great Mountains and the Ohio River and who are now very numerous, it will be out of the Indians' power to govern their young men, for we assure you the black clouds begin to gather fast in this country. And if something is not soon done those clouds will deprive us of seeing the sun. We desire you to give the greatest attention to

Public Record Office, C.O. 5/ 90:5; also Library of Congress transcript; reprinted in K. G. Davies, ed., *Documents of the American Revolution* (Shannon: Irish University Press, 1977–81), 3:254–55.

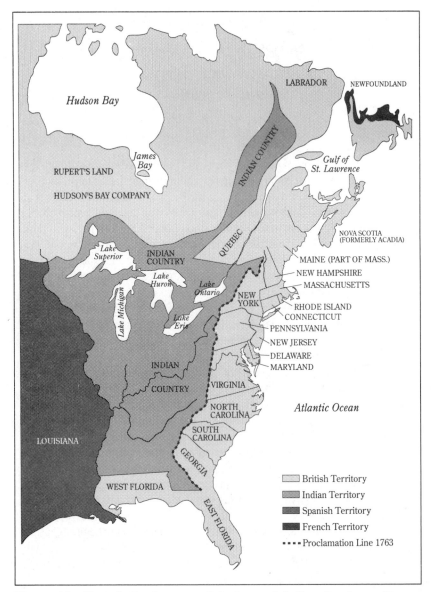

Figure 11. Boundaries between Colonies and Indian Territory, Proclaimed by the English in 1763

what we now tell you as it comes from our hearts and a desire we have to live in peace and friendship with our brethren the English. And therefore it grieves us to see some of the nations about us and your people ready to strike each other. We find your people are very fond of our rich land. We see them quarrelling every day about land and burning one another's houses. So that we do not know how soon they may come over the River Ohio and drive us from our villages, nor do we see you brethren take any care to stop them. It's now several years since we have met together in council, which all nations are surprised and concerned at. What is the reason you kindled a fire at Ohio for us to meet you (which we did and talked friendly together) that you have let your fire go out for some years past? This makes all nations jealous about us as we also frequently hear of our brethren the English meeting with Cherokees and with the Six Nations to strengthen their friendship, which gives us cause to think you are forming some bad designs against us who lives between the Ohio and Lakes. I have now told you everything that is in my heart and desire you will write what I have said and send it to the Great King. A belt. Killbuck, speaker.

NOTES

[1] *Pennsylvania Colonial Records* 4:559–86.

[2] Donald H. Kent, ed., *Pennsylvania Indian Treaties, 1737–1756,* in Alden T. Vaughan, gen. ed., *Early American Indian Documents: Treaties and Laws, 1607–1789,* (Frederick, Md.: University Publications of America, 1984), 2:291.

[3] E. B. O'Callaghan, ed., *Documents Relative to the Colonial History of the State of New York,* 15 vols. (Albany: Weed, Parsons, 1853–87), 4:893.

[4] David H. Corkran, *The Cherokee Frontier: Conflict and Survival* (Norman: University of Oklahoma Press, 1962), 14.

[5] Miantonomi's speech is in *Collections of the Massachusetts Historical Society,* 3rd ser. (1833), 3:154.

[6] King Charles I, who was executed in 1649 during the English Civil War.

[7] Samuel Gorton of Warwick, Rhode Island, was a religious radical frequently at odds with the Puritan authorities. He and his associates had settled on Narragansett land with Miantonomi's permission.

[8] The Narragansett sachems Pessicus and Canonicus were brother and uncle of Miantonomi, respectively.

[9] Kent, *Pennsylvania Indian Treaties,* 38.

[10] Corpus Christi is a feast of the Catholic Church.

[11] Jeremiah Langhorne was Chief Justice of the Pennsylvania Supreme Court.

[12] Tohickon is Tohickon Creek; the Blue Mountains are the Kittatinny Mountains; Mahoning Creek is a tributary of the Lehigh River.

[13] Old Weiser was a German immigrant, John Conrad Weiser, father of Conrad Weiser.

[14] The twitways were the Miamis; the Shawanahs Shawekelou probably refers to the Thwaegila division of the Shawnees; the Takkesaw were probably Nanticokes. (Kent, *Pennsylvania Indian Treaties,* 473 n. 30.)

[15] *Onas* means "feather" or "quill" and was thus an Iroquoian pun on Penn's name. The Iroquois used it to refer to William Penn and his successors as governors of Pennsylvania.

[16] Wyoming and Shamokin were Indian villages on the Susquehanna River.

[17] Julian P. Boyd and Carl Van Doren, eds., *Indian Treaties Printed by Benjamin Franklin, 1736–1762* (Philadelphia: Historical Society of Pennsylvania, 1938), xxxvii, xl.

[18] Strowds was a cheap trade cloth made from woolen rags, manufactured in Stroud, England, especially for the Indian trade.

[19] A note on the original says that *Cohongoroutas* means "Potomack." (Kent, *Pennsylvania Indian Treaties,* 477 n. 38.)

[20] *Assaraquoa* means "sword" or "big knife" and was the Iroquois title for governors of Virginia.

[21] *Tocarry-hogan* refers to Maryland.

[22] The Tennessee River was often referred to as the Cherokee.

4

In a World of Warfare:
Indians and the Wars for Empire

You both tell us to be Christians, you both make us madd we know not what side to choose.
> —Iroquois sachem Dekanissore to the governors
> of Canada and New York, 1701[1]

It is plain that you white people are the cause of this war; why do not you and the French *fight in the old country, and on the sea? Why do you come to fight on our land? This makes every body believe, you want to take the land from us by force, and settle it.*
> —Delaware Indians to Christian Frederick Post, 1758[2]

The contest for North America was not simply a battle between Indians and Europeans. Various European powers—England, France, Spain, Holland, Sweden, and even Russia on the northwest coast—had imperial ambitions on the continent and competed with one another at the same time as they endeavored to establish a hold on the lands of the Indians. By the late seventeenth century, the contest in eastern North America had boiled down to a struggle for empire among the French in Canada and the upper Ohio Valley, the English on the eastern seaboard, and the Spaniards in Florida and the lower Mississippi Valley. Competition between the European nations required that they compete in turn for the allegiance of different Indian nations. Indian nations thus had to pursue diplomatic negotiations with different English colonies as well as different European nations, and Indian people became entangled in European colonial wars fought in North America at the same time as they were fighting to keep their lands clear of European settlers.

Indian peoples living on the northern frontiers of Spain's American empire, from Florida to California, fought recurrent wars of resistance against the Iberian invaders. In 1680, for example, Pueblo Indians on the Rio Grande launched a synchronized assault on the Spaniards that won them a dozen years of freedom. In the eastern woodlands, Indians fought to preserve their lands from the growing threat of English settlers, but their struggle for independence was complicated and undermined by the fact that this area of the continent was also a cockpit of international rivalry. Several times France and England went head to head in open warfare: King William's War (1689–97), Queen Anne's War (1702–13), and King George's War (1744–48). Their struggle culminated in the Seven Years War (1756–63), a conflict that the English and later American historians often referred to as the French and Indian War. Fought in Europe, India, Africa, and the West Indies as well as on the American mainland and drawing in Spain, Prussia, and other European powers, the Seven Years War has been called the first world war. It certainly became a world war in Indian America as the tribes became caught up in the fighting, with even the Mohawks and Senecas breaking away from the policy of neutrality adopted by the Iroquois Confederacy.

Native Americans fought in these wars and in wars of their own, both against European invaders and against other Indian nations. As in the American Revolution that followed, much of the fighting was done in the frontier "backcountry," which usually meant on Indian lands. Indian warriors went on campaign, leaving their villages vulnerable to enemy attack and their families to bear the burden of feeding themselves. Warriors assumed unprecedented importance in Indian societies as French and British allies cultivated their friendship and bolstered their power base with supplies of gifts and guns. The wars disrupted cycles of planting, hunting, and gathering and the rituals that accompanied them. British and French armies burned Indian villages and cornfields.

By 1763, France was defeated and its New World empire lay in ruins. Those Indians who had fought for King Louis now had to come to terms with King George and his redcoats. Flushed with victory but drained by the expense of winning it, the British felt little need to conciliate the allies of their defeated foe with lavish gifts. British officers ignored longstanding traditions of respectful dealings with Indian nations, and British garrisons occupied posts formerly held by the French. Tensions exploded in Pontiac's War in 1763 when the Ottawa war chief led a multitribal assault on the British. The British worked to divide the tribes and quelled the revolt.

Confronted with almost endemic warfare, Indian peoples pursued a variety of strategies. They formed alliances with European powers who could supply the guns and trade goods they needed to survive in time of conflict. Some, like the Iroquois and Choctaw, also played off belligerent nations and kept some of their options open. Some migrated or sought refuge in mission villages. Those who fought usually did so for their own reasons, often took the opportunity to settle old scores, and regularly frustrated their allies by their independent behavior. Some were inspired by powerful revitalization movements that preached rejection of Europeans and their ways. As many of the documents in this chapter illustrate, Indians did not go to war without

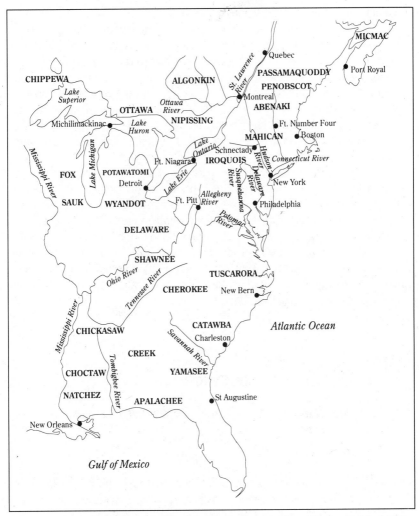

Figure 12. Indian America in the French and Indian Wars, 1689–1763

questioning the causes of conflict, weighing the commitment of their allies, or considering the consequences.

LA BARRE'S FAILED BLUFF

The Five Nations of the Iroquois were a thorn in the side of the French in Canada for much of the seventeenth century. They waged recurrent war against the settlers and disrupted French diplomatic and commercial endeavors with other tribes. The French retaliated by invading Iroquois country several times in what is now upstate New York, usually with little effect.

In 1684 Joseph Antoine Lefebre de La Barre, governor of New France, led an expedition that was intended to browbeat the Iroquois into stopping their practices of hunting in Canada and of trading with the English at Albany. Hunger and disease thinned the ranks of La Barre's army long before he reached Iroquois country, and he resorted to arranging a conference on the south shore of Lake Ontario in the hope that he could bluff the Iroquois into making concessions.

The Onondaga orator Otreouti also known as La Grand Gueule or Garangula, listened quietly, puffing on his pipe, while the Frenchman made his threats. When La Barre's speech was over, Garangula got up, walked around the assembled French and Indians for several minutes in apparent deep thought, and then delivered a humiliating rebuke to the French. He not only ridiculed the governor for his transparent bluff but also made it clear that the Iroquois were dependent on neither the French governor (Onontio or, here, Yonnondio) nor the English. La Barre was recalled to France the year after his humiliation by the Iroquois.

GARANGULA

Speech to New France Governor La Barre
1684

Yonnondio, I Honour you, and the Warriors that are with me all likewise honour you. Your Interpreter has finished your Speech; I now begin mine. My words make haste to reach your Ears. hearken to them.

Yonnondio, You must have believed when you left Quebeck, that the Sun had burnt up all the Forests which render our Country Unaccessible to the French, Or that the Lakes had so far overflown their Banks, that they had surrounded our Castles, and that it was impossible for us to get out of them. Yes, Yonnondio, surely you must have thought so, and the Curiosity of

Cadwallader Colden, *History of the Five Indian Nations,* pt. 1 (London, 1727), 53–55.

seeing so great a Country burnt up, or under Water, has brought you so far. Now you are undeceived, since that I and my Warriors are come to assure you that the Sennekas, Cayugas, Onnondagas, Oneydoes and Mohawks are all alive. I thank you, in their Name, for bringing back into their Country the Calumet which your Predecessor received from their hands. It was happy for you that you left under ground that Murdering Hatchet which has been so often dyed in the Blood of the French. Hear Yonnondio, I do not Sleep, I have my eyes Open, and the Sun which enlightens me discovers to me a great Captain at the head of a Company of Soldiers, who speaks as if he were Dreaming. He says that he only came to the Lake to smoke on the great Calumet with the Onnondagas. But Garangula says, that he sees the Contrary, that it was to knock them on the head, if Sickness had not weakned the Arms of the French.

I see Yonnondio Raving in a Camp of sick men, who's Lives the great Spirit has saved, by Inflicting this Sickness on them. Hear Yonnondio, Our Women had taken their Clubs, our Children and Old Men had carried their Bows and Arrows into the heart of your Camp, if our Warriors had not disarmed them, and retained them when your Messenger, Ohquesse appeared in our Castle. It is done, and I have said it.

Hear Yonnondio, we plundered none of the French, but those that carried Guns, Powder and Ball to the Twihtwies and Chictaghicks,[3] because those Arms might have cost us our Lives. Herein we follow the example of the Jesuits, who stave all the Barrels of Rum brought to our Castle, lest the Drunken Indians should knock them on the Head. Our Warriors have not Bevers enough to pay for all those Arms that they have taken, and our Old Men are not afraid of the War. *This Belt preserves my Words.*

We carried the English into our Lakes, to traffick there with the Utawawas and Quatoghies, as the Adirondacks[4] brought the French to our Castles, to carry on a Trade which the English say is theirs. We are born free, We neither depend upon Yonnondio nor Corlaer.[5]

We may go where we please, and carry with us whom we please, and buy and sell what we please. If your Allies be your Slaves, use them as such, Command them to receive no other but your People. *This Belt Preserves my Words.*

We knockt the Twihtwies and Chictaghiks on the head, because they had cut down the Trees of Peace,[6] which were the Limits of our Country. They have hunted Bevers on our Lands: They have acted contrary to the Custom of all Indians; for they left none of the Bevers alive, they kill'd both Male and Female. They brought the Satanas[7] into their Country, to take part with them, and Arm'd them, after they had concerted ill Designs against us. We have done less than either the English or French, that have usurp'd the Lands of so many Indian Nations, and chased them from their own Country. *This Belt Preserves my Words.*

Hear Yonondio, What I say is the Voice of all the Five Nations. Hear what they Answer, Open your Ears to what they Speak. The Sennekas, Cayugas, Onnondagas, Oneydoes and Mohawks say, That when they buried the Hatchet at Cadarackui[8] (in the presence of your Predecessor) in the middle of the Fort, they planted the Tree of Peace, in the same place, to be there carefully preserved, that, in place of a Retreat for Soldiers, that Fort might be a Rendevouze of Merchants; that in place of Arms and Munitions of War, Bevers and Merchandize should only enter there.

Hear, Yonondio, Take care for the future, that so great a Number of Soldiers as appear here do not choak the Tree of Peace planted in so small a Fort. It will be a great Loss, if after it had so easily taken root, you should stop its growth, and prevent its covering your Country and ours with its Branches. I assure you, in the Name of the Five Nations, That our Warriors shall dance to the Calumet of Peace under its leaves, and shall remain quiet on their Mats, and shall never dig up the Hatchet till their Brethren, Yonnondio or Corlaer shall either joyntly or seperately endeavour to attack the Country which the great Spirit has given to our Ancestors. *This Belt preserves my Words, and this other, the Authority which the Five Nations have given me.*

IROQUOIS LOYALTY
TURNS TO DISENCHANTMENT

The Iroquois suffered their first losses at the hands of the French in 1609 when Samuel de Champlain and his companions shot down several Mohawk chiefs on the shores of the lake that bears his name. Tied to the English at Albany by their need for trade and guns, the Iroquois generally sided with them against the French as Anglo-French imperial rivalry gathered momentum in the late seventeenth century. The Iroquois paid a heavy price for their involvement, however.

In 1692, the English met with the Five Nations at Albany and accused them of not prosecuting the war with sufficient vigor. In their response, given by an Oneida sachem named Cheda, the Iroquois promised to uphold the Covenant Chain, the metaphor of their allegiance to the English, but they showed increasing resentment at bearing such a heavy proportion of the fighting.

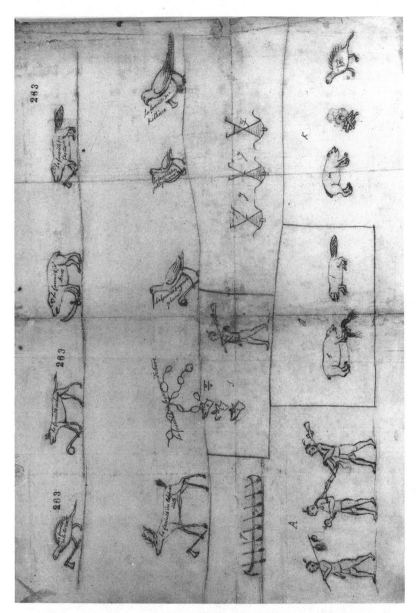

Figure 13. Drawings Made on a Tree by a Passing Iroquois War Party
In this French composite of drawings (the figure is sideturned), each member of the war party drew the totem animal of his clan (Turtle, Wolf, Bear, Beaver, Deer, Snipe, Hawk) holding a weapon. The number of paddles in the canoe represents the size of the war party; the three inverted figures at right indicate the number of enemies killed (one woman, two men). The panels at the bottom center and right show war councils between the Bear and Beaver clans and between the Bear and Turtle clans. The drawing at bottom left is a French depiction of warriors returning with a captive and two scalps.[9]

By 1700, the Iroquois had suffered devastating losses from their involvement in European conflicts. Some estimates say their population had been halved. In an attempt to halt the downward spiral, they decided to opt out of involvement in the Europeans' wars, declaring a policy of formal neutrality and leaving the French and English to fight their own battles. They sent ambassadors to meet with distant Indian nations, with the French in Montreal, and with the English in Albany to inform them of the new policy. Their new strategy enabled the Iroquois to recover some of the power and population they had lost in the endemic warfare of the seventeenth century, but their neutral stance would be finally and irrevocably shattered in the American Revolution.

CHEDA

Promise to Uphold the Covenant Chain

1692

Brother Corlear,

The Sachems of the Five Nations have with great Attention heard Corlear speak; we shall make a short Recital, to shew you with what Care we have hearkened. After the Recital he continued.

We heartily thank Corlear, for his coming to this Place to view the Strength thereof, for his bringing Forces with him, and for his Resolution of putting Garisons into the Frontier Places. Giving five Bevers and a Belt.

Brother Corlear, as to what you blame us for, let us not reproach one another, such Words do not savour well among Friends. They gave nothing with this Article.

Brother Corlear, be patient under the Loss of your Men, as we are of the Mohawks our Brethren, that were killed at the same Time. You take no Notice of the great Losses we have suffered. We designed to have come to this Place to have condoled with you in your Loss, but the War took up all our Time, and employed all Hands. They gave five Bevers, four Otters, and one Belt, as a Gift of Condolence.

Cadwallader Colden, *History of the Five Indian Nations,* pt. 2 (London, 1747), 124–27.

Brother Corlear, we are all Subjects of one great King and Queen, we have one Head, one Heart, one Interest, and are all ingaged in the same War. You tell us, that we must expect no Peace while the Kings are at War on the other Side the great Water. We thank you for being so plain with us. We assure you we have no Thoughts of Peace. We are resolved to carry on the War, though we know we only are in danger of being Losers. Pray do you prosecute the War with the same Resolution. You are strong and have many People. You have a great King, who is able to hold out long. We are but a small People, and decline daily, by the Men we lose in this War, we do our utmost to destroy the Enemy; but how strange does it seem to us! How unaccountable! that while our great King is so inveterate against the French, and you are so earnest with us to carry on the War, that Powder is now sold dearer to us than ever? We are poor, and not able to buy while we neglect hunting; and we cannot hunt and carry on the War at the same Time: We expect, that this Evil we so justly complain of be immediately remedied. Giving nine Bevers.

Brother Corlear, you desire us to keep the Enemy in perpetual Alarm, that they may have no Rest, till they are in their Graves; Is it not to secure your own Frontiers? Why then not one Word of your People that are to join us? We assure you we shall continue to carry on the War into the Heart of the Enemies Country. Giving eight Bevers.

We the Five Nations, Mohawks, Oneydoes, Onondagas, Cayugas, and Senekas, renew the Silver Chain whereby we are linked fast with our Brethren of Assarigoa (Virginia) and we promise to preserve it as long as the Sun shall shine in the Heavens. Giving ten Bevers.

But Brother Corlear, How comes it, that none of our Brethren fastened in the same Chain with us, offer their helping Hand in this general War, in which our great King is engaged against the French? Pray Corlear, how come Maryland, Delaware River, and New-England, to be disengaged from this War? You have always told us, that they are our Brethren, Subjects of the same great King. Has our King sold them? Or do they fail in their Obedience? Or do they draw their Arms out of our Chain? Or has the great King commanded, that the few Subjects he has in this Place, should make War against the French alone? Pray make plain to us this Mystery? How can they and we be Brethren, and make different Families? How can they and we be Subjects of the same great King, and not be engaged in the same War? How can they and we have the same Heart, the same Head, and the same Interest, as you tell us, and not have the same Thoughts? How comes it, that the Enemy burns and destroys the Towns in New-England, and they make no Resistance? How comes our great King to make War, and not to destroy his

Enemies? When, if he would only command his Subjects on this Side the great Lake to joyn, the Destruction of the Enemy would not make one Summer's Work.

You need not warn us of the Deceit and Treachery of the French, who would probably insinuate Thoughts of Peace; but Brethren, you need not fear us, we will never hearken to them: Tho' at the same Time, we must own, that we have not been without Thoughts of your being inclined to Peace, by Reason of the Brethrens Backwardness in pushing on the War. The French spread Reports among us to this Purpose, and say, that they had in a Manner concluded the Matter with you. We rejoice to be now assured of this Falshood. We shall never desist fighting the French as long as we shall live. And gave a Belt of Wampum.

We now renew the old Chain, and here plant the Tree of Prosperity and Peace. May it grow and thrive, and spread its Roots even beyond Canada. Giving a Belt.

We make the House clean, where all our Affairs of Importance are transacted with these five Otters.

We return you Thanks for the Powder and Lead given us; but what shall we do with them without Guns, shall we throw them at the Enemy? We doubt they will not hurt them so. Before this we always had Guns given us. It is no Wonder the Governor of Canada gains upon us, for he supplies his Indians with Guns as well as Powder; he supplies them plentifully with every Thing that can hurt us. Giving five Otters.

INTERTRIBAL CONFLICT
FOSTERED BY COLONISTS

Intertribal wars continued and sometimes escalated at the same time as Indians were fighting the Europeans' wars. The speech of the Cayuga warrior and chief Gachadow, or Gachradodon, delivered at the Treaty of Lancaster in June 1744, shows the European hand in fomenting and perpetuating intertribal conflict from New York to the Carolinas.

Gachadow's speech illustrates the range of techniques and metaphors employed by Indian orators. He depicts the Catawbas as warlike, treacherous, and intransigently hostile. In reality, the Catawbas loved peace as much as anyone else and needed it so that they could hunt and trade. When peace was made in 1752, they embraced it with joy "by Reason it enables us to pay our Debts, and to cloth ourselves and Families."[10]

GACHADOW

Speech to the Virginia Commissioners
at the Treaty of Lancaster
1744

Brother Assaraquoa:[11]

The World at the first was made on the other side of the Great water different from what it is on this side, as may be known from the different Colour of Our Skin and of Our Flesh, and that which you call Justice may not be so amongst us. You have your Laws and Customs and so have we. The Great King might send you over to Conquer the Indians, but looks to us that God did not approve of it, if he had, he would not have Placed the Sea where it is, as the Limits between us and you.

Brother Assaraquoa:

Tho' great things are well remembered among Us, Yet we don't remember that we were ever Conquered by the Great King, or that we have been employ'd by that Great King to conquer others; if it was so it is beyond our Memory. We do remember we were employed by Maryland to Conquer the Conestogo's,[12] and that the Second time we were at War with them we carry'd them all off.

Brother Assaraquoa:

You Charge us with not acting agreeable to our Peace with the Catawbas; we will repeat truly to you what was done: The Governor of New York at Albany, in behalf of Assaraquoa, gave us several Belts from the Cherickees and Catawbas, and we agreed to a Peace if those Nations would send some of their Great men to Us to confirm it face to face, and that they would Trade with us, and desired that they would appoint a time to meet at Albany for this Purpose, but they never came.

Brother Assaraquoa:

We then desired a Letter might be sent to the Catawbas and Cherikees to desire them to come and confirm the Peace. It was long before an Answer came, but we met the Cherikees and Confirmd the Peace, and sent some of Our People to take care of them untill they returned to their own Country.

Colonial Records of Pennsylvania, 4:720–21.

The Catawbas refused to come, and sent us word that we were but Women; that they were men and double men for they had two P——s; that they could make Women of Us, and would be always at War with us. They are a deceitful People; Our Brother Assaraquoa is deceived by him; we don't blame him for it, but are sorry he is so deceived. . . .

Brother Assaraquoa:
We have confirm'd the Peace with the Cherikees, but not with the Cataw-bas. They have been Treacherous, and know it, so that the War must continue till one of Us is destroyed. This we think Proper to tell you, that you may not be Troubled at what we do to the Catawbas.

Brother Assaraquoa:
We will now Speak to the Point between us. You say you will agree with us to the Road. We desire that may be the Road which was last made (the Waggon Road). It is always a custom among Brethren or Strangers to use each other kindly. You have some very ill-natured People living up there, so that we desire the Persons in Power may know that we are to have reason-able Victuals when we are in want.

You know very well when the White People came first here they were poor; but now they have got our Lands and are by them become Rich, and we are Now poor. What little we had for the Land goes soon away, but the Land lasts forever. You told us you had brought with you a Chest of Goods, and that you have the Key in your Pockets; But we have never seen the Chest nor the Goods that are said to be in it. It may be smal and the Goods few. We want to see them, and are desirous to come to some Conclusion. We have been sleeping here these Ten Days past, and have not done any thing to the Purpose.

THE ABENAKIS DEFY THE ENGLISH

When the United States held treaties with Indian tribes in the nineteenth century, American commissioners often dictated terms and spoke down to Indian delegates with the arrogance of power. In colonial times the power balance was much more equal and Indian speakers frequently "gave as good as they got" in their negotiations with Europeans, as this speech illustrates.

In 1752 the governor of Massachusetts sent Phineas Stevens to Canada as his emissary to meet with the Abenaki Indians. The Abenakis knew Stevens well and seem to have respected him. He had been captured as a boy in Massachusetts by an Abenaki raiding party, spent several years living with them, and learned their language and customs. On his return from captivity, he ran a trading post at Fort Number Four on the Connecticut River near Charlestown, New Hampshire and, as commander of that little fort, withstood French and Indian attacks during King George's War.

Stevens met with Abenakis from the village of St. Francis (Odanak) at Montreal in July 1752. Many of these people had migrated from northern New England to Canada to escape the pressure of English settlement. In the presence of the governor of Montreal and of Indian deputies from the neighboring villages of Caughnawaga (Kahnawake) and Lake of the Two Mountains (Oka), the Abenaki speaker Atiwaneto made clear to Stevens the Abenakis' determination to resist English expansion and their contempt for English claims to sovereignty.

ATIWANETO

Speech Resisting Colonial Expansion
1752

Brother, We speak to you as if we spoke to your Governor of Boston. We hear on all sides that this Governor and the Bostonians say that the Abenakis are bad people. 'Tis in vain that we are taxed with having a bad heart. It is you, brother, that always attack us; your mouth is of sugar but your heart of gall. In truth, the moment you begin we are on our guard.

Brothers, We tell you that we seek not war, we ask nothing better than to be quiet, and it depends, brothers, only on you English, to have peace with us.

We have not yet sold the lands we inhabit, we wish to keep the possession of them. Our elders have been willing to tolerate you, brothers Englishmen, on the seabord as far as Sawakwato, as that has been so decided, we wish it to be so.

But we will not cede one single inch of the lands we inhabit beyond what has been decided formerly by our fathers.

You have the sea for your share from the place where you reside; you can

E. B. O'Callaghan, ed., *Documents Relative to the Colonial History of the State of New York*, 15 vols. (Albany: Weed, Parsons, 1853–87), 10:252–54.

trade there. But we expressly forbid you to kill a single beaver, or to take a single stick of timber on the lands we inhabit. If you want timber we'll sell you some, but you shall not take it without our permission.

Brothers, Who hath authorized you to have those lands surveyed? We request our brother, the Governor of Boston, to have those surveyors punished, as we cannot imagine that they have acted by his authority.

Brother, You are therefore masters of the peace that we are to have with you. On condition that you will not encroach on those lands we will be at peace, as the King of France is with the King of Great Britain.

By a Belt.

I repeat to you Brothers, by this belt, that it depends on yourselves to be at peace with the Abenakis.

Our Father who is here present has nothing to do with what we say to you; we speak to you of our own accord, and in the name of all our allies. We regard our Father, in this instance, only as a witness of our words.

We acknowledge no other boundaries of yours than your settlements whereon you have built, and we will not, under any pretext whatsoever, that you pass beyond them. The lands we possess have been given us by the Master of Life. We acknowledge to hold only from him.

We are entirely free. We are allies of the King of France, from whom we have received the Faith and all sorts of assistance in our necessities. We love that monarch, and we are strongly attached to his interests.

Let us have an answer to the propositions we address you, as soon as possible. Take this message in writing to give to your Governor. We also shall keep a copy of it to use in case of need.

Without stirring a step it is easy for you Governor to transmit his answer to us; he will have merely to address it to our Father who will have the goodness to send it to us.

THE CHICKASAWS APPEAL FOR HELP

The Chickasaw Indians of what is today northern Mississippi were a small tribe. Recurrent warfare with the French and their Choctaw allies reduced them to little more than four hundred warriors in the eighteenth century. Nevertheless, they had a reputation as formidable fighters and consistently frustrated French attempts to invade their territory. The English looked upon them as loyal allies up to the end of the Revolution. The following speech from Chickasaw headmen to the governor of South Carolina illustrates the hardships the Chickasaw faced as a result of almost continual warfare.

CHICKASAW HEADMEN

Speech to the Governor of South Carolina
April 5, 1756

From the Headmen and Warriours of the Chekesaws Nation to the King of Carolina and His Beloved Men, This is to let you know we are daily cut oft by our Enemies the French and their Indians who seems to be resolved to drive us from this Land. Therefore we beg of you, our best Friends, to send back our People that are living in other Nations in order to enable us to keep our Lands from the French and their Indians. We hope you will think on us in our Poverty as we have not had the Liberty of Hunting these 3 Years but have had enough to do to defend our Lands and prevent our Women and Children from being Slaves to the French. Our Traders that come here are not willing to trust us Gun Powder and Bulletts to hunt and defend ourselves from our Enemies, neither are we able to buy from them. Many of our Women are without Flaps and many of our young Men without Guns which renders them uncapable of making any Defence against such a powerful Enemy. We are very thankful to you for your last Presents without which it would not have been possible for us to keep Possession of this Land. We have not forgotten all your old good Talks, they are stil fresh in our Minds and we shall always look upon the English as our best Friends and will always endeavour to hinder the French from incroaching on our Lands either to build Forts or make any other Improvments. We will never give up this Land but with the Loss of our Lives. We look upon your Enemies as ours and your Friends as our Friends. The Day shall never come while Sun shines and Water runs that we will join any other Nation but the English. We hope you will stil take Pity on us and give us a Supply of Powder and Bullets and Guns &c. to enable us to outlive our Enemies and revive a dying Friend. We have had no less than four Armies against us this Winter and have lost 20 of our Warriours and many of our Wives and Children carried of alive, our Towns sett on Fire in the Night and burnt down, many of our Houses &c. destroyed our Blanketts &c. We were out a hunting at the Time where we was all attacked by the Back Enemy at our Hunting Camp where we lost several of our Warriours, Women and Children so that we were obliged to

William L. McDowell, Jr., ed., *Colonial Records of South Carolina: Documents Relating to Indian Affairs, 1754–1765* (Columbia: University of South Carolina Press, 1970), 109–10. Copyright South Carolina Department of Archives and History.

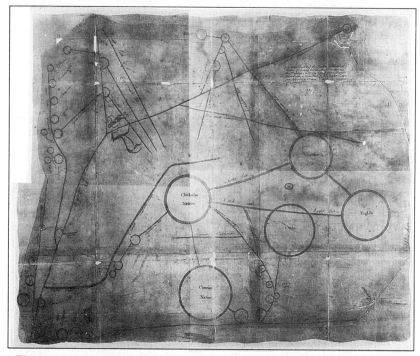

Figure 14. English and French Copies of Chickasaw Deerskin Maps (ca. 1723 and 1737)

Europeans often used maps as instruments of conquest. European cartographers commonly replaced Indian names with European names, labeled Indian country as "empty land," and ignored the presence of Indian peoples, towns, and lands as they marked out boundaries. The net result was to contribute to the dispossession of Indian people by creating documents in which they did not exist. However, though Indian peoples were often what geographer Brian Harley called "victims of a map," they were capable mapmakers themselves. They possessed extensive geographical knowledge, served as guides for Europeans, and showed them the lay of the land in a variety of ways. Indians at Cape Ann, Massachusetts, drew a map of the coastline in charcoal for French explorer Samuel de Champlain in 1605, placing pebbles to indicate the location of Indian villages. John Lawson, who traveled among the Indians of North Carolina in the first decade of the eighteenth century, said they drew very accurate maps. He had only to put pen and ink into an Indian's hand "and he has drawn me the Rivers, Bays, and other Parts of a Country, which afterwards I have found to agree with a great deal of Nicety."[13] Other travelers agreed that Indians were reliable and accurate mapmakers.

Not all maps, however, were intended to convey geographical information. The purpose of these two maps was to show social and political relationships between the Chickasaw Indians and surrounding nations and tribes. The first map *(above)*, painted on a deerskin by a Chickasaw headman and presented to Governor Francis Nicholson of South Carolina in the early 1720s, covers a huge area, from Texas in the

(Continued on p. 132)

NATIONS AMIES ET ENNEMIES DES TCHIKACHAS.

Ces Figures ont etées Tirrées, d'apres l'original qui etoient Sur une peau que
Mingo-Ouma, Grand chef de Guerre de la Nation Tchikachas à donné au
Capitaine de Pakana, Pour apporter à Sa Nation, et aux François, a fin qu'ils
Vissent le nombre de leurs Amis et aussy leurs Ennemis, les premiers Sont marqués
en Noir et le Seconds en Rouge. Les Ronds maques des villages et Nations Entieres.
A. Les Anglois, B. Les Kaouitas, C. Les Kachétas D. Les Vtchité, E. Les Toukaulou charaki
F. Les Charakis Ceux cy parlent une langue différente de E, G. Les Affasqués Abékas,
H Les Alybamons, I. La Mobille ou les Francois, K. Les Tchakts, L. Toute la Nation.
Tchikachas, qui est blanche en dedans, mais d'on les Environs ne Sont que de Sang
elle est blanches, parce qu'ils pretendent, qu'il ne Sort que de bonnes parolles de
leur Villages, mais que ceux des Environs perdent l'Esprit en ne l écoutant point,
ce qui rend Ses Terres Teinte de Sang. M. Les Villages et Nations Huronnes Iroquoises.
et ceux qu'ils appellent Nantouaguó N. Les Villages et Nations des Tamarois
Peanquichias, &c. o. Les Arkansas ou Okappa, P. Les chakchouma Sur lesqu'els
ils doivent aller Frapper incessament Q. ce Sont des chemins de Guerre, qui
ne Se rendent pas jusques aux Villages, Parce qu'ils esperent qu'ils deviendrons
blancs, en faisant la paix avec Ceux Vers ou ils tendent R. Riviere des
Alybamons et chemin de cette Nation à la Mobille, il narrive pas jusque à
la Mobilla, par ce qu'ils disent quils noseroient y aller, mais que
maigré cela est blanc pour nous S. Chemin blancs qui vont chez leurs Amis
T. Chemins de Guerre, V. Chemin de chasse des
Alybamons, Blancs. le Sept 7bre 1737.

DeBat

Figure 14 (continued)

west to Florida and New York in the east. The forty-three circles represent villages or tribes; rivers and paths are depicted only as arteries of communication radiating from the Chickasaw Nation.

The second map *(p. 131)* is a French copy, dated 1737, of a deerskin map brought back by an Alabama Indian who had been sent as an emissary to the Chickasaws. The circles and lines portray the disposition of the Chickasaws' friends and enemies. The captions identify the various tribes and nations (for example, A = the English; F = the Cherokees; H = the Alabamas; I = Mobile or the French; K = the Choctaws; L = the Chickasaws) and explain whether the paths between the nations are warpaths or white paths of peace and friendship.

These two maps give an insight to the Chickasaws' view of their position in the world as, for much of the eighteenth century, they found themselves surrounded by French and Indian enemies who threatened to sever their trade relations with the English in Charleston.[14]

---

leave our Hunting Camps and return to our Nation. Our Traders can tell you all this is true, if you think we tell Lies. We have told you the greatest of our Wants and are in hopes you will not forget us and leave us to be cutt of by our Enemies. Pray send all our People that lives amongst you to our Nation for we think they must be troublesome to you and would be of great Service to us for we are now reduced to small a Number we can hardly spare Men to guard our Traders to and from our Nation. We have no more to say at Present but hope you will pity us for we are very poor.

Tuska Chickamobbey (his Mark)	Pia Mattaha (his Mark)
Pia Hagego (his Mark)	Tanna Puskemingo (his Mark)
Tiske Omastabey (his Mark)	War King (his Mark)
Mucklassau Mingo (his Mark)	Pia Haggo (his Mark)
Mingo Opya (his Mark)	Funne Mingo Mas Habey (his Mark)

FRENCH AND INDIAN WARS, OR FRENCH AND ENGLISH WARS?

Our history books traditionally refer to the imperial conflicts of the eighteenth century as the French and Indian Wars, since English colonists in North America found themselves fighting French soldiers and their Indian allies. From the Indians' point of view, as from the French point of view, the title represents an Anglo-centric distortion of reality. Christian Frederick

Post, a Moravian serving as an ambassador from Pennsylvania, made two trips to the Ohio country in 1758 in an effort to bring peace. In September he met with Shingas, his brother Tamaqua or King Beaver, and other Delawares. Both Virginia and Pennsylvania offered rewards for Shingas's scalp, but the Indians made clear exactly who they thought responsible for these wars.

DELAWARE INDIANS

Response to the Moravian Ambassador

1758

The land is ours, and not theirs; therefore, we say, if you will be at peace with us, we will send the *French* home. It is you that have begun the war, and it is necessary that you hold fast, and be not discouraged, in the work of peace. We love you more than you love us; for when we take any prisoners from you, we treat them as our own children. We are poor, and yet we clothe them as well as we can, though you see our children are as naked as at the first. By this you may see that our hearts are better than yours. It is plain that you white people are the cause of this war; why do not you and the *French* fight in the old country, and on the sea? Why do you come to fight on our land? This makes every body believe, you want to take the land from us by force, and settle it. . . .

Brother, your heart is good, you speak always sincerely; but we know there are always a great number of people that want to get rich; they never have enough; look, we do not want to be rich, and take away that which others have. God has given you the tame creatures; we do not want to take them from you. God has given to us the deer, and other wild creatures, which we must feed on; and we rejoice in that which springs out of the ground, and thank God for it. Look now, my brother, the white people think we have no brains in our heads; but that they are great and big, and that makes them make war with us: we are but a little handful to what you are; but remember, when you look for a wild turkey you cannot always find it, it is so little it

Reuben G. Thwaites, ed., *Early Western Travels* (Cleveland: Arthur H. Clark, 1904), 1:214–16.

hides itself under the bushes: and when you hunt for a rattlesnake, you cannot find it; and perhaps it will bite you before you see it. However, since you are so great and big, and we so little, do you use your greatness and strength in compleating this work of peace. This is the firft time that we saw or heard of you, since the war begun, and we have great reason to think about it, since such a great body of you comes into our lands. It is told us, that you and the *French* contrived the war, to waste the *Indians* between you; and that you and the *French* intended to divide the land between you: this was told us by the chief of the *Indian* traders; and they said further, brothers, this is the last time we shall come among you; for the *French* and the *English* intend to kill all the *Indians,* and then divide the land among themselves. . . .

Brother, I suppose you know something about it; or has the Governor stopped your mouth, that you cannot tell us?

A NEW ERA FOR ALGONKIANS
AND ENGLISHMEN

General James Wolfe captured Quebec for the British in 1759. The next year Montreal fell to the redcoats. By 1761, the French were effectively defeated in North America, although the formal peace treaty was not signed until 1763. Most of the Algonkian Indian tribes living around the Great Lakes had been allies of the French for generations. They now confronted a harsh new era as the British replaced their French "father" as the dominant European power in the region.

In 1761, the Chippewa or Ojibwa chief Minavavana, also known as the Grand Sauteur, met British trader Alexander Henry on Michilimackinac, an island at the junction of Lake Huron and Lake Michigan. Speaking through interpreters and at the head of a body of painted Indians, the chief looked "steadfastly" at Henry as he spoke. His speech rejects the British pretensions to Indian lands by virtue of defeating the French. It also reveals the importance of gift giving in Indian diplomacy, something the French knew well and the English were soon to learn. The English regarded Indians as mercenary in their requests for presents and cut back on gifts to the Indians at the end of the Seven Years War; this retrenchment convinced the Indians that the English cared for them only so long as there was a war on and was a major cause of Pontiac's War in 1763. Gift giving was an essential lubricant in Indian diplomacy, indicating sincerity and cementing relationships.

The Chippewa's words were not idle boasting: In 1763 the Indians captured the British post at Michilimackinac, along with their other forts west of Detroit and Fort Pitt.

Figure 15. Detail from Benjamin West's *The Death of General Wolfe*
West's dramatic picture shows the heroic death of Wolfe at the capture of Quebec, the key to Canada, in 1759. The Indian, watching reflectively, is no doubt West's invention, but his presence symbolizes the larger involvement of Indian peoples in the wars for empire in North America. Some warriors served the British; many others from Canada, the Great Lakes, and the Ohio Valley fought several times in the campaigns of the French general the Marquis de Montcalm, who also died in the fight for Quebec.

MINAVAVANA

Speech to Alexander Henry
1761

Englishman, it is to you that I speak, and I demand your attention!

Englishman, you know that the French king is our father. He promised to be such; and we in return promised to be his children. This promise we have kept.

Englishman, it is you that have made war with this our father. You are his enemy; and how then could you have the boldness to venture among us, his children? You know that his enemies are ours.

Englishman, we are informed that our father, the King of France, is old and infirm; and that being fatigued with making war upon your nation, he is fallen asleep. During his sleep you have taken advantage of him and possessed yourselves of Canada. But his nap is almost at an end. I think I hear him already stirring and inquiring for his children, the Indians; and when he does awake, what must become of you? He will destroy you utterly!

Englishman, although you have conquered the French, you have not yet conquered us! We are not your slaves. These lakes, these woods and mountains were left to us by our ancestors. They are our inheritance; and we will part with them to none. Your nation supposes that we, like the white people, cannot live without bread—and pork—and beef! But you ought to know that He, the Great Spirit and Master of Life, has provided food for us in these spacious lakes and on these woody mountains.

Englishman, our father, the King of France, employed our young men to make war upon your nation. In this warfare many of them have been killed, and it is our custom to retaliate until such time as the spirits of the slain are satisfied. But the spirits of the slain are to be satisfied in either of two ways; the first is by the spilling of the blood of the nation by which they fell; the other by *covering the bodies of the dead,* and thus allaying the resentment of their relations. This is done by making presents.

Englishman, your king has never sent us any presents, nor entered into any treaty with us, wherefore he and we are still at war; and until he does these things we must consider that we have no other father, nor friend

Alexander Henry, *Travels and Adventures in the Years 1760–1776* (Chicago: R. R. Donnelley, 1921), 43–45.

among the white men than the King of France; but for you we have taken into consideration that you have ventured your life among us in the expectation that we should not molest you. You do not come armed with an intention to make war; you come in peace to trade with us and supply us with necessaries of which we are in much want. We shall regard you, therefore, as a brother; and you may sleep tranquilly, without fear of the Chipewa. As a token of our friendship we present you with this pipe to smoke.

PONTIAC'S WAR

Indian warfare traditionally combined spiritual as well as military dimensions. Warriors consulted dreams and visions before embarking on expeditions, prepared ritually for conflict, and often went to war to appease the spirits of the dead and assuage the grief of bereaved relatives. Not surprisingly, resistance to white expansion sometimes combined spiritual and moral revival with political and military opposition as Indians tried to recover the world they had lost. In 1763, in the wake of France's defeat and with British redcoats occupying forts formerly held by the French, the Indians of the Ohio Valley and the Great Lakes mounted such a campaign. Historians have labeled the ensuing war "Pontiac's conspiracy," after the Ottawa war chief whom contemporaries identified as its most prominent leader. In fact, it was not a conspiracy so much as a widespread revolt by the Indians against the inroads of European culture and against British soldiers.

A Delaware Indian prophet by the name of Neolin preached rejection of European ways and values among the tribes of the Ohio Valley and Great Lakes. In a speech delivered in the form of a parable to assembled Indians from various tribes in the spring of 1763, Pontiac related how the Master of Life, appearing to the Wolf (the French applied the name *loup* or "wolf" to the Delaware and other Indians), reminded the Indians that they had become weak and dependent on Europeans. The speech originally was recorded in French, possibly by a priest.

Pontiac's War ultimately failed, but it had far-reaching consequences. In an effort to prevent future Indian wars, the British government by the Royal Proclamation of 1763 placed the lands west of the Appalachian Mountains off limits to settlers. Colonists and land speculators who resented this imposition of royal authority began to contemplate independence from Great Britain.

PONTIAC

The Master of Life Speaks to the Wolf
1763

I am the Master of Life, whom thou desirest to know and to whom thou wouldst speak. Listen well to what I am going to say to thee and all thy red brethren. I am He who made heaven and earth, the trees, lakes, rivers, all men, and all that thou seest, and all that thou hast seen on earth. Because [I have done this and because] I love you, you must do what I say and [leave undone] what I hate. I do not like that you drink until you lose your reason, as you do; or that you fight with each other; or that you take two wives, or run after the wives of others; you do not well; I hate that. You must have but one wife, and keep her until death. When you are going to war, you juggle, join the medicine dance, and believe that I am speaking. You are mistaken, it is to Manitou to whom you speak; it is a bad spirit who whispers to you nothing but evil; and to whom you listen because you do not know me well. This land, where you live, I have made for you and not for others. How comes it that you suffer the whites on your lands? Can't you do without them? I know that those whom you call the children of your Great Father supply your wants, but if you were not bad, as you are, you would well do without them. You might live wholly as you did before you knew them. Before those whom you call your brothers came on your lands, did you not live by bow and arrow? You had no need of gun nor powder, nor the rest of their things, and nevertheless you caught animals to live and clothe yourselves with their skins, but when I saw that you went to the bad, I called back the animals into the depths of the woods, so that you had need of your brothers to have your wants supplied and cover you. You have only to become good and do what I want, and I shall send back to you the animals to live on. I do not forbid you, for all that, to suffer amongst you the children of your father. I love them, they know me and pray to me, and I give them their necessities and all that they bring to you, but as regards those who have come to trouble your country, drive them out, make war to them! I love them not, they know me not, they are my enemies and the enemies of your brothers! Send them back to the country which I made for them! There let them remain.

Michigan Pioneer and Historical Collections (1886), 8:270–71.

THE PLEAS AND PLIGHT
OF THE CHOCTAW CHIEFS

In the eighteenth century, the powerful Choctaw Indians of Mississippi played a key role in the competition among France, Spain, and England for control of the lower Mississippi Valley. They generally sided with France

Figure 16.   Outacite, Cherokee Chief, 1762
By the eighteenth century, Indians throughout the eastern woodlands were involved in European contests for empire in North America. Europeans cultivated client chiefs and bestowed medals on them to symbolize their allegiance; Indian leaders looked to Europeans to provide them with the trade goods their people had come to depend on. This eighteenth-century engraving of Outacite, or Mankiller, shows the Cherokee chief wearing traditional facial tattoos and scalp lock, together with a gorget around his neck displaying the royal arms of George III.

against the English and their Chickasaw allies, but different parties within the Choctaw Nation favored different strategies and allegiances. This factionalism disrupted Choctaw society but allowed the Choctaws to survive in a world of intense rivalry and maintain a constant supply of European trade goods. The French in particular made annual gifts an integral part of their Indian diplomacy. These gifts allowed the Choctaw "medal" chiefs (Europeans gave Indian chiefs large and small medals as symbols of their rank and allegiance) to carry out one traditional function of a chief, redistributing wealth among the people.

In 1763, at the end of the Seven Years War, France ceded the Choctaw homeland to Britain. In reality, France ceded only its *claims* to Choctaw territory; the Choctaws continued to own and control the area. Nevertheless, the Choctaws no longer could play off rival European powers and had to look to the British alone for their supplies. The British, however, preferred to exchange merchandise in trade or as payment for direct services rather than to give gifts as a standard procedure. At a time when the white-tailed deer population, on which the Choctaws relied for trade, was in decline in Choctaw territory, the new regime hit the Indians hard. Traders came into Choctaw towns, peddling alcohol, cheating the Indians with short weights, and causing unprecedented social chaos. The chiefs were unable either to maintain peace or to counter the power of the traders by distributing merchandise to their people.

The Choctaws first met British superintendent for the southern Indians John Stuart in conference at Mobile, Alabama, in 1765, but the problems remained unresolved. They met him again at Mobile in December 1771 and January 1772. At first glance, the speeches the chiefs from the various Choctaw towns made to Stuart that winter look like confessions of abject dependence on the British. But the situation was more complex than that. The chiefs were campaigning for a resumption of the practice of annual gift giving so that they would have goods to distribute to their followers and halt the downward spiral in their influence and the chaos in their towns. As Mingo Emmitta, the great chief of the Choctaw nation, indicates at the start of his speech, many chiefs had been killed in the social turmoil. The Choctaw chiefs at Mobile were, in fact, pleading for their political lives.[15]

CHOCTAW CHIEFS

Speeches to John Stuart, Mobile, Alabama

1772

Mingo Emmitta Speaks

Chiefs and white Brethren

Many of our great Chiefs who attended the last Congress are dead, Since that time we have lost Five great Medal Chiefs and other leading men, the Dead cannot Speak Such as are living and Present have now an opportunity to Speak for their Nation.

Addressing the Superintendant

You are the father and Chief of the Red men, you are returned after a long absence to See us and Supply our wants, you Fixed no time for returning to meet us, you made us no Promise of a Congress at any Particular Period, but you told us That the Seas were dangerous and your return was uncertain, but That if you never returned Some other Person would be appointed by the Great King to take care of us, you are at last come, heaven has preserved you in great danger and the sight of you makes us Glad, I once lost a Father but I found one dearer and greater in you, at the last Congress we met you naked and Miserable, you sent us home Cloathed and Comforted, during your absence I was like a Sick man you have returned to Cheer my Spirits and administer relief and I hope you will be attentive to relieve our necessities, This day I see you are a just and Good Father, and have not forgotten your Children, you are like a Great Doctor who can Cure all distempers, the Sight of whom Comforts and Chears the Spirits of His Patients; We have been used to meet Great Chiefs, this day we meet Greater Chiefs we rejoyce

Proceedings of the Mobile Congress, reprinted in *Publications of the Mississippi Historical Society* 5 (1925): 147–51.

in the Sight of our Father and gratefully Thank the great King for Sending him to relieve our Wants? what can Red men ask of their Father? but arms and ammunition to defend them and Cloathing to keep them warm, what can make a Red man Rich and powerfull? a Gun and ammunition, it is in the power of our Father to make his Children Rich and happy by giving us arms and Cloathing.

When I return to my Nation It will be asked what have you Seen? I will answer That I Saw my Father the Cheif of the Red men the Great Governor and Chief of the white men in this Country and the Chief Leader and General of the Great Kings Warriors who received me kindly and as a proof I will Show them what I shall receive from my Father, what can we ask or Expect from our white Brethren but to Supply our wants.

Our Father is Like a Turkey perched upon the Top of a High Tree we are his Brood of Chickens eagerly looking up at but cannot reach him at our return to our Houses our Young our Old our Fathers our Wives our Children will all rejoyce and be happy in having their wants Supplied.

What can our White Brethren think of us by giving us such narrow Flaps, they dont cover our Secret parts, and we are in danger of being deprived of our Manhood, by every Hungry dog That approaches us, these Flaps are too narrow I hope this will be altered.

I must Complain of the great Quantities of Rum carried into our Towns it is what distracts our Nation we wish to see a Stop put to this pernicious Practice and That the Traders be allowed to Carry no more then a Small Quantity Sufficient to procure some Provisions and pay for the building Stores or Houses. When the Clattering of the Packhorse Bells are heard at a Distance our Town is Immediately deserted young and old run out to meet them Joyfully crying Rum Rum; they get Drunk, Distraction Mischief Confusion and Disorder are the Consequences and this the Ruin of our Nation.

I have no Complaint to make against the Traders residing in my Town, but I desire Such of my people as have Complaints to make of their Traders to speak out and be particular.

Illepotapo of the Chickesawhays
Great Medal Chief Desires all the
Red men present to attend to his Speech

I am Glad to See my Father and Brothers here to day, and Glad to take them by the Hand, I am a red man and very poor, my hand is Black and Soils their white hands Chickesaws and Chactaws behold your white Brethren who have come at last to Supply our Wants. The day is now come That I much longed for, but allmost despaired of seeing, Brothers Chickesaws you and we

Chactaws will Share between us the Presents which our Father has brought us as we are Brothers.

I am not come here to beg, and enumerate Particular Articles, I know my father the Superintent, is Just and knows what things are fitting for Red Men and will Supply our wants accordingly he knows us to be poor and Incapable of making Necessaries for ourselves.

Father, I beg to be Furnished with a Copy of the Tarriff to carry into my Town, That I may Show it to the Traders who Supply us with Flaps so Scanty that they are Insufficient to cover our Nakedness.

When Mr. John McIntosh arrived amongst us the Trade was well regulated but the Chickesaws took him from us since which time the measure by which the Traders sell their Goods is Shortned and the weights by which they take our Skins are grown hevier. I hope therefore to have Standard weights and measures which cannot be altered given me to carry into my Town which may prevent Quarrels between us and our Traders; for why Should we be obliged to Quarrel with our white Brethren when my people return from hunting and carry their Skins to Barter for Goods, the Traders hold them between them and the Light, and carefully Examine them before they take them but they are not equally carefull to do them Justice my Warriors Reproach me and ask me why I who am their Chief do not obtain Justice for them? This makes me ashamed and Diminishes my Consequence in the Nation.

When Mr. Smith (who stands here) First came into my Town he acted honestly and Traded Fairly, but he afterwards fell off his measure, Shortned and his weights grew hevier; then Mr. Sims (who I see here also) Settled in my Town also and Traded Justly and Fairly I reasoned with Mr. Smith and recommended to him to follow Mr. Sym's Example but he rejected my Council which occasioned such a Quarrel That we had almost gone to blows, I have no more to say, but to beg that the Superintendant will order my old Drum to be mended or give me a new one.

Captain Ouma of Seneacha Great Medal Chief

All the Chiefs of the Six Towns except myself are dead and I am happy in having lived to See my Father and white Brethren.

It is very long Since I last saw my Father we are very poor and in want of ammunition we are Ignorant and helpless as the Beasts in the woods Incapable of making Necessaries for our selves our sole dependance is upon you.

In my part of the nation people have Sometime been murmering and Jarring, they used to reproach me, and Say, you have no Father to assist you in taking care of your people. Your Father is dead. But this day I have the happiness to See you alive, and I hope you will Supply my wants, and those of my people That we may return with Gladness of heart, my wife and Family are here I recommend them to your care they want Cloathing.

I am now to tell you the Cause of all disorder and Quarreling between us and our white men. It is Rum. It pours in upon our nation Like a great Sea from Mobille and from all the Plantations and Settlements round about Particularly from the House of Simon Favre who is Settled upon this River. I am not a bad Man ask all the Traders and white men who go into our Nation if I am a bad man. I may be sometimes Cross but whenever That happens Rum is the Cause I beg some regulation may be made to prevent the profuse Importation of Rum amongst us and I will engage That our white People and us will live in Harmony like Brothers.

Mr. Taitt (who I see here) is my Trader. I have no Complaint against him, but nevertheless I beg to be Furnished with Standard weights and measures, and a Copy of the Tarriff to carry with me which will greatly Contribute to the maintenance of Peace, and if the Trade is laid under Proper Regulations you will never hereafter be Troubled with any Complaints of or from us but we Will live in Friendship Harmony and ease.

Appapaye of the Town of Olitachas Small Medal

We are poor Ignorant Red men Incapable of Assisting ourselves our dependance is upon our Father; look at us we are poor Red men, it is true, yet are we men and not Beasts my white Brethren can tame Bears Tiges and other Savage Beasts you Certainly can tame us and make us look like men by Cloathing us a Poor Chactaw miserably wraped up in a Bear Skin for Cloathes, is despicable but Cloath us and Let the great King be told that his Children the Chactaws look like men.

I hope our father the Superintendant will Consider our Situation and not Send us home with Tears in our Eyes and destitute of all necessaries I speak for my people, Send them home Sattisfied I shall follow with a Chearfull Heart.

NOTES

[1] E. B. O'Callaghan, ed., *Documents Relative to the Colonial History of the State of New York*, 15 vols. (Albany: Weed, Parsons, 1853–87), 4:893.
[2] Reuben G. Thwaites, ed., *Early Western Travels* (Cleveland: Arthur H. Clark, 1904), 1:214–16.

[3] The Miami and Illinois Indians, respectively.

[4] The Ottawa, Huron, and Algonkin Indians, respectively.

[5] *Corlaer* (or *Corlear*) was the Iroquois title for the governor of New York.

[6] A metaphor for bringing war into Iroquois country.

[7] The Shawnees.

[8] Cadarackui or Cadaraqui refers to Fort Frontenac on Lake Ontario, present-day Kingston, Ontario.

[9] William N. Fenton, "Northern Iroquoian Culture Patterns," in Bruce G. Trigger, ed., *Handbook of North American Indians,* Vol. 15, *Northeast* (Washington, D.C.: Smithsonian Institution, 1978), 299.

[10] William L. McDowell, Jr., ed., *Colonial Records of South Carolina: Documents Relating to Indian Affairs 1750–1754* (Columbia: University of South Carolina Press, 1958), 358.

[11] *Assaraquoa* means "sword" or "big knife" and was the Iroquois title for the governors of Virginia.

[12] The Conestogas were the Susquehannock Indians.

[13] Hugh Talmage Lefler, ed., *A New Voyage to Carolina by John Lawson* (Chapel Hill: University of North Carolina Press, 1967), 214.

[14] Gregory A. Waselkov, "Indian Maps of the Colonial Southeast," in Peter H. Wood, Gregory A. Waselkov, and M. Thomas Hatley, eds., *Powhatan's Mantle: Indians in the Colonial Southeast* (Lincoln: University of Nebraska Press, 1989), 292–343.

[15] Richard White, *The Roots of Dependency* (Lincoln: University of Nebraska Press, 1983), chap. 4, esp. 69–75.

5

American Indians and the American Revolution, 1775–1783

On the one hand we are forgotten, abandoned; on the other hand we are solicited and at times threatened by the English; in such a situation what can we do, what ought we to do?
—Indians in the Great Lakes region
to French emissary Godfrey de Linctot, 1780[1]

That event was for us the greatest blow that could have been dealt us, unless it had been our total destruction.
—Indian Leaders to Spanish Governor Cruzat, St. Louis, 1784[2]

Scholars of Indian history have often neglected the impact of the American Revolution on American Indians, preferring to lump the Revolution together with the other wars and calamities of the late eighteenth century and pointing out that replacing King George III with President George Washington meant little to Indian peoples whose struggle to preserve their lands and cultures continued. But the Revolution was a devastating experience for many Indian people and marked the beginning of a new era in their history.

The outbreak of the American Revolution took many Native Americans by surprise. At first, most tried to keep out of it, regarding it as a family quarrel between the king and his children. As each side pressed them to get involved, however, Indians often found that they had to choose sides. In general, most tribes eventually supported the British: The British had more of the trade goods on which they had become dependent, they had an Indian department whose personnel were experienced and well connected among the tribes, and they had demonstrated in the past that they would try to restrain trespass onto Indian lands. The Americans, by contrast, were frequently short of supplies and could do little to stop their backcountry settlers encroaching on Indian lands. In fact, American militia, who apparently regarded all Indians as "savages," murdered influential Indian leaders like White Eyes of the Delawares and Cornstalk of the Shawnees who had been working for peace, thereby driving their people into the arms of the British.

Not all Indians joined the British cause, however. Indians from Stockbridge, Massachusetts, enlisted as minutemen in the American army; the Oneidas of New York fought for the Americans even though that entailed fighting against relatives in other Iroquois tribes; the Micmacs, Passamaquoddies, and Penobscots of Maine and Nova Scotia supported the Americans, as did the Catawbas of South Carolina. Even in tribes that allied with the British, there were pro-American factions and plenty of people who just wanted to keep out of it. The Revolution split the ancient unity of the Iroquois Confederacy, turning Mohawks, Onondagas, Cayugas, and Senecas against Oneidas and Tuscaroras; the Cherokee Nation divided along generational lines, with older chiefs trying to preserve peace and friendship with the Americans while younger warriors joined the British in an effort to win back their lands. Just as colonial society split into Loyalist and Patriot factions, with perhaps a majority of people trying to remain neutral, so, throughout the length and breadth of Indian country, the Revolution divided tribes and communities.

Indian warriors raided the American frontier in New York, Pennsylvania, Kentucky, Georgia, and the Carolinas, sometimes in company with British troops and Loyalist Rangers. Indian raids sapped American resources and diverted American energies, and stories of Indian "massacres," such as at Cherry Valley in New York in 1778, sent terror through American settlements. But the Revolution was also fought in Indian country. The Americans responded to Cherokee attacks in 1776 by dispatching expeditions from Virginia, Georgia, and the Carolinas to carry fire and sword through Cherokee country.

In 1779, in an effort to cripple the Iroquois war effort by striking at their home base, George Washington ordered invasions of Iroquois country that destroyed forty towns, burned countless crops, and cut down orchards. Homeless and hungry Iroquois fled to the British at Fort Niagara for food and shelter and ever after remembered George Washington as "Town Destroyer." Thomas Jefferson, who was governor of Virginia during the Revolution, urged a war of extermination against the Shawnees in Ohio, and the Shawnees saw their villages burned time and again by Kentucky militia who crossed the Ohio River. Armies and war parties crossed back and forth through Indian country. Individuals and communities were caught up in the fighting, and neutrals sometimes suffered more than others: In 1782, at Gnadenhutten in Ohio, American militia murdered ninety-six Delaware Indians who had converted to the Moravian faith and as pacifists refused to participate in the fighting.

American Indians made great sacrifices and suffered great losses as a result of the American Revolution. White Americans remember the event as securing their liberty; for Native Americans it represented another step toward the loss of their freedom. At the end of the war, the British and the Americans signed the Peace of Paris, ignoring the Indians who had been their allies and their enemies. Britain handed Indian lands to the United States and left Indian people to confront the renewed American assaults on their land and culture. The Cherokee chief Keniteta, or Rising Fawn, making his peace with the Virginians in 1783, threw a handful of ashes into the air to symbolically cast off his allegiance to the British. "They have been the ruin of my People," he said.[3] Indians who had supported the American cause fared little better. While Mahicans from Stockbridge were away fighting with the American army, their lands continued to slip into the hands of covetous neighbors. By the end of the Revolution, Stockbridge ceased to exist as an Indian town. The Mahicans petitioned their former allies for help, but to no avail. They migrated first to New York and then to new homes in Wisconsin.

The selections in this chapter contain many themes familiar to Indians in colonial times—protests over loss of land, distrust of allies, and anguish at their people's plight. They also show Indian people struggling to come to terms with a new era and new challenges. Although Indian people fought for their freedom, too, in the Revolutionary War, they would enjoy few liberties in the new society born out of that conflict.

THE ONEIDAS DECLARE NEUTRALITY

The Declaration of Independence implies that all Indians were willing and ruthless allies of a tyrannical king. ("He [the king] . . . has endeavoured to bring on the inhabitants of our frontiers, the merciless Indian Savages, whose known rule of warfare, is an undistinguished destruction of all ages, sexes, and conditions.") In fact, most tried to stand apart from what they saw as a "family" quarrel. As the following speech to Governor John Trumbull of Connecticut demonstrates, the Oneidas initially hoped to remain neutral. But the Revolution was a conflict that tolerated no neutrality. Eventually, owing in large measure to the efforts of their Presbyterian missionary Samuel Kirkland, most Oneidas decided to support the Americans. Their action split the Iroquois Confederacy as Oneidas clashed in battle with warriors from other Iroquois tribes, and their allegiance to the Americans caused them tremendous suffering. British and Iroquois war parties burned their villages in retaliation, and many Oneidas sought shelter in squalid refugee camps around Schenectady, New York.

ONEIDA INDIANS

Speech to Governor Trumbull

1775

As my younger brothers of the New England Indians, who have settled in our vicinity, are now going down to visit their friends, and to move up parts of their families that were left behind—with this belt by them, I open the road wide, clearing it of all obstacles, that they may visit their friends and return to their settlements here in peace.

We Oneidas are induced to this measure on account of the disagreeable situation of affairs that way; and we hope, by the help of God, they may return in peace. We earnestly recommend them to your charity through their long journey.

Now we more immediately address you, our brother, the Governor, and the chiefs of New England.

Brothers: We have heard of the unhappy differences and great contention between you and Old England. We wonder greatly, and are troubled in our minds.

Brothers: Possess your minds in peace respecting us Indians. We cannot intermeddle in this dispute between two brothers. The quarrel seems to be unnatural. You are *two brothers of one blood.* We are unwilling to join on either side in such a contest, for we bear an equal affection to both you Old and New England. Should the great king of England apply to us for aid, we shall deny him; if the Colonies apply, we shall refuse. The present situation of you two brothers is new and strange to us. We Indians cannot find, nor recollect in the traditions of our ancestors, the like case, or a similar instance.

Brothers: For these reasons possess your minds in peace, and take no umbrage that we Indians refuse joining in the contest. We are for peace.

Brothers: Was it an alien, a foreign nation, who had struck you, we should look into the matter. We hope, through the wise government and good pleasure of God, your distresses may be soon removed and the dark clouds be dispersed.

Brothers: As we have declared for peace, we desire you will not apply to our Indian brethren in New England for their assistance. Let us Indians be all of one mind, and live with one another; and you white people settle your own disputes between yourselves.

American Archives, 4th ser., vol. 2, 1116–17.

Brothers: We have now declared our minds; please to write to us, that we may know yours. We, the sachems and warriors, and female governesses of *Oneida,* send our love to you, brother governor, and all the other chiefs in New England.

JOSEPH BRANT ADDRESSES
HIS MAJESTY'S SECRETARY OF STATE

Joseph Brant, or Thayendanegea (1742–1807), was a Mohawk Indian who had been educated in Eleazar Wheelock's school and was a protégé of Sir William Johnson. He was instrumental in securing Mohawk support for the British war effort in the Revolution. In 1776 Brant, together with a warrior named Oteroughyanento, Colonel Guy Johnson, and other members of the British Indian department, sailed to England. There, Brant met the king and queen, enjoyed London's night life with the prince of Wales, and had his portrait painted by the well-known artist George Romney. However, as shown by this letter to Secretary of State Lord Germain (to whom he gave the Iroquois name Gorah), Brant was in London on business of vital importance to his people.

JOSEPH BRANT

Address to Lord Germain

1776

Brother Gorah:

We have cross'd the great Lake and come to this kingdom with our Superintendant Col. Johnson from our Confederacy the Six Nations and their Allies, that we might see our Father the Great King, and joyn in informing him, his Councillors and wise men, of the good intentions of the Indians our bretheren, and of their attachment to His Majesty and his Government.

Brother: The Disturbances in America give great trouble to all our Na-

E. B. O'Callaghan, ed., *Documents Relative to the Colonial History of the State of New York,* 15 vols. (Albany: Weed, Parsons, 1853–87), 8:670–71.

Figure 17. Joseph Brant
Portrait of the Mohawk painted by George Romney when Brant was in London in 1776.

tions, as many strange stories have been told to us by the people in that country. The Six Nations who alwayes loved the King, sent a number of their Chiefs and Warriors with their Superintendant to Canada last summer, where they engaged their allies to joyn with them in the defence of that country, and when it was invaded by the New England people, they alone defeated them.

Brother: In that engagement we had several of our best Warriors killed and wounded, and the Indians think it very hard they should have been so deceived by the White people in that country, the enemy returning in great numbers, and no White people supporting the Indians, they were oblidged to retire to their vilages and sit still. We now Brother hope to see these bad children chastised, and that we may be enabled to tell the Indians, who have always been faithfull and ready to assist the King, what His Majesty intends.

Brother: The Mohocks our particular Nation, have on all occasions shewn their zeal and loyalty to the Great King; yet they have been very badly treated by his people in that country, the City of Albany laying an unjust claim to the lands on which our Lower Castle is built, as one Klock and others do to those of Conijoharrie our Upper Viliage.[4] We have been often assured by our late great friend Sr William Johnson who never deceived us, and we know he was told so that the King and wise men here would do us justice; but this notwithstanding all our applications has never been done, and it makes us very uneasie. We also feel for the distress in which our Bretheren on the Susquehanna are likely to be involved by a mistake made in the Boundary we setled in 1768. This also our Superintendant has laid before the King, and we beg it may be remembered. And also concerning Religion and the want of Ministers of the Church of England, he knows the designs of those bad people and informs us he has laid the same before the King. We have only therefore to request that his Majesty will attend to this matter: it troubles our Nation & they cannot sleep easie in their beds. Indeed it is very hard when we have let the Kings subjects have so much of our lands for so little value, they should want to cheat us in this manner of the small spots we have left for our women and children to live on. We are tired out in making complaints & getting no redress. We therefore hope that the Assurances now given us by the Superintendant may take place, and that he may have it in his power to procure us justice.

Brother: We shall truly report all that we hear from you, to the Six Nations at our return. We are well informed there has been many Indians in this Country who came without any authority, from their own, and gave much trouble. We desire Brother to tell you this is not our case. We are warriors known to all the Nations, and are now here by approbation of many of them, whose sentiments we speak.

Brother: We hope these things will be considered and that the King or his great men will give us such an answer as will make our hearts light and glad before we go, and strengthen our hands, so that we may joyn our Superintendant Col. Johnson in giving satisfaction to all our Nations, when we report to them, on our return; for which purpose we hope soon to be accomodated with a passage.

Dictated by the Indians and taken down by

Jo: CHEW. Sec^y

CHEROKEES FIGHT
FOR THEIR SURVIVAL

Indian peoples who fought on the British side in the Revolution did so for their own reasons rather than as pawns of the British. In 1776, British Indian agents tried to restrain the southern Indians until they could coordinate their attacks with British campaigns. However, when a delegation of northern Indians carrying a nine-foot war belt spoke in the council house at the "beloved town," or capital, of the Overhill Cherokees at Chota in eastern Tennessee, younger warriors seized the moment and went to war against colonists who had settled their lands illegally. The Americans responded quickly and decisively with devastating invasions of Cherokee country, burning towns and crops and forcing the Cherokees to petition for peace. A young Cherokee chief named Dragging Canoe continued the fight and accused those Cherokees who made peace of becoming "Virginians," a derogatory term in Cherokee eyes. However, at the treaty talks held at Fort Patrick Henry near Long Island on the Holston River in 1777, some of the older chiefs continued their own resistance in words. Having made peace with Virginia, the Cherokee chief Corn Tassel, or Old Tassel, turned to answer the North Carolinians' request for land, returning their wampum belt to them in symbolic rejection of their proposals. As Tassel points out, preserving Cherokee lands and hunting culture was essential to Cherokee survival and identity.

CORN TASSEL

Speech at Treaty Talks with Virginia and North Carolina

1777

Now the beloved men of North Carolina shall hear my reply to what they said to me last night. The talks you gave me came from the Governor to make a path from your Country to mine and was verry good till you came to talk of the boundary line. My beloved man and the beloved man of Virginia have taken hold of each other fast high up the arm.

It may be the same by my brothers of North Carolina. But by their asking so much land it seems as if they want to see what we would say, that we might refuse something, and they might catch us in a trap for an excuse. I left people both at home and in the woods far beyond there, who are waiting and listening to hear what I do. As you are talking of much land I dont know how they would like that part of your proposal. As I said before the beloved men are here together. My beloved Man has been to see the Great beloved man of Virginia who I suppose wrote to your Great beloved man to send you here, and talk about making Peace. I want to know whether he wrote anything to him to require so much land as you seem to do. I am talking to my Brothers so I call you all. as to land I did not expect any thing on that subject; but only concerning peace. The man above hath ordered it so that the white benches shall be set down for us, and I hope nothing will enter either of our hearts but good thoughts. I would leave it to the beloved man of Virginia to settle all things (about Lands) between us. I am talking with my elder Brothers on a subject I cannot clearly comprehend. I did not expect it would have been put to me at this time; for my elder Brothers have imposed much on me in the land way. If this and another house was packed full of goods they would not make satisfaction. But I will leave the difference between us to the great Warrior of all America. It seems misterious to me why you should ask so much land so near me. I am sensible that if we give up these lands they will bring you more a great deal than hundreds of pounds. It spoils our hunting ground; but always remains good to you to raise families and stocks on, when the goods we receive of you are rotten and gone to nothing.

North Carolina Historical Review 8 (1931): 90–91.

Your stocks are tame and marked; but we dont know ours they are wild. Hunting is our principle way of living. I hope you will consider this and pity me. Here is my old friend the Elk (meaning Col°. Preston)[5] and two particular from Virginia hearing the answer I make to my brothers of North Carolina. you require a thing I cannot do, for which reason I return you the string of Beads to consider upon again.

In my talks at Chote Town house there shall be nothing bad towards my elder Brothers. I will hold them fast and strong. I have been often told that my elder Brothers were naked and had nothing. I said if so I will be naked also. I looked for nothing but to raise my children in peace and safety. My former friend who is now my Brothers enemy told me if I listened to you I should wear hickory bark shirts; but that Talk I do not mind.

returned the String

THE DELAWARES AND THE TREATY OF FORT PITT

The Delaware Indians in the Ohio Valley occupied a precarious position during the Revolution, caught between the British at Detroit with their Indian allies to the north and west and the Americans at Fort Pitt to the east. For a long time the Delawares tried to preserve their neutrality, and Chief White Eyes cultivated good relations with George Morgan, the American Indian agent at Fort Pitt, whom the Delawares called Taimenend.

In 1778, White Eyes and the Delawares signed a treaty with the United States at Fort Pitt (reproduced in Appendix II). In return for the right to cross Delaware lands, the Americans guaranteed the territorial rights of the Delawares and even suggested the possibility of an Indian state with representation in Congress. The final version of the treaty committed the Delawares to a military alliance with the United States. George Morgan, who was not present at the treaty, denounced it as a fraud, and Delawares who saw the written document were vociferous in their complaints to Morgan, as this letter of January 1779 attests.

Most Delawares eventually sided with the British after American militia murdered White Eyes, who was killed even as he carried out his treaty commitment to guide American troops through the Ohio country. Captain Pipe, or Hopocan, who attended the treaty, made common cause with the British. In 1782, in retaliation for the murder of their relatives at the Moravian mission of Gnadenhutten, the Delawares captured and ritually tortured Colonel William Crawford, who had been present as a witness at the treaty.

DELAWARE INDIANS

Letter to George Morgan

1779

Brother Taimenend:

Since the Treaty last Fall at Fort Pitt I have observed that some matters have been spoken of which I & the Commissioners should have agreed to, but which are quite strange to me & to which I never agreed & though I never could find out right how matters was I yet thought a time would come when the truth would be known—I have now looked over the Articles of the Treaty again & find that they are wrote down false, & as I did not understand the Interpreter what he spoke I could not contradict his Interpretation, but now I will speak the truth plain & tell you what I spoke.

The following are the complaints made by the Delaware Council of Coochocking which they lay before Colonel George Morgan (their much beloved Brother and faithfull Agent, granted to them by the great Council of the United States) in order that an enquiry be made in the same. . . .

Brother Taimenend:

I remember very well that when I was at the Treaty at Fort Pitt, I throwed down every thing that was bad, & which came from our Enemies the English to my Brothers the Americans; my heart became quite easy, & I was determined to continue in that what I was so often told to do by you, which was to sit quite still & let you & the English make out the matter together; but was very much surprized when I found after my return from the Treaty, that I was looked upon as a Warrior, & which was the cause of so much confusion among my People.

The Tomhawk was handed to me at Fort Pitt but not in a Warlike manner, we all standing & at no Council Fire, neither did I understand the meaning of it. I neither desired any Implements of War, all what I agreed to was to pilot the Army 'till beyond our bounds, & my great Capt White Eyes with several others to go before the Army & convey them to the Enemy in order to be of use to both Parties, in case they should desire to speak or treat with one another.

Louise P. Kellogg, ed., *Frontier Advance on the Upper Ohio* (Madison: Wisconsin State Historical Society, 1916), 202–05.

THE REVOLUTION THROUGH
THE EYES OF A SENECA WOMAN

The life story of Mary Jemison, the white woman who spent most of her life with the Senecas, affords a rare glimpse into the impact of the Revolution on the Indians' home front, as seen through the eyes of a wife and mother (Mary gave birth to a daughter in the first year of the war). Mary Jemison saw the Iroquois delegates return from the German Flats council in 1775 believing they were secure in their neutrality; she observed the shift toward hostilities after the Oswego council in 1777; she saw Seneca warriors return from the bloody battle at Oriskany near Fort Stanwix in 1777; and she saw General John Sullivan's army march through Iroquoia destroying towns and crops in 1779. The American Revolution, celebrated in the nation's history and mythology, meant something different for Indian women who lived and suffered through it.

MARY JEMISON

A View of the Revolution
1775–1779

Thus, at peace amongst themselves, and with the neighboring whites, though there were none at that time very near, our Indians lived quietly and peaceably at home, till a little before the breaking out of the revolutionary war, when they were sent for, together with the Chiefs and members of the Six Nations generally, by the people of the States, to go to the German Flats, and there hold a general council, in order that the people of the states might ascertain, in good season, who they should esteem and treat as enemies, and who as friends, in the great war which was then upon the point of breaking out between them and the King of England.

Our Indians obeyed the call, and the council was holden, at which the pipe of peace was smoked, and a treaty made, in which the Six Nations solemnly agreed that if a war should eventually break out, they would not take up

James Seaver, ed., *The Narrative of the Life of Mary Jemison* (1824 and various editions).

arms on either side; but that they would observe a strict neutrality. With that the people of the states were satisfied, as they had not asked their assistance, nor did not wish it. The Indians returned to their homes well pleased that they could live on neutral ground, surrounded by the din of war, without being engaged in it.

About a year passed off, and we, as usual, were enjoying ourselves in the employments of peaceable times, when a messenger arrived from the British Commissioners, requesting all the Indians of our tribe to attend a general council which was soon to be held at Oswego. The council convened, and being opened, the British Commissioners informed the Chiefs that the object of calling a council of the Six Nations, was, to engage their assistance in subduing the rebels, the people of the states, who had risen up against the good King, their master, and were about to rob him of a great part of his possessions and wealth, and added that they would amply reward them for all their services.

The Chiefs then arose, and informed the Commissioners of the nature and extent of the treaty which they had entered into with the people of the states, the year before, and that they should not violate it by taking up the hatchet against them.

The Commissioners continued their entreaties without success, till they addressed their avarice, by telling our people that the people of the states were few in number, and easily subdued; and that on the account of their disobedience to the King, they justly merited all the punishment that it was possible for white men and Indians to inflict upon them; and added, that the King was rich and powerful, both in money and subjects: That his rum was as plenty as the water in lake Ontario: that his men were as numerous as the sands upon the lake shore:—and that the Indians, if they would assist in the war, and persevere in their friendship to the King, till it was closed, should never want for money or goods. Upon this the Chiefs concluded a treaty with the British Commissioners, in which they agreed to take up arms against the rebels, and continue in the service of his Majesty till they were subdued, in consideration of certain conditions which were stipulated in the treaty to be performed by the British government and its agents.

As soon as the treaty was finished, the Commissioners made a present to each Indian of a suit of clothes, a brass kettle, a gun and tomahawk, a scalping knife, a quantity of powder and lead, a piece of gold, and promised a bounty on every scalp that should be brought in. Thus richly clad and equipped, they returned home, after an absence of about two weeks, full of the fire of war, and anxious to encounter their enemies. Many of the kettles which the Indians received at that time are now in use on the Genesee Flats. . . .

Previous to the battle at Fort Stanwix, the British sent for the Indians to come and see them whip the rebels; and, at the same time stated that they did not wish to have them fight, but wanted to have them just sit down, smoke their pipes, and look on. Our Indians went, to a man; but contrary to their expectation, instead of smoking and looking on, they were obliged to fight for their lives, and in the end of the battle were completely beaten, with a great loss in killed and wounded. Our Indians alone had thirty-six killed, and a great number wounded. Our town exhibited a scene of real sorrow and distress, when our warriors returned and recounted their misfortunes, and stated the real loss they had sustained in the engagement. The mourning was excessive, and was expressed by the most doleful yells, shrieks, and howlings, and by inimitable gesticulations.

During the revolution, my house was the home of Col's Butler[6] and Brandt, whenever they chanced to come into our neighborhood as they passed to and from Fort Niagara, which was the seat of their military operations. Many and many a night I have pounded samp for them from sun-set till sun-rise, and furnished them with necessary provision and clean clothing for their journey. . . .

At that time I had three children who went with me on foot, one who rode on horse back, and one whom I carried on my back.

Our corn was good that year; a part of which we had gathered and secured for winter.

In one or two days after the skirmish at Connissius lake, Sullivan and his army arrived at Genesee river, where they destroyed every article of the food kind that they could lay their hands on. A part of our corn they burnt, and threw the remainder into the river. They burnt our houses, killed what few cattle and horses they could find, destroyed our fruit trees, and left nothing but the bare soil and timber. But the Indians had eloped and were not to be found.

Having crossed and recrossed the river, and finished the work of destruction, the army marched off to the east. Our Indians saw them move off, but suspecting that it was Sullivan's intention to watch our return, and then to take us by surprize, resolved that the main body of our tribe should hunt where we then were, till Sullivan had gone so far that there would be no danger of his returning to molest us.

This being agreed to, we hunted continually till the Indians concluded that there could be no risk in our once more taking possession of our lands. Accordingly we all returned; but what were our feelings when we found that there was not a mouthful of any kind of sustenance left, not even enough to keep a child one day from perishing with hunger.

The weather by this time had become cold and stormy; and as we were destitute of houses and food too, I immediately resolved to take my children and look out for myself, without delay. With this intention I took two of my little ones on my back, bade the other three follow, and the same night arrived on the Gardow flats, where I have ever since resided. . . .

. . . The snow fell about five feet deep, and remained so for a long time, and the weather was extremely cold; so much so indeed, that almost all the game upon which the Indians depended for subsistence, perished, and reduced them almost to a state of starvation through that and three or four succeeding years. When the snow melted in the spring, deer were found dead upon the ground in vast numbers; and other animals, of every description, perished from the cold also, and were found dead, in multitudes. Many of our people barely escaped with their lives, and some actually died of hunger and freezing.

THE REVOLUTION THROUGH CAPTAIN PIPE'S EYES

Although he attended the Treaty of Fort Pitt in 1778, Captain Pipe, or Hopocan, became one of the principal Delaware advocates of siding with the British. He was not, however, a pliant tool of King George, as he demonstrated in this speech to Colonel Arent Schuyler DePeyster, the British commander at Detroit, in November 1781. In fact, Pipe made it clear that he regarded the British as usurpers to the title of "Father," which rightly belonged to the French, and that only economic necessity drove the Delawares to take up arms in a "white man's" war.

The Revolution was a disaster for the Delawares. Those who had converted to the Moravian faith tried to sit out the war at their village of Gnadenhutten, only to be murdered in cold blood by American militia who suspected them of carrying out raids. At the same time, Indians who supported the Crown were regarded as expendable by their British allies. As Pipe realized, the Indians had much to lose and little to gain by getting involved in this war.

The Moravian missionary John Heckewelder, who recorded this speech, was extremely impressed with Pipe's oratorical power. Given his own pro-American sympathies, however, it is likely that Heckewelder was most impressed by the anti-British sentiments expressed by one of Britain's Indian allies, and he may have embellished the anti-British tenor of the speech.

CAPTAIN PIPE

Speech to British Colonel DePeyster
November 1781

Father! I have said *Father,* tho indeed I am ignorant of the cause for so calling him having never known of any other Father than the French, and considering the English as Brothers. But as *this* Name is now also imposed upon us, I therefore make use of it and say:

Father! Some time ago You put a War hatchet into my hands, saying: take this Weapon, and try it on the heads of my Enemies, the Long Knives (the American People) and let me afterwards know if it was sharp and good.

Father! Altho at the time You gave me this Weapon, I had neither cause nor inclination to go to War against a People who had done me no injury: yet out of obedience to You, who *say* You are my Father, and call me your child, I received the Hatchet, well knowing, that if I did *not* obey, he would withhold from the necessaries of life, without which I could not subsist, and which were not elsewhere to be procured and had, but at the House of my Fathers!

Father! Withal You may perhaps think me a fool, in risking my life at your call! and in a cause too, by which I have no prospect of gaining any thing; for it is *your* cause, and *not* mine to fight the Long Knives (the Virginians or American People). You both have raised the quarrel within yourselves; and by right, you ought to fight it out *Yourselves* and *not* compel Your Children, the Indians, to expose themselves to Danger for *Your* sake!

Father! Many lives have already been lost on *your* account! Nations have suffered and been weakened! Children have lost Parents, brothers, and relatives! Wifes have lost Husbands! It is not known how many more *may* perish before *Your* war will be at end!

Father! I have said: that You may perhaps think me a fool, rushing thoughtless on Your Enemy! Do *not* believe this Father! Think not that I lack sense *sufficient to convince me,* that altho You *now* pretend to keep up a perpetual enmity to the Long Knives (American People); you may, e'er long, conclude a Peace with them!

Father! You say you love your children the Indians! This You have often

James H. O'Donnell, ed., "Captain Pipe's Speech: A Commentary on the Delaware Experience, 1775–1781," *Northwest Ohio Quarterly* 64 (1992): 126–33.

told them; and indeed it is your interest to say so to them, in order to have them at your service!

But Father! who of us can believe, that you could love a People differing in Colour to that of Yours, more than those (of such) who have a *white* Skin like unto that of Yours!

Father! Pay attention to what I now shall say! While *You! Father!* are setting me on Your Enemy, much in the same manner as a hunter sets on his Dogs at the game—while *I* be in the act of rushing *on* this Enemy of Yours, with the bloody destructive Weapon You gave me: I May *perchance* happen to look back, from whence you started me: and *what may I see?* I shall probably see my Father shaking hands with the Long Knives. *Yes!* with *those very People* he now calls his Enemys! *and* while doing this: he may be laughing at *my* folly, and having *obeyed* him and am *now* risking *my* life at his command. *Father!* keep what I have said in remembrance!

Now *Father! here* is what hath been done with the Hatchet you gave me! (The Pipe hands DePeyster the stick with the one scalp attached) I have done what you bid me to do with the Hatchet, and found it sharp. Nevertheless I did *not* do all what I *might* have done! *No!* I did *not!* my *heart* failed me! I felt compassion for *Your* Enemy! Innocence has *no* share in *Your* quarrels; therefore I distinguished! I *spared!* I took some live flesh (prisoners) which, while bringing on to You, I espied one of Your large Canoes on which I put the same for You! In a few days You will receive this flesh, and find, that the Skin is of the same colour as Yours!

Father! I hope you will not destroy what I have saved! You! *Father!* have the means of keeping *alive* what with me would have to *starve for want!* The Warriors Cabin is generally empty! *Your House is always full.*

ADJUSTING TO NEW REALITIES: THE CHICKASAWS' REVOLUTION

The Chickasaw Indians controlled an important strategic location on the banks of the Mississippi River in northern Mississippi. Throughout the eighteenth century they had been firm allies of the British, who had armed and supported them against the French and their Choctaw allies. During the Revolution, the Chickasaws conducted small-scale operations, mainly patrolling the banks of the Ohio and Mississippi rivers. When the Americans sent them a message in the spring of 1779 threatening destruction if they did not make peace, the Chickasaw chiefs Mingo Houma, Payamataha, and Tuskau Pautapau sent a defiant reply:

We desire no other friendship of you but only desire you will inform us when you are Coming and we will meet you half Way, for we have heard so much of it that it makes our heads Ach[e]. Take care that we dont serve you as we have served the French before with all their Indians, send you back without your heads. We are a Nation that fears or Values no Nation as long as our Great Father King George stands by us for you may depend as long as life lasts with us we will hold him fast by the hand. . . . This is our Talk to you and we desire that you may not keep it hid but have it printed in your News Papers that all your people may see it and know who it was from; We are men & Warriors and dont want our Talks hidden.[7]

During the Revolution, Spain won West Florida from the British, and the geopolitical landscape of the Mississippi Valley took on a very different appearance. Instead of unquestioned support from the British, the Chickasaws now found themselves without allies in the midst of competition among Spain, the new United States government, and several states. Different factions within the Chickasaw Nation cultivated relations with Spaniards and Americans in an attempt to secure the trade Britain previously had supplied. Realizing that the end of the Revolution meant the beginning of a new era, the formerly defiant and independent Chickasaw chiefs attempted to mend diplomatic fences by sending the following message to Congress.

CHICKASAW CHIEFS

Message to Congress

July 1783

To His Excellency the President of the
Honorable Congress of the
United American States

Friend & Brother,

This is the first talk we ever sent you—we hope it will not be the last. We desire you to open your Ears to hear, and your heart to understand us, as we shall always be ready to do to your talks, which we expect will be good, as you are a great and wise man.

Brother,

When our great father the King of England called away his warriors, he told us to take your People by the hand as friends and brothers. Our hearts were always inclined to do so & as far as our circumstances permitted us, we evinced our good intentions as Brothers the Virginians can testify—It makes our hearts rejoice to find that our great father, and his children the Americans have at length made peace, which we wish may continue as long as the Sun and Moon, And to find that our Brothers the Americans are inclined to take us by the hand, and Smoke with us at the great Fire, which we hope will never be extinguished.

Brother,

Notwithstanding the Satisfaction all these things give us we are yet in confusion & uncertainty. The Spaniards are sending talks amongst us, and inviting our young Men to trade with them. We also receive talks from the Governor of Georgia to the same effect—We have had Speeches from the Illinois inviting us to a Trade and Intercourse with them—Our Brothers, the Virginians Call upon us to a Treaty, and want part of our land, and we

Calendar of Virginia State Papers, 3:515–17.

expect our Neighbors who live on Cumberland River, will in a Little time Demand, if not forcibly take part of it from us, also as we are informed they have been marking Lines through our hunting grounds: we are daily receiving Talks from one Place or other, and from People we Know nothing about. We Know not who to mind or who to neglect. We are told that the Americans have 13 Councils Compos'd of Chiefs and Warriors. We Know not which of them we are to Listen to, or if we are to hear some, and Reject others, we are at a loss to Distinguish those we are to hear. We are told that you are the head Chief of the Grand Council, which is above these 13 Councils: if so why have we not had Talks from you,—We are head men and Chiefs and Warriors also: and have always been accustomed to speak with great Chiefs & warriors—We are Likewise told that you and the Great men of your Council are Very Wise—we are glad to hear it, being assured that you will not do us any Wrong, and therefore we wish to Speak with you and your Council, or if you Do not approve of our so Doing, as you are wise, you will tell us who shall speak with us, in behalf of all our Brothers the Americans, and from whare and whome we are to be supplyed with necessarries in the manner our great father supplied us—we hope you will also put a stop to any encroachments on our lands, without our consent, and silence all those People who sends us Such Talks as inflame & exasperate our Young Men, as it is our earnest desire to remain in peace and friendship with our Br: the Americans for ever.

Brother,

The King our Common father always left one of his beloved Men among us, to whom we told anything we had to say, and he soon obtained an answer—and by him our great Father, his Chiefs & headmen spoke to us.

Our great father always gave him goods to cover the nakedness of our old men who could not hunt, our women and our children, and he was as one mouth, and one tongue between us, and was beloved of us all. Such a man living among us particularly at this time, would rescue us from the darkness and confusion we are in. By directing us to whom we should speak, and putting us in the right Path that we should not go wrong.

We have desired our Br. Mr. Donne, who brought talks from General Clark,[8] and has been some time among us, to deliver this talk to you, and speak it in our behalf to your Grand Council, that you may know our want, and as you are wise, that you may direct us what to do for the best. He has Promised, at our desire to take it to your great council fire & to bring as your answer, that you may be no more in the dark—beleive what he tells you from us; we have told him all that is in our hearts.

Brothers, we are very poor for necessaries, for Amunition particularly. We can supply ourselves from the Spaniards but we are averse to hold any intercourse with them, as our hearts are always with our Brothers the Americans. We have advised our young men to wait with patience for the answer to this talk, when we rest assured of having supplies, and every thing so regulated that no further confusion may ensue. We wish that this land may never again be stained with the blood of either white or Red men, that piece may last forever and that both our women and children may sit down in safety under their own shade to enjoy without fear or apprehension the Blessing which the good Spirit enriches them with. Brother, we again desire you and your cheifs to Listen to what we say that we shall not have to Repeat it again, and as you are all Wise, you will know what to do.

Done at Chuck-ul-issah our Great Town the 28th Day of July, 1783.

> Minghoma,
> Pyamathahaw,
> Kushthaputhasa,
> Pyamingoe of Christhautra,
> Pyamingo of Chuckaferah.[9]

BRANT DEMANDS THE TRUTH

At the Peace of Paris in 1783, British diplomats recognized the independence of their thirteen former colonies and ceded to the new United States all territory between the Atlantic Ocean and the Mississippi River, from north of Florida to the Great Lakes. Florida, which had remained loyal to Britain, was transferred to Spain. Despite the fact that most of this territory was still Indian country, Britain made these concessions without any reference to or discussion with her Indian allies, who would be devastated by the changes in sovereignty. As rumors of the peace terms filtered into Indian country, Native Americans reacted in anger, bewilderment, and disbelief. Joseph Brant sent a long message to Governor Frederick Haldimand of Quebec, reminding him of the Mohawks' longstanding loyalty to the Crown and asking for the "real truth." Britain's Indian allies in the South were equally alarmed at the news of peace. Some reacted in anger, accusing the British of betraying them; others asked to accompany the redcoats as they evacuated the mainland, rather than stay and come to terms with the Americans or Spaniards.

Message to Governor Frederick Haldimand

1783

Brother Asharekowa and Representatives of the King, the sachems and War Chieftains of the Six United Nations of Indians and their Allies have heard that the King, their Father, has made peace with his children the Bostonians. The Indians distinguish by Bostonians, the Americans in Rebellion, as it first began in Boston, and when they heard of it, they found that they were forgot and no mention made of them in said Peace, wherefore they have now sent me to inform themselves before you of the real truth, whether it is so or not, that they are not partakers of that Peace with the King and the Bostonians.

Brother, listen with great attention to our words, we were greatly alarmed and cast down when we heard that news, and it occasions great discontent and surprise with our People; wherefore tell us the real truth from your heart, and we beg that the King will be put in mind by you and recollect what we have been when his people first saw us, and what we have since done for him and his subjects.

Brother, we, the Mohawks, were the first Indian Nation that took you by the hand like friends and brothers, and invited you to live amongst us, treating you with kindness upon your debarkation in small parties. The Oneidas, our neighbors, were equally well disposed towards you and as a mark of our sincerity and love towards you we fastened your ship to a great mountain at Onondaga, the Center of our Confederacy, the rest of the Five Nations approving of it. We were then a great people, conquering all Indian Nations round about us, and you in a manner but a handfull, after which you increased by degrees and we continued your friends and allies, joining you from time to time against your enemies, sacrificing numbers of our people and leaving their bones scattered in your enemies country. At last we assisted you in conquering all Canada, and then again, for joining you so firmly and faithfully, you renewed your assurances of protecting and defending ourselves, lands and possessions against any encroachment whatsoever, procuring for us the enjoyment of fair and plentiful trade of your people, and sat contented under the shade of the Tree of Peace, tasting the favour and

Public Record Office, C.O. 42/44, 133–35; reprinted in Charles M. Johnston, ed., *Valley of the Six Nations* (Toronto: Champlain Society, 1964), 38–41.

friendship of a great Nation bound to us by Treaty, and able to protect us against all the world.

Brother, you have books and records of our mutual Treaties and Engagements, which will confirm the truth of what I have been telling, and as we are unacquainted with the art of writing, we keep it fresh in our memory by Belts of Wampum deposited in our Council House at Onondaga. We have also received an ornament for the Head, i.e. a crown, from her late Majesty, Queen Ann,[10] as a token of her mutual and unalterable friendship and alliance with us and our Confederacy. Wherefore, we on our side have maintained an uninterrupted attachment towards you, in confidence and expectation of a Reciprocity, and to establish a Perpetual Friendship and Alliance between us, of which we can give you several instances, to wit, when a few years after the Conquest of Canada, your people in this country thought themselves confined on account of their numbers with regard to a Scarcity of Land, we were applied to for giving up some of ours, and fix a Line or mark between them and Us. We considered upon it, and relinquished a great Territory to the King for the use of his Subjects, for a Trifling consideration, merely as a Confirmation of said Act, and as a proof of our sincere Regard towards them. This happened so late as the year 1768 at Fort Stanwix, and was gratefully Accepted and Ratified by the different Governors and Great men of the respective Colonies on the Sea Side, in presence of our Late Worthy Friend and Superintendent, Sir William Johnson, when we expected a Permanent, Brotherly Love and Amity, would be the Consequence, but in vain. The insatiable thirst for Power and the next Object of dissatisfaction to the King's Subjects on the Sea Coast, and they to blind our Eyes, Sent Priests from New England amongst us, whom we took for Messengers of Peace, but we were Surprisingly undeceived when we found soon after, that they came to sow the Seeds of discord among our People, in order to alienate our ancient attachments and Alliance from the King our Father, and join them in Rebellion against him, and when they stood up against him, they first endeavored to ensnare us, the Mohawks, and the Indians of the Six Nations living on the Susquehanna River, and the Oneidas, by which division they imagined the remainder of the Confederacy would soon follow, but to not the Least effect.

About this Sad Period we lost our Greatest Friend, Sir William Johnson,[11] notwithstanding we were unalterably determined to stick to our Ancient Treaties with the Crown of England and when the Rebels attempted to insult the Families and Descendents of our late Superintendent, on whom the management of our affairs devolved, we stuck to them and Protected them as much as in our Power, conducting them to Canada with a determined

Resolution inviolably to adhere to our Alliance at the Risque of our Lives Families and Property, the rest of the Six Nations finding the Firmness and Steadiness of us, the Mohawks, and Aughuagos,[12] followed our Example and espoused the King's cause to this Present Instant.

It is as I tell you, Brother, and would be too tedious to repeat on this Pressing Occasion the many Proofs of Fidelity we have given the King our Father.

Wherefore Brother, I am now Sent in behalf of all the King's Indian Allies to receive a decisive answer from you, and to know whether they are included in the Treaty with the Americans, as faithful Allies should be or not, and whether those Lands which the Great Being above has pointed out for Our Ancestors, and their descendants, and Placed them there from the beginning and where the Bones of our forefathers are laid, is secure to them, or whether the Blood of their Grand Children is to be mingled with their Bones, thro' the means of Our Allies for whom we have often so freely Bled.

NOTES

[1] Clarence W. Alvord, ed., *Kaskaskia Records, 1778–1790,* in *Collections of the Illinois State Historical Society* (1909): 5:163–65.

[2] Lawrence Kinnaird, ed., *Spain in the Mississippi Valley,* vol. 3, pt. 2, 117, in *Annual Report of the American Historical Association* (1945).

[3] *Calendar of Virginia State Papers* 3:420–21.

[4] The Lower Mohawk castle or village was near Fort Hunter on the Mohawk River.

[5] Colonel William Preston, one of Virginia's Indian commissioners.

[6] Colonel John Butler of the British Indian Department. Based at Fort Niagara, Butler and Joseph Brant made frequent forays against the American frontier.

[7] Papers of the Continental Congress, National Archives, item 51, vol. 2, 41–42.

[8] George Rogers Clark had sent John Donne as an emissary to the Chickasaws to arrange peace between them and Virginia.

[9] Kushthaputhasa is probably a garbled spelling of Tuskau Pautaupa, Payamataha's brother. Piomingo of the town of Tchoukfala emerged as the leader of the pro-American party in the Chickasaw Nation after the Revolution.

[10] Brant's grandfather had been among the delegation who visited Queen Anne in 1710.

[11] Sir William Johnson died in council with the Iroquois in 1774. His death on the eve of the Revolution added to the turmoil in Iroquois society.

[12] The Aughuagos were the inhabitants of Oquaga or Onaquaga, a mixed Iroquois settlement on the upper Susquehanna River. The Americans destroyed their village in 1778.

6

Indian Voices from the New Nation

The Americans, a great deal more ambitious and numerous than the English, put us out of our lands, forming therein great settlements, extending themselves like a plague of locusts in the territories of the Ohio River which we inhabit.
—Indian leaders to Spanish Governor Cruzat, St. Louis, August 1784[1]

I observe in every Treaty we Have had that a bound is fixt, but we always find that your people settle much faster shortly after a Treaty than Before. It is well known that you have taken almost all our Country from us without our consent. . . . Truth is, if we had no Land we should have Fewer Enemies.
—Corn Tassel, 1787[2]

As American Patriots celebrated the victory that brought them independence from Britain, Native Americans braced themselves for the invasion of their lands that was sure to come. Faced with an empty treasury after a long war, the new government hoped to sell off Indian lands to pay its bills and looked to Indian lands as the basis of the new Republic's empire. But state governments, land companies, and individual speculators also had their eyes on Indian lands. The years following the Revolution thus witnessed renewed competition for land. At first, the United States took the position that it had acquired the Indians' territory from Britain by right of conquest. American commissioners dictated treaties, demanding that the tribes give up vast amounts of land as the price of peace. But the Indians soon recovered from their shock and began to unite in resistance to American demands. A new round of wars began in the late 1780s, although to many Indians the conflict was simply a continuation of their long struggle to defend their cultural and territorial boundaries.

Some in the new American government also wrestled with the question of where Indian people fit in the new society that was developing in America. Thomas Jefferson, James Madison, Henry Knox, and others advocated a policy of extending to Indian people "the blessings of civilization," by which they meant Christianity and a settled, agricultural way of life. Some Native Americans accepted these "blessings" and attempted to learn new ways;

others rejected them outright. Many tribes united in opposition to American expansion, forcing the United States to modify its policies.

Whatever their response, however, Indian people found they could do little to stem the tide of expansion. Oneida Indians, who had fought for the Americans in the Revolution, lost their lands in New York. Cherokees who made great efforts to adopt the new way of life were unable to preserve their homelands in Georgia, Tennessee, and North Carolina. American officials might talk of "civilizing" Indian people, but Indians realized that land lay at the root of American Indian policy and of United States–Indian relations.

ALEXANDER McGILLIVRAY
REJECTS AMERICAN PRETENSIONS

During colonial times, Scottish and English traders active in the southeastern deerskin trade frequently married Indian women. Those unions produced children of mixed heritage who often grew up to play influential roles as cultural intermediaries between Indian and European societies. Alexander McGillivray was the son of a Scottish father and a Creek-French mother. Because Creek society was matrilineal, he inherited membership in his mother's clan, the Wind clan. His father gave Alexander an English education in Charleston, and the young man served the British during the Revolution, but his first allegiance was always to the Creeks.

After the Revolution, McGillivray emerged as the most prominent southeastern Indian of his day. Confronted with aggression from Georgia and South Carolina, the Creeks and other southern tribes cultivated relations with Spain as a potential ally against American expansion. At Pensacola in 1784, they placed themselves under Spanish protection and secured assurances of trade, thereby freeing themselves from dependence on the Americans. Educated in European ways and experienced in Indian diplomacy, McGillivray was well equipped to conduct Creek foreign policies in the turbulent years after the Revolution. As this speech, delivered to the Spanish governor Arturo O'Neill, illustrates, he was also able to expose the fraudulence of American claims to his people's lands.

Plagued by ill health, McGillivray died in his early thirties in 1793. By 1795, Spain began to pull back from the Mississippi Valley, and the southern Indians found themselves left alone to deal with the expanding American Republic.

ALEXANDER McGILLIVRAY

Letter to Governor Arturo O'Neill

July 10, 1785

Whereas We the Cheifs and Warriors of the Creek Chickesaw and Cherokee Nations having received information that an Envoy has been appointed by his Most Catholic Majesty the King of Spain for the purpose
of settling the boundarys of his territorys and those of the States of
America, and as we have reason to Apprehend that the American Congress in those important matters will endeavour to avail themselves of
the Late treaty of peace between them & the British Nation and that they
will aim at getting his Majesty the King of Spain to confirm to them that
Extensive Territory the Lines of which are drawn by the Said treaty and
which includes the whole of our hunting Grounds to our Great injury and
ruin—It behoves us therefore to object to, and We Cheifs and Warriors of
the Creek Chickesaw and Cherokee Nations, do hereby in the most solemn
manner protest against any title claim or demand the American Congress
may set up for or against our lands, Settlements, and hunting Grounds in
Consequence of the Said treaty of peace between the King of Great Brittain and the States of America declaring that as we were not partys, so
we are determined to pay no attention to the Manner in which the British
Negotiators has drawn out the Lines of the Lands in question Ceded to
the States of America—it being a Notorious fact known to the Americans, known to every person who is in any ways conversant in, or acquainted with American affairs, that his Brittannick Majesty was never
possessed either by session purchase or by right of Conquest of our Territorys and which the Said treaty gives away. On the contrary it is well
known that from the first Settlement of the English colonys of Carolina
and Georgia up to the date of the Said treaty no tittle has ever been or
pretended to be made by his Brittanic Majesty to our lands except what
was obtained by free Gift or by purchase for good and valuable Consider-
ations.

We can urge in Evidence upon this occasion the Cessions of Lands made
to the Carolinians and Georgians by us at different periods and one so late
as June 1773 of the Lands lying on the bank of the River OGeechee for which

John Walton Caughey, ed., *McGillivray of the Creeks* (Norman: University of Oklahoma
Press, 1938), 90–93.

we were paid a Sum not less than one hundred and twenty thousand pounds Stg. nor has any treaty been held by us Since that period for the purpose of granting any land to any people whatever nor did we the Nations of Creeks, Chickesaws and Cherokees do any act to forfeit our Independance and natural Rights to the Said King of Great Brittain that could invest him with the power of giving our property away unless fighting by the side of his soldiers in the day of battle and Spilling our best blood in the Service of his Nation can be deemed so.

The Americans altho' sensible of the Injustice done to us on this occasion in consequence of this pretended claim have divided our territorys into countys and Sate themselves down on our land, as if they were their own. Witness the Large Settlement called Cumberland and others on the Mississippi which with the Late attempts on the Occonnee Lands are all encroachments on our hunting Grounds.

We have repeatedly warned the States of Carolina and Georgia to desist from these Encroachments and to confine themselves within the Lands [granted] to Brittain in the Year 1773. To these remonstrances we have received friendly talks and replys it is true but while they are addressing us by the flattering appellations of Friends and Brothers they are Stripping us of our natural rights by depriving us of that inheritance which belonged to our ancestors and hath descended from them to us Since the beginning of time.

As His most Gracious Majesty was pleased to Express his favorable disposition toward all those Nations of Indians who implored his favor and protection and which we the Cheifs and Warriors of the Nations aforesaid did do in General Congress, held at Pensacola in June 1784 receiving at the same time his Gracious assurances of protection to us, our respective propertys and Hunting Grounds—Relying thereupon and having the greatest Confidence in the Good faith, humanity and Justice of His Most Gracious Majesty the King of Spain we trust that he will enter into no terms with the American States that may Strengthen their claims or that may tend to deprive us of our Just inheritance.

And we request that your Excellency will have the Goodness to forward this Memorial and representation so that it may reach the foot of his Majestys throne. Humbly entreating that He will be pleased to take the same into his Royal consideration and that he will give his Said Envoy at the Americans Congress such orders respecting the premises as he in his great wisdom and Goodness may think fitte.

We conclude with the Sincerest assurances of our firmest attachment to Him and Gratitude for any favor His Most Gracious Majesty may procure us on this occasion.

Done at Little Tallassie in the Upper Creek Nation
This 10th July 1785
by order and in behalf of the Said Indian Nations

(Signed) Alex: McGillivray

THE UNITED INDIAN NATIONS
ANNOUNCE A NEW POLICY

As the new American nation grew and flexed its muscles, it committed itself to expansion across the area of the Old Northwest, bordered by the Ohio River, the Great Lakes, and the Mississippi. Indian people found themselves fighting a desperate holding action as the by now familiar pressures on their lands intensified. At the Treaty of Fort Stanwix in 1784, American commissioners browbeat Iroquois delegates into ceding large amounts of their territory. When those delegates returned home, they were scorned by their people, who disavowed their actions. At the Treaty of Fort McIntosh in 1785, Delawares, Wyandots (also known as Hurons), Miamis (whom the English and Americans often called Twightwees), and other tribes from the Ohio region were coerced into making similar cessions. The Shawnees, who refused to attend the Fort McIntosh treaty, met the Americans the next year at Fort Finney and received similar treatment.

By 1786, however, the northern tribes were coming to realize what was happening and how they could prevent it. As in colonial times, Indian lands were being lost piecemeal in sales and agreements made by individuals, unauthorized speakers, and single tribes. Only by taking a united stance could the Indians hope to halt the loss of their lands. As the newly independent states tried to form themselves into a new, united nation, so Indian nations strove to present a united front against American expansion. The following message from the united tribes to Congress gave the United States clear warning that the Indians regarded the Ohio River as the boundary between Indian lands and American settlers and that henceforth they would consider no land sales as valid without the unanimous agreement of all the tribes. This united opposition checked American expansion beyond the Ohio River for almost ten years.

UNITED INDIAN NATIONS

Speech at the Confederate Council
November 28 and December 18, 1786

Present:—The Five Nations, the Hurons, Delawares, Shawanese, Ottawas, Chippewas, Powtewattimies, Twichtwees, Cherokees, and the Wabash confederates

To the Congress of the United States of America:

Brethren of the United States of America: It is now more than three years since peace was made between the King of Great Britain and you, but we, the Indians, were disappointed, finding ourselves not included in that peace, according to our expectations: for we thought that its conclusion would have promoted a friendship between the United States and Indians, and that we might enjoy that happiness that formerly subsisted between us and our elder brethren. We have received two very agreeable messages from the thirteen United States. We also received a message from the King, whose war we were engaged in, desiring us to remain quiet, which we accordingly complied with. During the time of this tranquillity, we were deliberating the best method we could to form a lasting reconciliation with the thirteen United States. Pleased at the same time, we thought we were entering upon a reconciliation and friendship with a set of people born on the same continent with ourselves, certain that the quarrel between us was not of our own making. In the course of our councils, we imagined we hit upon an expedient that would promote a lasting peace between us.

Brothers: We still are of the same opinion as to the means which may tend to reconcile us to each other; and we are sorry to find, although we had the best thoughts in our minds, during the beforementioned period, mischief has, nevertheless, happened between you and us. We are still anxious of putting our plan of accommodation into execution, and we shall briefly inform you of the means that seem most probable to us of effecting a firm and lasting peace and reconciliation: the first step towards which should, in our opinion, be, that all treaties carried on with the United States, on our parts, should be with the general voice of the whole confederacy, and carried on in the most open manner, without any restraint on either side; and especially as landed matters are often the subject of our councils with you, a matter of the

American State Papers, Class II: Indian Affairs (Washington, 1832), 1:8–9.

greatest importance and of general concern to us, in this case we hold it indispensably necessary that any cession of our lands should be made in the most public manner, and by the united voice of the confederacy; holding all partial treaties as void and of no effect.

Brothers: We think it is owing to you that the tranquillity which, since the peace between us, has not lasted, and that that essential good has been followed by mischief and confusion, having managed every thing respecting us your own way. You kindled your council fires where you thought proper, without consulting us, at which you held separate treaties, and have entirely neglected our plan of having a general conference with the different nations of the confederacy. Had this happened, we have reason to believe every thing would now have been settled between us in a most friendly manner. We did every thing in our power, at the treaty of fort Stanwix, to induce you to follow this plan, as our real intentions were, at that very time, to promote peace and concord between us, and that we might look upon each other as friends, having given you no cause or provocation to be otherwise.

Brothers: Notwithstanding the mischief that has happened, we are still sincere in our wishes to have peace and tranquillity established between us, earnestly hoping to find the same inclination in you. We wish, therefore, you would take it into serious consideration, and let us speak to you in the manner we proposed. Let us have a treaty with you early in the spring; let us pursue reasonable steps; let us meet half ways, for our mutual convenience; we shall then bring [bury] in oblivion the misfortunes that have happened, and meet each other on a footing of friendship.

Brothers: We say let us meet half way, and let us pursue such steps as become upright and honest men. We beg that you will prevent your surveyors and other people from coming upon our side the Ohio river. We have told you before, we wished to pursue just steps, and we are determined they shall appear just and reasonable in the eyes of the world. This is the determination of all the chiefs of our confederacy now assembled here, notwithstanding the accidents that have happened in our villages, even when in council, where several innocent chiefs were killed when absolutely engaged in promoting a peace with you, the thirteen United States.

Although then interrupted, the chiefs here present still wish to meet you in the spring, for the beforementioned good purpose, when we hope to speak to each other without either haughtiness or menaces.

Brothers: We again request of you, in the most earnest manner, to order your surveyors and others, that mark out lands, to cease from crossing the Ohio, until we shall have spoken to you, because the mischief that has recently happened has originated in that quarter; we shall likewise prevent our people from going over until that time.

Brothers: It shall not be our faults if the plans which we have suggested to you should not be carried into execution; in that case the event will be very precarious, and if fresh ruptures ensue, we hope to be able to exculpate ourselves, and shall most assuredly, with our united force, be obliged to defend those rights and privileges which have been transmitted to us by our ancestors; and if we should be thereby reduced to misfortunes, the world will pity us when they think of the amicable proposals we now make to prevent the unnecessary effusion of blood. These are our thoughts and firm resolves, and we earnestly desire that you will transmit to us, as soon as possible, your answer, be it what it may.

Done at our Confederated Council Fire, at the Huron village, near the mouth of the Detroit river, December 18th, 1786.

> The Five Nations,
> Hurons, Ottawas, Twichtwees, Shawanese,
> Chippewas, Cherokees, Delawares,
> Powtewatimies, The Wabash Confederates.

THE WORLD TURNED UPSIDE DOWN

By the time the American colonists had won their independence and created a new nation, the original inhabitants of this country had seen truly revolutionary changes in their own lives. Many Indian people in New England were reduced to petitioning state legislatures for relief from the poverty that now afflicted them. As two Mohegan speakers, Henry Quaquaquid and Robert Ashpo, explain in this petition to the Connecticut State Assembly in May 1789, the forces that had disrupted their world were not only political. The Mohegans may have been playing to their audience by admitting their own responsibility for many of the changes, and nostalgia certainly colored their view of past days as a golden age. Nevertheless, their words convey the bewilderment many Indian people must have felt as their world changed around them.

HENRY QUAQUAQUID
AND ROBERT ASHPO

Petition to the
Connecticut State Assembly

May 1789

We beg leave to lay our concerns and burdens at your excellencies' feet. The times are exceedingly altered, yea the times are turned upside down; or rather we have changed the good times, chiefly by the help of the white people. For in times past our forefathers lived in peace, love and great harmony, and had every thing in great plenty. When they wanted meat, they would just run into the bush a little way, with their weapons, and would soon return, bringing home good venison, raccoon, bear and fowl. If they chose to have fish, they would only go to the river, or along the seashore; and they would presently fill their canoes with variety of fish, both scaled and shell-fish. And they had abundance of nuts, wild fruits, ground nuts and ground beans; and they planted but little corn and beans. They had no contention about their lands, for they lay in common; and they had but one large dish, and could all eat together in peace and love. But alas! it is not so now; all our hunting and fowling and fishing is entirely gone. And we have begun to work our land, keep horses and cattle and hogs; and we build houses and fence in lots. And now we plainly see that one dish and one fire will not do any longer for us. Some few there are that are stronger than others; and they will keep off the poor, weak, the halt and blind, and will take the dish to themselves. Yea, they will rather call the white people and the mulattoes to eat out of our dish; and poor widows and orphans must be pushed aside, and there they must sit, crying and starving, and die. And so we are now come to our good brethren of the Assembly, with hearts full of sorrow and grief, for immediate help. And therefore our most humble and earnest request is, that our dish of suckutash may be equally divided amongst us, so that every one may have his own little dish by himself, that he may eat quietly and do with his dish as he pleases, that every one may have his own fire.

The original is in the Connecticut State Library, Hartford. The version reprinted here is from John W. DeForest, *History of the Indians of Connecticut* (Hartford, 1852); other versions elsewhere.

JOSEPH BRANT WEIGHS INDIAN
AND WHITE CIVILIZATIONS

Mohawk Joseph Brant has been described as a "man of two worlds." He was prominent in the councils of the Six Nations and as a leader of Iroquois warriors; he was also well connected in Britain and twice crossed the Atlantic. Perhaps more than any other Indian of his time, he was adept at functioning in both Indian and white society and was uniquely qualified to weigh the merits of each way of life. There is a long literary tradition of attributing to native speakers penetrating criticisms of so-called civilized society: The words of a "noble savage" proved effective weapons for cutting to the heart of the hypocrisy, corruption, and greed that many writers saw in their own society. Brant is supposed to have been asked whether he thought Indians living in a "state of nature" were more or less happy than white people living in "civilization." His long reply is fairly conventional in its criticisms, but Brant was well schooled in the conventions of the people for whom his reply was intended.

JOSEPH BRANT

Indian vs. White Civilization

1789

I was, sir, born of Indian parents, and lived while a child, among those you are pleased to call savages; I was afterwards sent to live among the white people, and educated at one of your schools; since which period, I have been honoured, much beyond my deserts, by an acquaintance with a number of principal characters both in Europe and America. After all this experience, and after every exertion to divest myself of prejudice, I am obliged to give my opinion in favour of my own people. . . . I will not enlarge on an idea so singular in civilized life, and perhaps disagreeable to you; and will only observe, that among us, we have no law but that written on the heart of every rational creature by the immediate finger of the great Spirit of the

Quoted in Isabel Thompson Kelsay, *Joseph Brant* (Syracuse: Syracuse University Press, 1984), citing *American Museum* 6 (September 1789): 226–27.

universe himself. We have no prisons—we have no pompous parade of courts; and yet judges are as highly esteemed among us, as they are among you, and their decisions as highly revered; property, to say the least, is as well guarded, and crimes are as impartially punished. We have among us no splendid villains, above the controul of that law, which influences our decisions; in a word, we have no robbery under the colour of law—daring wickedness here is never suffered to triumph over helpless innocence—the estates of widows and orphans are never devoured by enterprising sharpers. Our sachems, and our warriors, eat their own bread, and not the bread of wretchedness. No person, among us, desires any other reward for performing a brave and worthy action, than the consciousness of serving his nation. Our wise men are called fathers—they are truly deserving the character; they are always accessible—I will not say to the meanest of our people—for we have none mean, but such as render themselves so by their vices.

. . . We do not hunger and thirst after those superfluities of life, that are the ruin of thousands of families among you. Our ornaments, in general, are simple, and easily obtained. Envy and covetousness, those worms that destroy the fair flower of human happiness, are unknown in this climate.

The palaces and prisons among you, form a most dreadful contrast. Go to the former places, and you will see, perhaps, a deformed piece of earth swelled with pride, and assuming airs, that become none but the Spirit above. Go to one of your prisons—here description utterly fails!—certainly the sight of an Indian torture, is not half so painful to a well informed mind. Kill them [the prisoners], if you please—kill them, too, by torture; but let the torture last no longer than a day. . . . Those you call savages, relent—the most furious of our tormentors exhausts his rage in a few hours, and dispatches the unhappy victim with a sudden stroke.

But for what are many of your prisoners confined? For debt! Astonishing! and will you ever again call the Indian nations cruel?—Liberty, to a rational creature, as much exceeds property, as the light of the sun does that of the most twinkling star: but you put them on a level, to the everlasting disgrace of civilization. . . . And I seriously declare, that I had rather die by the most severe tortures ever inflicted by any savage nation on the continent, than languish in one of your prisons for a single year. Great Maker of the world! and do you call yourselves christians? . . . Does then the religion of him whom you call your Saviour, inspire this conduct, and lead to this practice? Surely no. It was a sentence that once struck my mind with some force, that "a bruised reed he never broke." Cease then, while these practices continue among you, to call yourselves christians, lest you publish to the world your hypocrisy. Cease to call other nations savage, when you are tenfold more the children of cruelty, than they.

THE CONTINUING CONFLICT OVER LAND

In 1791, warriors of the northwestern Indian confederacy, led by the Miami war chief Little Turtle and the Shawnee Blue Jacket, inflicted a smashing defeat on the United States, destroying an American army under General Arthur St. Clair, governor of the Northwest Territory. In the wake of that defeat the United States dispatched commissioners to meet with the Indians and negotiate a settlement, but the Americans would not agree to the Indian demand that the Ohio River remain the boundary to their lands.

In a general council held at the foot of the Miami Rapids in northwestern Ohio in August 1793, delegates from the Wyandots, Seven Nations of Canada,[3] Delawares, Shawnees, Miamis, Ottawas, Chippewas, Senecas, Potawatomis, Conoys, Munsees, Nanticokes, Mahicans, Mississaguas, Creeks, and Cherokees met with the American commissioners. The Indian speakers reviewed the history of their relations with the United States, showing how past treaties had failed to stop white expansion onto their lands, and then offered their own solution to the problem.

INDIAN REPRESENTATIVES

Proposal to Maintain Indian Lands

1793

Brothers;—

Money, to us, is of no value, & to most of us unknown, and as no consideration whatever can induce us to sell the lands on which we get sustenance for our women and children; we hope we may be allowed to point out a mode by which your settlers may be easily removed, and peace thereby obtained.

Brothers;—

We know that these settlers are poor, or they would never have ventured to live in a country which have been in continual trouble ever since they crossed the Ohio; divide therefore this large sum of money which you have

---

E. A. Cruikshank, ed., *The Correspondence of Lieut. Governor John Graves Simcoe,* 5 vols. (Toronto: Ontario Historical Society, 1923–31) 2:17–19.

offered to us, among these people, give to each also a portion of what you say you would give us annually over and above this very large sum of money, and we are persuaded they would most readily accept of it in lieu of the lands you sold to them, if you add also the great sums you must expend in raising and paying Armies, with a view to force us to yield you our Country, you will certainly have more than sufficient for the purposes of repaying these settlers for all their labour and improvements.

Brothers;—

You have talked to us about concessions. It appears strange that you should expect any from us, who have only been defending our just Rights against your invasion; We want Peace; Restore to us our Country and we shall be Enemies no longer.

Brothers;—

You make one concession to us, by offering us your money, and another by having agreed to do us justice, after having long and injuriously withheld it. We mean in the acknowledgement you have now made, that the King of England never did, nor never had a right, to give you our Country, by the Treaty of peace, and you want to make this act of Common Justice, a great part of your concessions, and seem to expect that because you have at last acknowledged our independence, we should for such a favor surrender to you our Country.

Brothers;—

You have talked also a great deal about pre-emption and your exclusive right to purchase Indian lands, as ceded to you by the King at the Treaty of peace.

Brothers;—

We never made any agreement with the King, nor with any other Nation that we would give to either the exclusive right of purchasing our lands. And we declare to you that we consider ourselves free to make any bargain or cession of lands, whenever & to whomsoever we please, if the white people as you say, made a treaty that none of them but the King should purchase of us, and that he has given that right to the U. States, it is an affair which concerns you & him & not us. We have never parted with such a power.

Brothers;—

At our General Council held at the Glaize[4] last Fall, we agreed to meet Commissioners from the U. States, for the purpose of restoring Peace, provided they consented to acknowledge and confirm our boundary line to be the Ohio; and we determined not to meet you until you gave us satisfaction on that point; that is the reason we have never met.

We desire you to consider Brothers, that our only demand, is the peaceable possession of a small part of our once great Country. Look back and view the lands from whence we have been driven to this spot, we can retreat no further, because the country behind hardly affords food for its present inhabitants. And we have therefore resolved, to leave our bones in this small space, to which we are now confined.

Brothers;—

We shall be persuaded that you mean to do us justice if you agree, that the Ohio, shall remain the boundary line between us, if you will not consent thereto, our meeting will be altogether unnecessary.

NOTES

[1] Lawrence J. Kinnaird, ed., *Spain in the Mississippi Valley,* Annual Report of the American Historical Association for 1945 (Washington, D.C.), vol. 3, pt. 2, 117.

[2] *Calendar of Virginia State Papers* 4 (1886): 306.

[3] The Seven Nations of Canada was a confederacy of the mission communities along the St. Lawrence River. Centered at Caughnawaga, it included Oka, Odanak, Akwesasne, and other groups.

[4] The Glaize was the area at the junction of the Auglaize and Maumee rivers in northwestern Ohio. By this time many Indian peoples had congregated in the region as American expansion pushed them from their traditional homelands.

EPILOGUE

Surviving as Vanishing Americans

The Indians' hope that the United States might forgo expansion in return for peace and agree to the Ohio as a permanent boundary was not to be realized. The 1793 meeting broke up, the Americans split the Indian confederacy by playing on different tribal interests, and a year later General Anthony Wayne defeated the Indians at the Battle of Fallen Timbers in northwestern Ohio. At the Treaty of Greenville in 1795, tribal leaders ceded most of Ohio to the United States. Indian resistance shifted westward. In the first decade of the nineteenth century, the Shawnee war chief Tecumseh and his brother the Shawnee Prophet revived Indian resistance in the North and preached a message of pan-Indian unity throughout the eastern woodlands; from 1813 to 1814 the Creeks fought a bloody war against American expansion in the South. But it was too little and too late. The Indians' war for independence was lost. They now had to find ways to continue being Indians in the midst of a society that insisted that Indians were a "vanishing race."

For more than two hundred years, Indian peoples in the eastern woodlands of North America had adjusted to massive changes in their world generated by the European invasion of America. Amid the chaos, they dealt with the newcomers in a variety of ways. They traded with them and negotiated with them; they listened to their teachings and offered them alternative ways of life; they made war and made love; they avoided them and lived alongside them. However, as Americans in the new nation looked back across the long span of colonial history, they rarely saw anything but instances of Indian hostility. All Indians came to be regarded as warlike "savages" who had fought against the pioneers and had resisted "civilization" every step of the way. The struggles of Indian peoples to defend their lands and cultures provided their conquerors with further justification to take what was left of their land and destroy what remained of their traditional ways of life. Indian people had been virtually everywhere in colonial America, but there could be no place for "savages" in the new society Americans hoped to create.

In 1830, Congress passed the Indian Removal Act, and thousands of Indian people were driven from their ancestral homes in eastern America to seek new homes beyond the Mississippi. Americans assumed that Indians were doomed to extinction. They were wrong, of course, and the removal policies of the 1830s simply opened another chapter in the history of Indian peoples. The 1990 census recorded almost two million Indian people in the United States. There are 510 federally recognized tribes in the country and perhaps as many as 200 groups who are not recognized. Contrary to popular notions that Indians inhabit rural reservations in the West, more than half of Indian people live in cities, and many continue to live in the eastern United States. Some tribes, like the Penobscots and Passamaquoddies in Maine, have brought and won substantial lawsuits for lands taken from them illegally in the past; others, like the Mashpees on Cape Cod or the Abenakis in Vermont, have little or no land. Some, like the Iroquois in New York and Canada, are involved in recurrent conflict with state and federal governments over issues that affect their sovereignty; others, like the Abenakis of Vermont or the Lumbees of North Carolina, struggle simply to achieve state and federal recognition of their status as Indian tribes. Some, like the Mashantucket Pequots in Connecticut, have achieved unprecedented economic success through operating bingo halls and gambling casinos; many more live in poverty. Some Indian people live in communities that are distinctly Indian; others live and work alongside other Americans. Some Indian people have successfully demanded their rights in twentieth-century America. Many others, like indigenous people elsewhere in the world, still struggle to have their voices heard.

APPENDIX I

Treaty between the Abenaki Indians and the English at Casco Bay, 1727

The Submission and Agreement of the Delegates of the Eastern Indians

Whereas the several Tribes of the Eastern Indians Viz. The Penobscot, Nerridgawock, St. Johns, Cape Sables, and other Tribes Inhabiting within His Majesties Territories of *New England* and *Nova Scotia,* who have been engaged in the present War, from whom we, Saguaarum alias Loron, Arexis, Francois Xavier, & Meganumbee, are Delegated and fully Impowered to enter into Articles of Pacification with His Majesties Governments of the *Massachusetts-Bay, New-Hampshire* and *Nova Scotia,* have contrary to the several Treaties they have Solemnly entred into with the said Governments, made an Open Rupture, and have continued some Years in Acts of Hostility against the Subjects of His Majesty King GEORGE within the said Governments.

They being now sensible of the Miseries and Troubles they have involved themselves in, and being desirous to be restored to His Majesties Grace and Favour, and to Live in Peace with all His Majesties Subjects of the said Three Governments, and the Province of *New York* and Colonies of *Connecticut* and *Rhode Island* and that all former Acts of Injury be forgotten, have Concluded to make, and we do by these Presents in the Name and Behalf of the said Tribes, make Our Submission unto His most Excellent Majesty GEORGE by the Grace of GOD of *Great Britain, France* and *Ireland,* KING Defender of the Faith, &c. in as Full and Ample Manner, as any of our Predecessors have heretofore done.

"Indian Treaties," *Collections of the Maine Historical Society* (1856), 4:118–84.

And we do hereby promise and engage with the Honourable WILLIAM DUMMER Esq; as he is Lieutenant Governour and Commander in Chief of His Majesties Province of the *Massachusetts Bay* and with the Governours or Commanders in Chief of the said Province for the Time being, *That is to say.*

We the said Delegates for and in behalf of the several Tribes abovesaid, Do Promise and Engage, that at all times for Ever, from and after the Date of these Presents, We and They will Cease and Forbear all Acts of Hostility, Injuries and Discords towards all the Subjects of the Crown of *Great Britain,* and not offer the least Hurt, Violence or Molestation to them or any of them in their Persons or Estates, But will hence forward hold and maintain a firm and constant Amity and Friendship with all the English, and will never confederate or combine with any other Nation to their Prejudice.

That all the Captives taken in this present War, shall at or before, the Time of the further Ratification of this Treaty be restored without any Ransom or Payment to be made by them or any of them.

That His Majesty's Subjects the English shall and may peaceably and quietly enter upon, improve and for ever enjoy all and singular their Rights of Land and former Settlements, Properties and Possessions within the Eastern parts of the said Province of the *Massachusetts Bay,* together with all Islands, Isletts, Shoars, Beaches and Fishery within the same, without any Molestation or Claims by us or any other Indians, and be in no ways Molested, Interrupted or Disturbed therein. Saving unto the *Penobscot, Nerridgawock,* and other Tribes within His Majesties Province aforesaid, and their Natural Decendants repectively, all their Lands, Liberties and Properties not by them conveyed or Sold to or Possessed by any of the English Subjects as aforesaid, as also the Priviledge of Fishing, Hunting, and Fowling as formerly.

That all Trade and Commerce which hereafter may be Allowed betwixt the English and Indians, shall be under such Management and Regulation as the Government of the *Massachusetts* Province shall Direct.

If any Controversie or Difference at any time hereafter happen to arise between any of the English and Indians for any real or supposed Wrong or Injury done on either side, no Private Revenge shall be taken for the same but proper Application shall be made to His Majesties Government upon the place for Remedy or Redress thereof in a due course of Justice.

We Submitting Our selves to be Ruled and Governed by His Majesty's Laws, and desiring to have the Benefit of the same.

We also the said Delegates, in Behalf of the Tribes of Indians, inhabiting within the French Territories, who have Assisted us in this War, for whom we are fully Impowered to Act in this present Treaty, Do hereby Promise and Engage, that they and every of them shall henceforth Cease and Forbear all Acts of Hostility Force and Violence towards all and every the Subjects of His Majesty the King of Great Britain.

We do further in Behalf of the Tribe of the *Penobscot* Indians, promise and engage, that if any of the other Tribes intended to be Included in this Treaty, shall notwithstanding refuse to Confirm and Ratifie this present Treaty entred into on their Behalf and continue or Renew Acts of Hostility against the English, in such case the said *Penobscot* Tribe shall joine their Young Men with the English in reducing them to Reason.

In the next place we the aforenamed Delegates Do promise and engage with the Honourable John Wentworth Esq; as He is Lieut. Governour and Commander in Chief of His Majesties Province of *New Hampshire,* and with the Governours and Commader in Chief of the said Province for the time being, that we and the Tribes we are deputed from will henceforth cease and forbear all Acts of Hostility, Injuries & Discords towards all the Subjects of His Majesty King GEORGE within the said Province. And we do understand and take it that the said Government of *New Hampshire* is also included and comprehended in all and every the Articles aforegoing excepting that respecting the regulating the Trade with us.

And further we the aforenamed Delegates do Promise and Engage with the Honourable Lawrance Armstrong Esq; Lieutenant Governour and Commander in Chief of His Majesties Province of *Nova Scotia* or *L'Acadie* to live in peace with His Majesties Good Subjects and their Dependants in that Government according to the Articles agreed on with Major Paul Mascarene commissioned for that purpose, and further to be Ratified as mentioned in the said Articles.

That this present Treaty shall be Accepted Ratified and Confirmed in a Publick and Solemn manner by the Chiefs of the several Eastern Tribes of Indians included therein at *Falmouth* in *Casco Bay* some time in the Month of *May* next. *In Testimony* whereof we have Signed these Presents, and Affixed Our Seals. Dated at the Council Chamber in *Boston* in *New England,* this Fifteenth Day of December, Anno Domini, One Thousand Seven Hundred and Twenty-five, Annoque Regni Regis GEORGIJ, Magnæ Britanniæ, &c. Duodecimo.

Sig.

Sauguaarum   alias Loron

Sig.

Arexrus

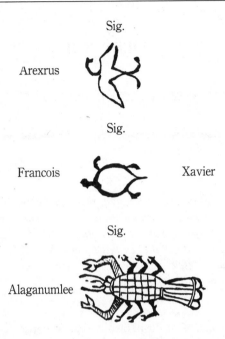

Sig.

Francois   Xavier

Sig.

Alaganumlee

Done in the presence of the Great and General Court or Assembly of the Province of the *Massachusetts Bay* aforesaid, being first Read distinctly, and Interpreted by Capt. *John Gyles,* Capt. *Samuel Jordan,* and Capt. *Joseph Bane,* Sworn Interpreters.

Attest J. Willard, Secr.

APPENDIX II

Treaty with the Delawares, 1778

Articles of agreement and confederation, made and entered into by Andrew and Thomas Lewis, Esquires, Commissioners for, and in Behalf of the United States of North-America of the one Part, and Capt. White Eyes, Capt. John Killbuck, Junior, and Capt. Pipe, Deputies and Chief Men of the Delaware Nation of the other Part.

Article I

That all offences or acts of hostilities by one, or either of the contracting parties against the other, be mutually forgiven, and buried in the depth of oblivion, never more to be had in remembrance.

Article II

That a perpetual peace and friendship shall from henceforth take place, and subsist between the contracting parties aforesaid, through all succeeding generations: and if either of the parties are engaged in a just and necessary war with any other nation or nations, that then each shall assist the other in due proportion to their abilities, till their enemies are brought to reasonable terms of accommodation: and that if either of them shall discover any hostile designs forming against the other, they shall give the earliest notice thereof. that timeous measures may be taken to prevent their ill effect.

Article III

And whereas the United States are engaged in a just and necessary war, in defence and support of life, liberty and independence, against the King of

Charles J. Kappler, ed., *Indian Treaties, 1778–1883* (Washington, D.C.: Government Printing Office, 1904).

England and his adherents, and as said King is yet possessed of several posts and forts on the lakes and other places, the reduction of which is of great importance to the peace and security of the contracting parties, and as the most practicable way for the troops of the United States to some of the posts and forts is by passing through the country of the Delaware nation, the aforesaid deputies, on behalf of themselves and their nation, do hereby stipulate and agree to give a free passage through their country to the troops aforesaid, and the same to conduct by the nearest and best ways to the posts, forts or towns of the enemies of the United States, affording to said troops such supplies of corn, meat, horses, or whatever may be in their power for the accommodation of such troops, on the commanding officer's, &c. paying, or engageing to pay, the full value of whatever they can supply them with. And the said deputies, on the behalf of their nation, engage to join the troops of the United States aforesaid, with such a number of their best and most expert warriors as they can spare, consistent with their own safety, and act in concert with them; and for the better security of the old men, women and children of the aforesaid nation, whilst their warriors are engaged against the common enemy, it is agreed on the part of the United States, that a fort of sufficient strength and capacity be built at the expense of the said States, with such assistance as it may be in the power of the said Delaware Nation to give, in the most convenient place, and advantageous situation, as shall be agreed on by the commanding officer of the troops aforesaid, with the advice and concurrence of the deputies of the aforesaid Delaware Nation, which fort shall be garrisoned by such a number of the troops of the United States, as the commanding officer can spare for the present, and hereafter by such numbers, as the wise men of the United States in council, shall think most conducive to the common good.

Article IV

For the better security of the peace and friendship now entered into by the contracting parties, against all infractions of the same by the citizens of either party, to the prejudice of the other, neither party shall proceed to the infliction of punishments on the citizens of the other, otherwise than by securing the offender or offenders by imprisonment, or any other competent means, till a fair and impartial trial can be had by judges or juries of both parties, as near as can be to the laws, customs and usages of the contracting parties and natural justice: The mode of such trials to be hereafter fixed by the wise men of the United States in Congress assembled, with the assistance of such deputies of the Delaware nation, as may be appointed to act in concert with them in adjusting this matter to their mutual liking. And it is further agreed between the parties aforesaid, that neither shall entertain or give countenance to the enemies of the other, or protect in their respective states, criminal fugitives, servants or slaves, but the same to apprehend, and secure and deliver to the State or States, to which such enemies, criminals, servants or slaves respectively belong.

Article V

Whereas the confederation entered into by the Delaware nation and the United States, renders the first dependent on the latter for all the articles of clothing, utensils and implements of war, and it is judged not only reasonable, but indispensably necessary, that the aforesaid Nation be supplied with such articles from time to time, as far as the United States may have it in their power, by a well-regulated trade, under the conduct of an intelligent, candid agent, with an adequate salary, one more influenced by the love of his country, and a constant attention to the duties of his department by promoting the common interest, than the sinister purposes of converting and binding all the duties of his office to his private emolument: Convinced of the necessity of such measures, the Commissioners of the United States, at the earnest solicitation of the deputies aforesaid, have engaged in behalf of the United States, that such a trade shall be afforded said nation, conducted on such principles of mutual interest as the wisdom of the United States in Congress assembled shall think most conducive to adopt for their mutual convenience.

Article VI

Whereas the enemies of the United States have endeavored, by every artifice in their power, to possess the Indians in general with an opinion, that it is the design of the States aforesaid, to extirpate the Indians and take possession of their country: to obviate such false suggestion, the United States do engage to guarantee to the aforesaid nation of Delawares, and their heirs, all their territorial rights in the fullest and most ample manner, as it hath been bounded by former treaties, as long as they the said Delaware nation shall abide by, and hold fast the chain of friendship now entered into. And it is further agreed on between the contracting parties should it for the future be found conducive for the mutual interest of both parties to invite any other tribes who have been friends to the interest of the United States, to join the present confederation, and to form a state whereof the Delaware nation shall be the head, and have a representation in Congress: Provided, nothing contained in this article to be considered as conclusive until it meets with the approbation of Congress. And it is also the intent and meaning of this article, that no protection or countenance shall be afforded to any who are at present our enemies, by which they might escape the punishment they deserve.

In witness whereof, the parties have hereunto interchangeably set their hands and seals, at Fort Pitt, September seventeenth, anno Domini one thousand seven hundred and seventy-eight.

Andrew Lewis,
Thomas Lewis,
White Eyes, his x mark,
The Pipe, his x mark,
Johnkill Buck, his x mark,

In presence of—
Lach'n McIntosh, brigadier-general, commander the Western Department.
Daniel Brodhead, colonel Eighth Pennsylvania Regiment,
W. Crawford, colonel,
John Campbell,
John Stephenson,
John Gibson, colonel Thirteenth Virginia Regiment,
A. Graham, brigade major,
Lach. McIntosh, jr., major brigade,
Benjamin Mills,
Joseph L. Finley, captain Eighth Pennsylvania Regiment,
John Finley, captain Eighth Pennsylvania Regiment.

Questions for Consideration

1. What value do Native American speeches, letters, and opinions have for better understanding (a) American Indian history and (b) United States history in general?

2. What problems and limitations might the following kinds of records contain for understanding Native American history?
   a. documents written about Indians by Europeans
   b. speeches by Indians
   c. Indian treaties
   d. oral traditions

3. How did Europeans and Native Americans differ in their appreciation for and use of spoken and written words, and how did this affect their relations?

4. The invasion of America has been described as creating a "new world" for Native American peoples. What was this new world like? What factors produced it? What do the documents tell us about Indian responses to the invasion and the changes?

5. Why and with what results did Indian people participate in the European fur and deerskin trades? What appear to have been the feelings of Indian people toward European traders and the products they brought into Indian villages?

6. Europeans claimed that their religion and "civilization" were inherently superior to those of the Indians. Government agents, teachers, and missionaries devoted tremendous efforts to convert Indians to their way of thinking, living, and worshiping. How do Indian people appear to have responded to these claims and these efforts? What criticisms did they in turn level against Euro-American society?

7. Land was a basic source of contention between Indians and colonists. How did they differ in their attitudes toward land? Why did competition for land so often lead to war?

8. What roles did Indians play in the "French and Indian War"? How did they regard their services and experiences? What were the results of their involvement?

9. Why and with what consequences did Indian people fight in the American Revolution?

10. How did the creation of the American Republic affect American Indians? What strategies did Indian peoples adopt in dealing with the United States?

11. What subjects do the Indian voices in this volume *not* mention? What might be the reasons for their silence?

12. Select one document and find out as much as possible about it and the circumstances in which it was created. What was the historical context of the document: What events led up to it and occurred in its aftermath? Who were the individuals involved and what were their goals? Is there any reason to suspect the authenticity of all or part of the document?

Selected Bibliography

PRINTED PRIMARY SOURCES

American Indians appear in documents recorded by travelers, traders, soldiers, missionaries, captives, Indian agents, and the governments of Britain, France, Spain, Holland, the United States, and the various colonies. Relevant manuscripts are scattered throughout Europe, the United States, and Canada. The following are some of the most useful collections of printed documents.

Colonial Records of South Carolina: Documents Relating to Indian Affairs, 1750–1754 and *Documents Relating to Indian Affairs, 1754–1765.* Edited by William L. McDowell, Jr. Columbia: University of South Carolina Press, 1958, 1970.

Dawnland Encounters: Indians and Europeans in Northern New England. Edited by Colin G. Calloway. Hanover, N.H.: University Press of New England, 1991.

Early American Indian Documents: Treaties and Laws, 1607–1789. 20 vols. projected. General editor Alden T. Vaughan. Frederick, Md.: University Publications of America, 1979–.

The Indian Peoples of Eastern America: A Documentary History of the Sexes. Edited by James Axtell. New York: Oxford University Press, 1981.

The Jesuit Relations and Allied Documents: Travels and Explorations of the Jesuit Missionaries in New France, 1610–1791. 71 vols. Edited by Reuben G. Thwaites. Cleveland, 1896–1901.

Native American Testimony: A Chronicle of Indian-White Relations from Prophecy to the Present, 1492–1992. Edited by Peter Nabokov. New York: Viking, 1991.

Native Writings in Massachusett. 2 vols. Edited and translated by Ives Goddard and Kathleen J. Bragdon. Philadelphia: American Philosophical Society, 1988.

The Papers of Sir William Johnson. 14 vols. Edited by James Sullivan et al. Albany, 1921–65.

Spirit of the New England Tribes: Indian History and Folklore, 1620–1984. Edited by William S. Simmons. Hanover, N.H.: University Press of New England, 1986.

SECONDARY SOURCES

Books and articles about American Indians before 1800 have proliferated in the last quarter century. The following represents a portion of this growing literature.

Axtell, James. *After Columbus: Essays in the Ethnohistory of Colonial North America.* New York: Oxford University Press, 1988.

———. *Beyond 1492: Encounters in Colonial North America.* New York: Oxford University Press, 1992.

———. *The European and the Indian: Essays in the Ethnohistory of Colonial North America.* New York: Oxford University Press, 1981.

———. *The Invasion Within: The Contest of Cultures in Colonial North America.* New York: Oxford University Press, 1985.

Bourne, Russell. *The Red King's Rebellion: Racial Politics in New England, 1675–1678.* New York: Oxford University Press, 1990.

Calloway, Colin G. *The Western Abenakis of Vermont, 1600–1800: War, Migration, and the Survival of an Indian People.* Norman: University of Oklahoma Press, 1990.

Cronon, William. *Changes in the Land: Indians, Colonists, and the Ecology of New England.* New York: Hill and Wang, 1983.

Dowd, Gregory Evans. *A Spirited Resistance: The North American Indian Struggle for Unity, 1745–1815.* Baltimore: Johns Hopkins University Press, 1992.

Graymont, Barbara. *The Iroquois in the American Revolution.* Syracuse: Syracuse University Press, 1972.

Hatley, Tom. *The Dividing Paths: Cherokees and South Carolinians through the Era of Revolution.* New York: Oxford University Press, 1993.

Jennings, Francis. *The Ambiguous Iroquois Empire: The Covenant Chain Confederation of Indian Tribes with English Colonies.* New York: W. W. Norton, 1984.

———. *Empire of Fortune: Crowns, Colonies, and Tribes in the Seven Years War in America.* New York: W. W. Norton, 1988.

———. *The Invasion of America: Indians, Colonialism, and the Cant of Conquest.* New York: W. W. Norton, 1976.

———, William N. Fenton, and Mary A. Druke, eds. *The History and Culture of Iroquois Diplomacy: An Interdisciplinary Guide to the Treaties of the Six Nations and Their League.* Syracuse: Syracuse University Press, 1985.

Martin, Calvin. *Keepers of the Game: Indian-Animal Relationships and the Fur Trade.* Berkeley: University of California Press, 1978.

Merrell, James H. *The Indians' New World: Catawbas and Their Neighbors from European Contact through the Era of Removal*. Chapel Hill: University of North Carolina Press, 1989.

Murray, David. *Forked Tongues: Speech, Writing, and Representation in North American Indian Texts*. Bloomington: Indiana University Press, 1991.

Richter, Daniel K. *The Ordeal of the Longhouse: The Peoples of the Iroquois League in the Era of European Colonization*. Chapel Hill: University of North Carolina Press, 1992.

Rountree, Helen C. *Pocahontas's People: The Powhatan Indians of Virginia through Four Centuries*. Norman: University of Oklahoma Press, 1990.

————. *The Powhatan Indians of Virginia*. Norman: University of Oklahoma Press, 1988.

Salisbury, Neal. *Manitou and Providence: Indians, Europeans, and the Making of New England, 1500–1643*. New York: Oxford University Press, 1982.

Szasz, Margaret Connell. *Indian Education in the American Colonies, 1607–1783*. Albuquerque: University of New Mexico Press, 1988.

Tanner, Helen H., ed. *Atlas of Great Lakes Indian History*. Norman: University of Oklahoma Press, 1987.

Thornton, Russell. *American Indian Holocaust and Survival: A Population History since 1492*. Norman: University of Oklahoma Press, 1987.

Trigger, Bruce G., ed. *Handbook of North American Indians*. Vol. 15, *Northeast*. Washington, D.C.: Smithsonian Institution, 1978.

Trigger, Bruce G. *Natives and Newcomers: Canada's "Heroic Age" Reconsidered*. Kingston and Montreal: McGill–Queens University Press, 1985.

Washburn, Wilcomb E., ed. *Handbook of North American Indians*. Vol. 4, *History of Indian-White Relations*. Washington, D.C.: Smithsonian Institution, 1988.

White, Richard. *The Middle Ground: Indians, Empires, and Republics in the Great Lakes Region, 1650–1815*. New York: Cambridge University Press, 1991.

————. *The Roots of Dependency: Subsistence, Environment, and Social Change among the Choctaws, Pawnees, and Navajos*. Lincoln: University of Nebraska Press, 1983.

Wood, Peter, Gregory A. Waselkov, and M. Thomas Hatley, eds. *Powhatan's Mantle: Indians in the Colonial Southeast*. Lincoln: University of Nebraska Press, 1989.

(*Continued from p. ii*)

"Agreement between Muttaak and his Councillors, 1681," "Petition from the Native Proprietors of Gay Head, 1749," and "The Will of Naomi Omaush, 1749." *Native Writings in Massachusetts,* edited by Ives Goddard and Kathleen J. Bragdon. Philadelphia: The American Philosophical Society, 1988. Reprinted by permission of the translator.

"The Iroquois Reject Wheelock's 'Benevolence,' 1772," and "Three Letters from One Narragansett Family, 1767, 1769, and 1771." *The Letters of Eleazar Wheelock's Indians,* edited by James Dow McCallum. Hanover, N.H.: Dartmouth College Publications, 1932. Reprinted with permission.

"The Chickasaw's Appeal for Help, 1756." *Colonial Records of South Carolina: Documents Relating to Indian Affairs, 1754–1765,* edited by William L. McDowell, Jr. Columbia: University of South Carolina Press, 1970. Reprinted with permission.

"The Creation of the World." *The Journal of Major John Norton, 1816,* edited by Carl F. Klinck and James J. Talman. Toronto: The Champlain Society, 1970, pp. 88–91. Reprinted by permission of the Champlain Society.

"Speech of Powhatan to Captain John Smith." Reprinted from *The Complete Works of John Smith,* edited by Philip Barbour. Published for the Institute of Early American History and Culture, Williamsburg, Virginia. Copyright © 1986 by the University of North Carolina Press.

ILLUSTRATIONS

Figure 1. Map of Indian peoples adapted from James Axtell, *Beyond 1492: Encounters in Colonial America,* copyright 1992. Reprinted by permission of Oxford University Press.

Figures 2, 11, 12. Maps of European invasions, Colonial and Indian boundaries, and the French and Indian Wars adapted from Carl Waldman, *Atlas of the North American Indian,* copyright 1985.

Figure 3. Indian Orator. Courtesy of the Rare Books and Manuscriptision, the New York Public Library; Astor, Lennox, and Tilden Foundations.

Figure 4. Hiawatha Wampum Belt. Courtesy of the Onondaga Nation and the New York State Museum.

Figure 5. Map of the Iroquois homeland adapted from Barbara Graymont, *The Iroquois,* copyright 1988. Reprinted by permission of the artist, Gary Tonge.

Figure 6. Detail from Willem Verelst's painting *Oglethorpe presenting Tomochichi and the Indians to the Lords Trustees of the Colony of Georgia.* Courtesy of the Smithsonian Institution National Anthropological Archives, Bureau of American Ethnology Collection.

Figure 7. Portrait of the Reverend Samson Occom. Courtesy of the Bowdoin College Museum of Art.

Figure 8. Founding of Dartmouth College. Wood engraving by Samuel E. Brown, 1839. Courtesy of Dartmouth College.

Figure 9. Portrait of Etow Oh Koam or Nicholas. Courtesy of the National Archives of Canada/C92421.

Figure 10. Portrait of Lapowinsa, by Gustavus Hesselius. Courtesy of the Historical Society of Pennsylvania.

Figure 13. Iroquois pictograms. Courtesy of the Archives Nationales, Paris; C11A.

Figure 14. English copy of a Chickasaw Map, 1723. Courtesy of the British Public Record Office. French copy of a Chickasaw Map, 1737. Courtesy of the Archives Nationales, Paris; C13A122.

Figure 15. Detail from Benjamin West's painting, *The Death of General Wolfe.* Courtesy of the National Gallery of Canada, Ottawa.

Figure 16. Outacite, Chief of the Cherokees, 1762. Engraving from an unknown source. Courtesy of the Smithsonian Institution National Anthropological Archives, Bureau of American Ethnology Collection.

Figure 17. Joseph Brant by Joshua Reynolds, 1776. Courtesy of the National Gallery of Canada, Ottawa.

Index